Management for Professionals

More information about this series at http://www.springer.com/series/10101

Mustafa F. Özbilgin • Fiona Bartels-Ellis •
Paul Gibbs
Editors

Global Diversity Management

A Fusion of Ideas, Stories and Practice

Foreword by Ciarán Devane

 Springer

Editors
Mustafa F. Özbilgin
Brunel University London
Middlesex, United Kingdom

Fiona Bartels-Ellis
British Council
London, United Kingdom

Paul Gibbs
Middlesex University
Cambridge, United Kingdom

ISSN 2192-8096 ISSN 2192-810X (electronic)
Management for Professionals
ISBN 978-3-030-19522-9 ISBN 978-3-030-19523-6 (eBook)
https://doi.org/10.1007/978-3-030-19523-6

This Springer imprint is published by the registered company Springer Nature Switzerland AG.
The registered company address is: Gewerbestrasse 11, 6330 Cham, Switzerland

Mustafa: In loving memory of Karsten Jonsen, my dear friend and coauthor. You are missed.
Fiona: Jane Franklin especially and other colleagues on the journey with us intent on making our cultural relations stronger and deeper, notably our Accredited Diversity Facilitators.
Paul. To the grandchildren in the knowledge they will continue to embrace diversity.

Foreword

To take equality, diversity and inclusion seriously must be in the interests of every organisation, public or private. The simplest reason is that it is the right thing to do. Why would one want to discriminate against some groups or individuals or preferentially favour others? A more self-interested reason is to be open to all the talent out there, rather than just a fraction. Capability must surely go up when one can select the best people from a larger talent pool. Linked to that is that a diverse work force with a diverse leadership reduces the likelihood of group-think, of monoculture, and of having a narrow range of experiences. With this you decrease the risk of missing what is really happening, rather than what one thinks is happening. However, this ought not to be mechanically but should be done with humanity and with compassion.

As a global organisation operating in well over a hundred countries, being sensitive to what works and does not in any given society is an essential competence for the British Council. The diversity of our staff is critical to having that insight and our collective openness to the diversity of the societies we work with is something we must be good at if we are to be effective in our task of building cultural relations on behalf of the UK. For this reason, Equality, Diversity and Inclusion (EDI) is something we track and measure through a rigorous Diversity Assessment Framework. Just as we keep a track on our finances or on the impact of our programmes, we track how we do on EDI across our global network. In some areas we do well and have some lessons to share. In others, such as consistency of leadership role modelling, we have more to learn and implement. We also seek to improve our own abilities through, for example, supporting research as a contribution to the enhancement of practice.

Sharing experiences is of course essential to our collective learning. This book gives a wider audience to our own and others' experiences and I thank our friends and colleagues who contributed. Bringing the insights of academics and practitioners together creates a unique blend of the two, reinforcing each.

Whatever the purpose of an organisation, delivering government services, meeting market needs or tackling social issues, values matter. Empathy, tolerance compassion, trust and understanding are just some of the skills modern leadership need to sustain the relations, knowledge and insight which drive positive impact commercially, socially and indeed in policy.

For all these reasons, this book is a valuable companion in debating and addressing EDI in the workplace. This is a book well worth taking our time to read. I commend the book, its contributors and of course its editors for all their observations and challenges which have made it so.

British Council   Sir Ciarán Devane
London, UK

Acknowledgements

Any level of progress and change that supports inclusion invariably involves the direct or indirect contributions of a range of people. For this book, there are two set of people who we would like to acknowledge. The first are those from the British Council, colleagues who funded the main research project. These include Jo Beall, Director of Education and Society until December 2018, and Emily Morrison Research, Project Manager. Many other colleagues have made a significant contribution giving generously of their time; these include colleagues from Ghana, Egypt, Jordan, Kenya and Saudi Arabia—Country Directors at the time who welcomed participation and those who shared honestly and with considerable insight and helped with arrangements. Of course the research team led by Paul Gibbs that undertook the study and converted the insights of the regions into evidence-based research.

The second half of the book also benefited from participants at conferences in London in Middlesex University in January 2018. We are grateful to all those colleagues in our workplaces for their support, views and contributions in various aspects of the research and practice reported in this book. We are grateful to Springer especially Ruth Milewski and Prashanth Mahagaonkar for their assistance in publishing this book. Finally, we are grateful to Alison Williamson for her contribution in moving a draft into a manuscript fit for publication.

Contents

**Introduction to the Challenges of International Diversity
Management**   1
Fiona Bartels-Ellis, Mustafa F. Özbilgin, and Paul Gibbs

Part I   Thinking About and Doing Large-Scale Projects

**What Do We Know About the Implementations of Equality,
Diversity and Inclusion in the Workplace?**   11
Alison Scott-Baumann, Paul Gibbs, Alex Elwick, and Kate Maguire

Global Diversity Management   25
Mustafa F. Özbilgin

Narrative Inquiry   41
Kate Maguire and Alison Scott-Baumann

Five Nations: A Diversity Study   55
Alex Elwick, Paul Gibbs, Kate Maguire, and Alison Scott-Baumann

Part II   Practitioners Reflecting on Practice

**What Makes You Successful at Diversity Management? A Personal
Journey**   81
Ágota Bíró

Diversity in Global Management   87
Patti Boulaye

**The Theatre of the Classroom: A Work in Progress. How Can I Meet
the Needs of Everyone in the Class When I Also Have to Deal with
the Pupils with Problems?**   93
David Crabtree

Training on and Exploring Cultural Approaches to Disability   103
Simon Minty

Tales from the Front 111
Wayne Mullen

Diversity in a Global Financial Organisation 121
Asif Sadiq MBE

How to Start an Emotion-Reflective Journey 129
Kathrin Tietze

**Making the Creative Case for Diversity Across Arts and Culture:
An Outsider Looking in** 137
Abid Hussain

**Promoting Cultural Awareness: A Means of Managing Global
Diversity** 145
Doirean Wilson

Part III   Conclusion

At the Core of Diversity Is Compassion 161
Paul Gibbs

A Reflection on Compassion 173
Jason De Santolo

Index 175

About the Authors

Fiona Bartels-Ellis is Global Head of Equality, Diversity and Inclusion at the British Council, the UK's principle international cultural relations organisation. She has the responsibility for setting and driving the strategic direction of equality, diversity and inclusion across the organisation's offices in 110 countries and territories. In this role she makes strenuous efforts to share the challenges and achievements of the UK journey towards a more inclusive and fair society for all and to learn from other societies and cultures.

Fiona is a member of the Higher Education Academy and her local Race Equality Council. She is a Fellow of the Royal Society of Arts and a Trustee of AGF supporting gifted and talented girls in science. Her qualifications include an Advanced Diploma in Social Work, a Postgraduate Certificate in Higher Education, an MPhil in Social Policy and a Doctorate in Professional Studies. Her contribution has been recognised through a number of awards and recognition in the Britain's most influential people of African and African Heritage Powerlists.

Ágota Bíró is HR Director at Emarsys and is currently working in Budapest in its R&D department as HR Director. She started her career as a teacher with a strong commitment to supporting children from a disadvantaged social background. She finished her postgraduate studies in Educational Management at Corvinus University of Budapest in 2008 and joined the British Council in 2009. During her seven years with the British Council, she worked internationally as a trainer, facilitator, projects and partnership manager and global diversity network representative in many projects, all somehow connected to mainstreaming diversity and inclusion. She finished her studies as an executive coach in 2014, from then on mainly focusing on leadership development with a wide range of clients, including public sector organisations, businesses and NGOs.

Ágota is a board member of the Hungarian Civil Liberties Union, an influential human rights organisation in Budapest. She is also one of the founders of Coch4Good, an initiative supporting leaders working for social change.

Patti Boulaye OBE is a Visiting Teaching Fellow at Middlesex University, with public speaking engagements at the Conference of World Scientists, the University of Oxford, the Royal Society of Arts, the Women's Federation for World Peace and the Houses of Parliament. She has released her autobiography, The Faith of a Child, and is a Patron of Eastside Educational Trust, Governor of the British American Drama Academy (affiliated with Oxford and Yale Universities), a member of the Creative Committee of Her Majesty the Queen's Golden Jubilee Celebrations, Advisory Board Member of IMAN Foundation Worldwide (peace forum for former heads of state and ministers). She was awarded an OBE for Charitable Work in the United Kingdom and Sub-Saharan Africa. Patti is Founder of BIPADA Academy and Support for Africa charity, which has built five healthcare clinics in West Africa and a school in Lesotho. She was awarded an Honorary Doctorate by the Joint Council of Churches and hosts her TV chat show, Life with Patti Boulaye.

David Crabtree has worked with schools, teachers in schools and national organisations in many countries, a journey that began at the Hornby Dyslexia Centre in London over 25 years ago with an international initiative to support learning outcomes for underperforming pupils. Later, as a founder member of a project based at the University of Westminster, David further devised methodologies for inclusion at classroom and whole-school level.

Continuing to constantly develop the 'AchieveAbility' model up until the present time, David has worked with the British Council on inclusive classroom practice for the neurodiverse in Africa, the Middle East, Latin America and Europe. David is a teacher, and holds the Postgraduate Diploma in SpLD (Dyslexia) and an MA in Education. His work includes the ground-breaking publication, 'A framework for whole institution inclusive teaching practice'. He is also the father of three children who learn differently, and is himself neurodiverse.

Alex Elwick is a lecturer at UCL Institute of Education and a researcher at Middlesex University, London. His work is concerned with education policy and social justice at national/regional (government) and local (institutional) levels. He has published on topics including the 'Prevent' policy in education, values and value statements in universities and urban school system reform. His doctorate explored learning in art galleries, and he has been a UK Research Council's Fellow at the Library of Congress, Washington DC.

Paul Gibbs is Director of Education Research at Middlesex University and Azerbaijan University. He is a Professor of the university, Founder of the Centre for Education Research and Scholarship and a Distinguished Professor at the Open University in Hong Kong. He recently completed two books: one on transdisciplinary higher education and one on happiness. He is also series editor of SpringerBriefs on Key Thinkers in Education and Debating Higher Education: Philosophical Perspectives for Springer Academic Press.

Abid Hussain is Director, Diversity at Arts Council England, the national development agency for arts and culture, leading the organisation's work on Equality, Inclusion and the Creative Case for Diversity. He is an alumnus of both the US International Visitor Leadership Programme (IVLP) and the Salzburg Global

Seminar, responding to themes of art and social change, migration, displaced artists and conflict transformation. Abid has led on the development of the Arts Council's strategic equality and diversity framework since 2014, which included the development and launch of the transformative Elevate and Change Makers programmes, which have made a significant contribution to diversifying the arts and cultural landscape in England. He has extensive experience of working with cultural institutions, academia, government and third-sector agencies across North America, Europe, East Asia, South Africa and Australasia.

Kate Maguire is Associate Professor of Professional Practice in the Faculty of Professional and Social Sciences at Middlesex University and head of its transdisciplinary research degree programmes. Her background is social anthropology of the Middle East and organisational psychology, both as a researcher and practitioner. Coming into higher education from careers in journalism, political research and trauma studies, she has engaged with anthropologically informed innovative research methodologies and research pedagogy relevant to professional practice research, with particular interest in bridging difference, embracing complexity and theorising professional practice, particularly ethics in practice to enhance professional learning and organisational change. She has led on fieldwork design and implementation for a number of projects and innovations.

Simon Minty is a Director of Sminty Ltd., a disability training and consultancy company which works with large international organisations. He is also a producer of the comedy troupe, Abnormally Funny People which he co-founded in 2005. He is the co-host of the BBC Ouch Talkshow. Simon has a Postgraduate Diploma in Disability Management at Work and a BSc (Joint Hons) in Philosophy and Sociology.

Wayne Mullen is the Global Head of Human Resources at The Workshop. Previously, Wayne held roles as Global Head of Leadership and Organisational Development at VTB Capital, and Head of Leadership and Development for Standard Bank's international investment banking business. Wayne has over two decades of leadership, diversity and organisational development experience across the globe for organisations such as the Bank of Tokyo-Mitsubishi, Barclays Capital, National Australia Bank, Ericsson, Vodafone, the Home Office, Siemens Business Services, King and Standard Bank. His work has featured in The Independent, Coaching at Work and Finance Week. He holds an MSc in Organisational Behaviour (Occupational Psychology) and a Doctorate in Leadership and Organisational Development. His research, which focused on the development of minority leaders, was awarded the Ken Goulding Prize for Research Excellence.

Mustafa F. Özbilgin is Professor of Organisational Behaviour at Brunel Business School, London. He also holds two international positions: Co-Chaire Management et Diversité at Université Paris Dauphine and Visiting Professor of Management at

Koç University in Istanbul. His research focuses on equality, diversity and inclusion at work from comparative and relational perspectives. He has conducted field studies in the United Kingdom and internationally, and his work is empirically grounded. His research is supported by international as well as national grants. His work has a focus on changing policy and practice in equality and diversity at work. He is an engaged scholar, driven by values of workplace democracy, equality for all and humanisation of work.

Asif Sadiq MBE is Head of Diversity, Inclusion and Belonging for the Telegraph, delivering the strategic plan to drive a co-ordinated approach across the business to focus both investment and intent on the broader inclusion agenda. He is a multi-award-winning diversity and inclusion expert with a proven track record in achieving operational and strategic targets, managing quality, performance, risk and change through promoting equal opportunities and diverse cultures. He is a passionate and inspirational leader with the ability to empower individuals and create a truly inclusive environment for all. Asif is key in implementing D&I activities and programmes, as well as connecting with stakeholders at all levels to build strong and influential relationships with business leaders and influencers. Asif acts as a role model, providing governance across the business on D&I and cultural change, and is committed to creating a strong sense of belonging for all.

Jason De Santolo (Garrwa and Barunggam) is a researcher, creative producer and father committed to forging a sustainable world for future generations through transformative research strategies, storytelling and practices of renewal. Born in Larrakia homelands—Darwin, he moved to Aoteaoroa/NZ at an early age and studied treaty and international environmental law. His unique research practice integrates video, creative practice and renewal strategies. In 2014 he received a UTS Research Excellence Scholarship and graduated in 2018 with a creative doctorate that explores the renewal of song traditions through his passion for filmmaking and collective aspirations for self-determination. Jason co-edited Decolonizing Research: Indigenous Storywork as Methodology with Jo-Ann Archibald and Jenny Lee-Morgan which will be available in April 2019 through Zed Books. His latest documentary Warburdar Bununu/Water Shield explores water contamination in Borroloola, NT, and is set to be released by Browncabs in 2019. Jason is currently Associate Professor in Design, School of Design, Faculty of Design Architecture & Building UTS.

Alison Scott-Baumann is Professor of Society and Belief, and Associate Director of Research (Impact and Engagement) at the School of Oriental and African Studies, University of London. She and her research team recently completed a three-year AHRC grant to analyse representations of Islam and Muslims on university campuses, and this complements her work on free speech on campus. In early 2019 she was commissioned by the government to work with Muslim community groups and improve young Muslims' access to higher education. She speaks on BBC

Radio 4, has written for the Guardian and several higher education blogs and applies Ricoeur's philosophy to social justice issues.

Kathrin Tietze holds a degree in Educational Studies, English linguistics and Psychology, studying in Germany and the United Kingdom. Early on, she developed a passion for and expertise in human rights, equality and inclusion. Previous positions include project coordinator at a city council, managing director at an NGO dealing with violence against women and children, and project manager with major focus on equality, diversity and inclusion development and implementation at the British Council. Currently Kathrin is building her portfolio as a freelance consultant and trainer for all things diversity and inclusion. She is constantly learning and exploring fresh ideas, new approaches and keen on building global networks.

Doirean Wilson is the Diversity Lead, HRM Senior Lecturer (Community Engagement and Practice) and Chair of Middlesex University's Race, Religion and Beliefs Forum. She is an award-winning diversity expert who has successfully led nine postgraduate programmes, including the Executive MBA. She is a Visiting Professor of Religion and Multiculturalism for the Joint Council of Churches for All Nation's School of Theology, Leadership and Management. She has several postgraduate qualifications, including a Master's degree in HRM and a Doctorate in Professional Practice. Doirean is a Chartered CIPD Fellow, Fellow of the Royal Society of Arts, Fellow of the Institute of Spirituality in Economics and Society and a Senior Fellow of the Higher Education Academy. She is a former business consultant and journalist, Chair of Nubian Jak Community and advisory board member for the Ghana UK-Based Awards (GUBA).

Introduction to the Challenges of International Diversity Management

Fiona Bartels-Ellis, Mustafa F. Özbilgin, and Paul Gibbs

Abstract

The introduction discusses the reason for the book, its development rationale and outlines the context of the chapters.

1   Summary

This book reflects the growth in global organisations and institutions and how they manage diversity across their operation within different cultural and value domains. In this respect, the book is located in a growing area of management. This work is contextualised by the leader in the field. We then report on a co-production project by researchers from Middlesex University, the School of Oriental and African Studies (SOAS) and the British Council. This brings into the limelight the issues that exploration of global diversity management can create and the promise it can provide. The study presents candidly empirical evidence not reported academically elsewhere. Professor Mustafa Özbilgin outlines the literature and contest of global diversity management.

F. Bartels-Ellis
British Council, London, UK
e-mail: fiona.bartels-ellis@britishcouncil.org

M. F. Özbilgin
Chair in Organisational Behaviour, Brunel Business School, Brunel University London, London, UK
e-mail: mustafa.ozbilgin@brunel.ac.uk

P. Gibbs (✉)
Centre for Education Research and Scholarship, Middlesex University, London, UK
e-mail: p.gibbs@mdx.ac.uk

© Springer Nature Switzerland AG 2019
M. F. Özbilgin et al. (eds.), *Global Diversity Management*, Management for Professionals, https://doi.org/10.1007/978-3-030-19523-6_1

The second section gives voice to practitioners involved in international diversity, with commentaries on how they might reflect issues for more generally the development of diversity management. This uses storytelling to bring the powerful accounts into the service of diversity. The various voices heard in these short chapters are passionate and bring the reality of diversity engagement to life. Together, these two sections address the complexity of diversity in a nuanced way that reflects the different realities of those involved in the implementation of diversity.

The short final section draws insights and conclusions by weaving academic research with practitioners' action in the field of education. It is located within the deposition of compassion; for that is one of the key emergent forces of all the studies offered in this book. It is this combination that gives it a unique positioning in the global management literature.

2   What Is the Context of This Book?

The range of research into diversity is significant and broad. It deals with the complex relationship between equality, diversity, inclusion and human rights through a plethora of theoretical, methodological and empirical viewpoints. 'Diversity and inclusion' seems to be a key policy area for organisations, with the vast majority having a written policy or set of guidelines. Often these policies cover the majority of protected characteristics through legislation. However, translating policy into action can be challenging. Although there has been substantial research into the role played by diversity in organisations, particularly around diversity theory, there has been a lack of attention to the implementation of diversity policy internally. Those studies that have focused on implementation and the practical aspects of engagement with diversity agendas are characterised by contextual limitations (e.g. Foster & Harris's (2005) study, which exclusively looks at a large retail company). Kirton et al. suggest that there is a gap between policy agendas around diversity and implementation on the ground, which they attribute to 'managerial agency', although recognising that the process of implementing any such agenda is necessarily complex and involves a range of stakeholders (2016: 321).

By comparing studies that have looked at the implementation of diversity agendas across a variety of contexts, it is possible to identify a number of factors that appear to inhibit the adoption of such practices. On a fundamental level, Dick and Cassell explored broad resistance to diversity and initiatives that promote diversity, challenging the discourse that promotes diversity as being in the interest of all groups (2002: 954) and recognising that some groups might rebel or push back against such initiatives, for instance, White males (Arnold, 1997). Dick and Cassell argue that:

> The power relations that exist in any organization. . . ensure that any initiatives that are designed to further the interests of some groups will be targeted with discrediting discourses. . . and thus will compromise the subjectivity of any individual who benefits through them, and ensures that the credibility of the initiative will always be called into question at some time or other. (Dick & Cassell, 2002: 972)

Similarly, Greene and Kirton (2009) suggest that increasing diversity could ultimately lead to greater divide or conflict within teams. Diversity and identity are densely intertwined in ways often not explicitly demonstrated in the practical application of how differences are and should be managed in organisations and to what ends (Tatli & Özbilgin, 2012).

As well as this fundamental hurdle that organisations are likely have to overcome, there are a number of further issues identified in the literature relating to the more practical or logistical concerns of implementation. While the business case for diversity is acknowledged, it can be a 'hard sell', because the benefits are sometimes difficult to observe (at least in the short term) (Kulik, 2014: 131). This is a directly observed feature of the study by Kirton et al. (2016: 333). This relates closely to the somewhat short-termist approach (e.g. Schneider & Northcraft, 1999) adopted among managers, founded upon a lack of incentives to pursue diversity in contrast to the immediate cost or disruption. Similarly, if managers are not encouraged both to understand and appreciate the longer-term benefits from diversity, other initiatives might suffer a similar fate: online diversity training was viewed as a superficial 'tick-box' exercise by the managers, in Kirton et al.'s research (2016: 328), because the benefits were not clear.

Implementation of diversity relies on a range of stakeholders, as suggested above, which can be compromised when there are differences of interpretation or under-standing among these stakeholder groups. Kirton et al., meanwhile, found that there was a distinction between an approach founded upon not discriminating and one that actually valued diversity and that this distinction was evident within the management structure. The environment at the information technology firm that they studied allowed managers autonomy in the composition of their teams; 'thus, the teamwork structure and managerial agency lay at the core of the implementation of the diversity policy'. However, this led to a dislocation between company/corporate policy and managerial implementation. In the seminal text by Özbilgin and Tatli (2008), they identify a need for context-specific frames to understand how diversity management may work across different cultural and economic settings. Further, they claim analyses of diversity management processes demand the attention of the individual professionals who carry out the daily activities of diversity management.

This is what this book project tries to achieve. It brings out the two macro- and micro-perspectives through a context-setting first section. This provides the voices of academics in the research of global diversity management with the British Council and then, in the second section of the book, offers ten short diversity case stories by practitioners in the voices that they adopt in their practice. We then, in the final chapter, introduce a theme of compassion that we believe underpins the analysis of academics and practitioners, revealed through the medium of narrative. In doing so, we believe that this book will provide a fusion of approaches that will have value to a range of audiences and impact positively on the understanding, theorising and practice of global diversity.

3   The Book's Structure

The first section of the book contains chapters that discuss the nature of diversity management in the appropriate literature, along with the fifth chapter by the academic research team that conducted the main project discussed in this chapter. The second is entitled *What Do We Know About the Implementations of Equality, Diversity and Inclusion in the Workplace*, and it highlights the way in which the academic literature has looked at the issue of diversity management. The third chapter, *Global Diversity Management* by Mustafa Özbilgin, discusses the three main challenges that face global diversity management, that is, individualism, deregulation and financialisation. In response to these challenges, the chapter introduces three innovative approaches as contemporary remedies: intersectional solidarity, global value chain and synchronicity. Intersectional solidarity can help organisations to overcome the individualist tendency that renders diversity management practices ineffectual. Global value chain approaches can help the organisations to have a more robust and truthful accounting of diversity interventions across their value chain. Finally, the synchronicity approach challenges the domination of financial decisions on business case arguments, alerting practitioners to the wider possibilities of utility in causal forms of togetherness.

Fourth chapter, *Narrative Enquiry,* by Kate Maguire and Alison Scott-Baumann, suggests that a global values framework gives the opportunity to strive to make a good business case for adherence to such principles. As principles are more challenging to enact than to formulate, research into how they can be enacted in everyday matters of the organisation is needed to support this values portfolio. Current literature highlights the use of storytelling as sense-making, and, as such, it has become a growing trend in the narrative approach across disciplines and professional sectors. Its contributors are from anthropology, education, linguistics, translation studies, literature, politics, psychology and sociology, organisation studies and history. This chapter surfaces the link between local and grand narratives through an ethno-narrative approach contextualised within a recent study of diversity[1] and specifically global diversity.

The fifth and substantive chapter deals with the main study that underpins the whole book. It is entitled *Five Nations: A Diversity Study* and describes how a project was designed and implemented to capture and disseminate good practice in the area of equality, diversity and inclusion (diversity) within the British Council and to influence others through a study of the stories that local and international staff tell. The aim of the fieldwork was to gather data in storytelling/narrative form on the experiences of staff in using the diversity principles as embedded features in their projects, teaching and other deliverables, as well as informing ways of being with each other as colleagues, in selected British Council offices. This is a report of the outcome of this aspect of the fieldwork, which took place in Egypt, Ghana, Kenya, Jordan and Saudi Arabia, as selected by the British Council.

---

[1]Equality, diversity and inclusion.

We then move to the second section, which takes a different focus, away from academic research and towards diversity management professionals and their own stories. We present ten voices that speak to these experiences.

4 Sixth Chapter: Agota Bíró—What Makes You Successful at Diversity Management? A Personal Journey

In this chapter, Agota shares her personal learning journey to diversity management and the various formal and non-formal learning experiences that widened her horizons in this area. In her opinion, and because the measurement of personal development is often vague, it is important to rely on personal stories that outline the various influences on a person that contributed to their becoming more empowered to be change makers in this field. In her case, one of the British Council's programmes (Intercultural Navigators) was a very important point, which was later supplemented by her work within the organisation as a diversity lead. As a diversity lead, she has had to understand the organisation's diversity strategy and framework, and this enabled her to think about mainstreaming. All these experiences contributed to who she has become and how she works now, on the individual, team and organisational levels, with diversity and inclusion.

5 Seventh Chapter: Patti Boulaye—A Personal Account of Diversity

Patti shares narratives based on reflections on her personal and career life-course journey of diversity from two cultural standpoints. These experiences had a significant impact on her understanding of people differences and how these can be harnessed so that others can benefit.

She offers a critical review of her early learning, born of her Nigerian upbringing, that helped to shape her beliefs. She compares this experience with the reality of finding herself in a culture different from her own, due to the horrors of the Biafra war, before her journey to Britain.

This voyage exposed her not only to the menace of bigotry but to the richness of people's differences. This is what enabled her to conclude that the pursuit of diversity and the acceptance of the differences of our fellow human beings are vital to our survival globally.

6 Eighth Chapter: David Crabtree—The Theatre of the Classroom

The focus of David's case study is the Theatre of the Classroom, and, by this, he means everything that happens between teachers and pupils during lessons. He uses this concept alongside reflective practice to help educators plan and prepare to meet the needs of all pupils especially those who learn differently. His work has taken him to Africa, Asia, the Middle East and Europe. The question that sparks most discussion is, 'How can I meet the needs of everyone in the class when I also have to deal with the pupils with problems? 'The content of the case study will spotlight the key characteristics for educators to focus their attention upon in order to create inclusive teaching and learning. David declares that, 'In this theatre, let us create stars'.

7 Ninth Chapter: Simon Minty—Training on and Exploring Cultural Approaches to Disability

Simon works as an independent trainer and consultant in field of disability rather than broader diversity, not always a bad thing, as disability is often seen as the more awkward of the equality strands. He has worked internationally for more than 15 years, visiting over 20 countries from Albania to Ukraine and China to Oman. Some trips have been with the British Council, but he also works with international corporations such as Google, Goldman Sachs, HSBC and McDonalds. His experiences have shown that a different country often means a different cultural view of disability and of disabled people. He aims to understand the local approach, enhancing it where it is useful to improve the independence and life chances of disabled people there. Where it is more of a hindrance, say where disabled people have not had input, he will show how it can be improved. As a disabled person himself, he can experience these differences from the moment he arrives which both fascinates him and can frustrate him. He recognises they cannot be ignored and there is diversity in disability.

8 Tenth Chapter: Wayne Mullen—Tales from the Front

This chapter contains a series of vignettes based on Wayne's experience of leadership development and diversity work globally. Examples might include launching a 360-degree feedback process globally with great results—apart from in Asia, where participation was low and scores lacked differentiation. A trip to Hong Kong uncovered cultural barriers that hindered the process: employees talked about the difficulties that they had with their managers yet struggled to give them feedback. How do you make upward feedback in cultures where 'losing face' is to be avoided? How do you help employees to give upward feedback?

Whistleblowing or informing? Delivering a workshop to colleagues in human resources about how we would handle whistleblowing, he was met with silence from a group of normally energetic, vocal human resources professionals. What happens when you try to implement whistleblowing policies in post-Soviet Russia, where calling someone an informer is one of the worst insults you can use?

9 Eleventh Chapter: Asif Sadiq—Diversity in a Global Financial Organisation

The chapter will discuss D&I from an international business perspective, looking at how large organisations work in various international settings and exploring how organisations embed their diversity and inclusion principles in international settings and countries where local views on certain elements of diversity can be different from those of the organisation. Asif explores how managing an international workforce works in practical terms and how this raises both challenges and opportunities for a business, with a view to see how we can work towards creating truly diverse and inclusive international workplaces of the future and manage the challenges and opportunities this brings.

10 Twelfth Chapter: Kathrin Tietze—How to Start an Emotion-Reflective Journey

This chapter deals with case studies in relation to human relationships, personal feelings, reflection and development in the area of diversity implementation. Through examples drawn from her experience as a professional in international diversity management implementation, lecturer of diversity management and process worker/deep democracy practitioner, she highlights the importance of empowering people to recognise and deal with their feelings, privileges and the ever-changing power structures they partake in. For example, what are the good learning outcomes on a semester-long seminar on diversity management? For her, they include a student writing that they have questioned their beliefs; that they have discovered a whole new world, which they see differently; and that they are also rather confused now about what is right and wrong. For her, this is the beginning of change and the successful start of an emotion-reflective journey on self, the other and organisations, specifically here in the field of diversity management yet also applicable to a wider context.

11 Thirteenth Chapter: Abid Hussain—Making the Creative Case for Diversity Across Arts and Culture: An Outsider Looking in

Abid tells the story of the Arts Council's Creative Case for Diversity, how it impacts on him and his role in its success.

12   Fourteenth Chapter: Doirean Wilson—Promoting Cultural Awareness: A Means of Managing Global Diversity

Global diversity is a topic of much debate and significant importance today, resulting in the growth in national and international laws fashioned as a means to address discrimination and the rise in high-profile cases against many international firms. These occurrences are indicative of an inability to understand different cultures, which is a must when doing business abroad in different cultural environments. Research evidence suggests that cultural misunderstandings can result in hostility and suspicion. This can affect an organisation's reputation, sustainability and quest for success, thus arguing a need to be culturally aware. This chapter draws on findings of a study that explored cultural meanings of respect and how these meanings manifest among culturally diverse business students in the classroom. The aim is to provide insight into the cultural awareness practices addressing team conflict that are used to manage diversity among national and international learners.

The book closes with two chapters. The first is *At the Core of Diversity is Compassion*, by Paul Gibbs. This draws upon both the main study and the experiences offered in the other chapters to propose that compassion underpins the nature of international diversity management and that this disposition has a multi-cultural and global appeal, providing a structure for all diversity engagement. This is followed by a short reflection on compassion by an indigenous scholar, Jason De Santolo, on compassion which reminds us of the reason for this book.

References

Arnold, J. (1997). *Managing careers into the 21st century*. London: Paul Chapman Publishing.

Dick, P., & Cassell, C. (2002). Barriers to managing diversity in a UK constabulary: The role of discourse. *Journal of Management Studies, 39*(7), 953–976.

Foster, C., & Harris, L. (2005). Easy to say, difficult to do: Diversity management in retail. *Human Resource Management Journal, 15*(3), 4–17.

Greene, A., & Kirton, G. (2009). *Diversity management in the UK: Organisational and stakeholder experiences*. London: Routledge.

Kirton, G., Robertson, M., & Avdelidou-Fischer, N. (2016). Valuing and value in diversity: The policy implementation gap in an IT firm. *Human Resource Management Journal, 26*(3), 321–336.

Kulik, C. (2014). Working below and above the line: The research–practice gap in diversity management. *Human Resource Management Journal, 24*(2), 129–144.

Özbilgin, M., & Tatli, A. (2008). *Global diversity management: An evidence-based approach*. Basingstoke: Palgrave Macmillan.

Schneider, S., & Northcraft, G. (1999). Three social dilemmas of workforce diversity in organisations: A social identity perspective. *Human Relations, 52*(11), 1445–1467.

Tatli, A., & Özbilgin, M. (2012). An emic approach to intersectional study of diversity at work: A Bourdieuan framing. *International Journal of Management Reviews, 142*, 180–200.

Part I

Thinking About and Doing Large-Scale Projects

What Do We Know About the Implementations of Equality, Diversity and Inclusion in the Workplace?

Alison Scott-Baumann, Paul Gibbs, Alex Elwick, and Kate Maguire

Abstract

This short literature review considers the academic literature that nests diversity management within an international context. It covers the issues in a general way before foregrounding the literature in diversity management and how this might be implemented in organisations. Its function is to give an overview which is built upon in the next chapter.

1   Scene Setting

Thinking about the underlying issue of diversity and open pathways to understanding shows us how the human condition is complicated by incompatible forces: the intellect cannot feel emotion fully, and our senses can never be rational. How, then, can we act in a just and fair manner towards each other? David Hume brilliantly asserted (1748/1998) that we respond to our senses' desires, act as we wish to and then rationalise our choices after the event. He believed humans to be bound together by natural affection for each other, but saw little natural justice in human nature or the will to follow shared rights, as that would mean having to abandon one's desires

A. Scott-Baumann (✉)
Department of Religions and Philosophies, SOAS, London, UK
e-mail: as150@soas.ac.uk

P. Gibbs · A. Elwick
Centre for Education Research and Scholarship, Middlesex University, London, UK
e-mail: p.gibbs@mdx.ac.uk; a.elwick@mdx.ac.uk

K. Maguire
Faculty of Professional and Social Sciences, Hendon Campus Middlesex University, London, UK
e-mail: k.maguire@mdx.ac.uk

© Springer Nature Switzerland AG 2019
M. F. Özbilgin et al. (eds.), *Global Diversity Management*, Management for
Professionals, https://doi.org/10.1007/978-3-030-19523-6_2

and one's habits for the common good. Bentham (1843) went even further and mocked the very idea that humans are entitled to natural rights, calling such a hope 'nonsense upon stilts'. Enlightenment thought, from Kant (1788/1996) onwards, has often proposed a third position, a place where intellect, abstract thought, and our senses, physical responses, can meet. In order to establish, recognise and maintain such a third term, it is necessary to accept insecurity, for it will be necessary to oscillate between the terms and accept provisionality and a degree of relativism: it is both rationally and emotionally impossible to have a clear and unambiguous understanding of diversity, because difference is what defines diversity.

The work of the British Council is informed by human rights principles that seek to guarantee freedom of thought, conscience and religion. Yet remaining flexible and relativist about our understanding of equality and diversity invites an element of subjectivity that is at odds with human rights and with organisational culture: flexibility implies that some may be treated differently from others, and this contradicts the ideas enshrined in equality legislation.

Indeed, the United Nations (UN) Global Compact principles exist to meet fundamental responsibilities in the areas of human rights, labour, environment and anti-corruption. Central to this development of diversity is the *Universal Declaration of Human Rights* (http://www.un.org/en/universal-declaration-human-rights/index.html) of the United Nations. This imperative and the consequential duties and responsibilities that fall upon countries and companies are monitored through the Office of the United Nations High Commissioner for Human Rights (OHCHR). Its work is important in raising issues of common compliance to international human rights systems and of the apparatus for the protection of human rights, in order to enhance and thus promote a fuller observance of those rights, in a just and balanced manner. These rights include the rights that directly impinge on the development of diversity. They include conventions on the rights of indigenous people and minorities, women, children, disabled and older persons, and the prevention of unjustified discrimination.

1.1   Foregrounding Diversity Management

The range of research into diversity is significant and broad. It deals with the complex relationship between equality, diversity, inclusion and human rights through a plethora of various theoretical, methodological and empirical viewpoints. It has, at its core, a business rationale of the effects of identity group upon the potential for organisational enhancement in processes and outcomes that has emerged in the United States but has spread to other Western countries (Zanoni & Janssens, 2008). Indeed, Tatli has suggested that diversity management originated in the late 1980s in the United States as a supposedly new management parading to 'deal with the issues of workplace inequality and diversity' (2011: 238).

This has led to studies that demonstrate that specific identities and diversity are constructed in distinct ways in distinctive social, historical and organisational contexts (Zanoni & Janssens, 2004). Identities are pre-defined, and the focus then tends to be on which identities are salient in the business process, rather than on the context shaping the meaning of identity itself. Significant numbers[1] of studies have shown the benefits of diversity and equality management for organisations. This literature shows that well-managed integrative approaches to equality and diversity have resulted in higher labour productivity, higher levels of employee innovation and lower voluntary turnover (Armstrong, Flood, Guthrie, Liu, MacCurtain, et al., 2010; Evans, 2014). Of specific relevance to this study with the British Council, Gotsis and Kortezi (2013) suggest that a strategy based upon ethical concepts of organisational virtue, care and human dignity will result in financial benefits for the organisation. Indeed, numerous studies have shown that top-management diversity positively influences a firm's performance and financial results (Baixauli-Soler, Belda-Ruiz, & Sanchez-Marin, 2015).

However, the literature on diversity management has also followed a path of what Oswick and Moon (2014) call 'management fashion', where each term has come to dominate the others in the literature, and this domination is enforced by a rhetoric of disparagement of previous work. They state that by 'dispensing with the rhetorical framing of new antidiscrimination approaches as "better" and instead re-presenting them as "different", it might be possible to move beyond the unhealthy marginaliza- tion of valuable approaches simply because they are not fashionable' (2014: 36). Yet diversity management is critiqued in much of the literature, not for its contribution to improving the context and engagement with others but for its lack of recognition of individual identity—in and for itself, diversity management institutionalises diver- sity and neglects issues of power. A recent overview concluded that critical diversity studies (Zanoni, Janssens, Benschop, & Nkomo, 2010) rest on three primary critiques of mainstream diversity management: a positivist ontology based on notions of a fixed identity, an inadequate theorisation of power and the minimal place given to the influences of context. Diversity and identity are profoundly intertwined in ways often not explicitly seen in the practical application of how differences are and should be managed in organisations and to what ends (Tatli & Özbilgin, 2012). This paradigm does have its critics, for it has tended to assume first that identities are conceptualised as fixed and unproblematic and taking a model of White, heterosexual, Western, middle-class able-bodied men as the reference point. Second, there is an inadequate theorisation of power and thirdly a tendency to downplay the organisational and societal context in shaping the meaning of diversity (Siebers, 2009). Indeed, Tatli and Özbilgin (2012) suggest an emergent Bourdieuan approach to diversity, where diversity is managed in response to the role that it plays in generating power, privilege advantage, disadvantage, discrimination and inequal- ity within the workforce. This is a dynamic view of the workplace as one that frames diversity management as a dynamic construction, which 'attends to temporal and geographic conceptuality of ructions of power, privilege, inequality and disadvan- tage' (2012: 181).

---

[1]See, for a comprehensive review, Davis, Frolova, & Callahan (2016).

2   Implementing Diversity Management: An Under-Researched Area

Diversity and inclusion seem to be a key policy area for organisations, and the vast majority have a written policy or set of guidelines. Often, as well, these policies cover the majority of characteristics protected through legalisation. However, translating policy into action can be challenging. Although there has been substantial research into the role played by diversity in organisations, particularly around diversity theory, there has been a lack of attention to the implementation of diversity policy internally. Those studies that have focused on implementation and the practical aspects of engagement with diversity agendas are characterised by contextual limitations (e.g. Foster & Harris' (2005) study, which exclusively looked at a large retail company). Kirton, Robertson and Avdelidou-Fischer suggested that there is a gap between policy agendas around diversity and implementation on the ground, which they attributed to 'managerial agency', although recognising that the process of implementing any such agenda is necessarily complex and involves a range of stakeholders (2016: 321).

By comparing studies that have looked at the implementation of diversity agendas across a variety of contexts, it is possible to identify a number of factors that appear to inhibit the adoption of such practices. On a fundamental level, Dick and Cassell explored broad resistance to diversity and initiatives that promote diversity, challenging the discourse that promotes diversity as being in the interest of all groups (2002: 954) and recognising that some groups might rebel or push back against such initiatives, for instance, White males (Arnold, 1997). Dick and Cassell argued that:

> The power relations that exist in any organization… ensure that any initiatives that are designed to further the interests of some groups will be targeted with discrediting discourses… and thus will compromise the subjectivity of any individual who benefits through them, and ensures that the credibility of the initiative will always be called into question at some time or other. (Dick & Cassell, 2002: 972)

Similarly, Greene and Kirton suggested that increasing diversity could ultimately lead to greater divide or conflict within teams (2009).

As well as this fundamental hurdle that organisations are likely to have to overcome, there are a number of issues identified in the literature, and these relate to the more practical or logistical concerns of implementation. While the business case for diversity is acknowledged (e.g. SHRM, 2009), it can be a 'hard sell' because the benefits are sometimes difficult to observe (at least in the short term) (Kulik, 2014: 131)—a directly observed feature of the study by Kirton et al. (2016: 333). This relates closely to a somewhat short-termist approach (e.g. Schneider & Northcraft, 1999) adopted among managers, founded upon a lack of incentives to pursue diversity in the face to the immediate cost or disruption. Similarly, if managers are not encouraged to both understand and appreciate the longer-term benefits from diversity, other initiatives might suffer a similar fate: online diversity training was viewed as a superficial 'tick-box' exercise by the managers in Kirton et al.'s research (2016: 328), because the benefits weren't clear.

Implementation of diversity relies on a range of stakeholders, as suggested above, which can be compromised when there are differences of interpretation or understanding among these stakeholder groups. Foster and Harris' research found that because the concept of diversity itself was ill-defined and open to interpretation, there was 'a lack of a common understanding', and this contributed to difficulties in implementation (2005: 10) as a result of 'inconsistencies and the dominance of expediency among those required to put the concept into practice' (2005: 5). Kirton et al., meanwhile, found that there was a distinction between an approach founded upon not discriminating and one that actually valued diversity and that this distinction was evident within the management structure (2016: 328). The environment at the IT firm that they studied allowed managers autonomy regarding the composition of their teams; 'thus, the teamwork structure and managerial agency lay at the core of the implementation of the diversity policy' (Kirton et al., 2016: 325). However, this led to a dislocation between company/corporate policy and managerial implementation.

A further failing on the part of organisations was often that diversity strategies were not fully embedded; instead, corporate policies employed rhetoric to imply value or appealed to managers' common sense and fairness (Kirton et al., 2016: 333). A series of studies, however, have shown that, on its own, rhetoric is largely unsuccessful (e.g. Foster & Harris, 2005; Greene & Kirton, 2009). As such, instead of being fully embedded, implementation of diversity feels superficial:

> The lack of clarity surrounding the concept of 'managing diversity' and the variable mix of contextual influences meant that for many operational managers managing diversity became whatever was deemed to be the most expedient solution at the time. (Foster & Harris, 2005: 13)

While there is clearly a host of difficulties associated with the implementation of diversity, the literature does suggest routes to success for organisations, and these clearly relate to the problems identified above. Of primacy was the ideal that managers—those ultimately responsible for activating processes—should feel that they owned these processes. Although human resources (HR) departments often play important roles, the diversity strategy should be led by managers themselves (Kirton et al., 2016: 328). Necessarily, this approach must be partnered by a strong accountability structure (Gilbert & Ivancevich, 2000).

Perhaps unsurprisingly, stakeholder engagement is another key marker of more successful approaches. Even when HR specialists do undertake much of the work around initiatives, 'management engagement' is absolutely vital to their success (Kirton et al., 2016: 328). Disseminating the business imperative to management enables them to recognise the importance of their role, and holistic training plans ensure that this is not just communicated but understood (SHRM, 2009). The SHRM report also suggested that it can be beneficial to offer 'appropriate management incentives' in order to show commitment to the process and to motivate managers

(2009: 28). Ultimately, a successful approach to the implementation of diversity in an organisation must be guided by an understanding and recognition of value in workforce diversity combined with the practical aspects of engaging managers in the corporate agenda for diversity (Kirton et al., 2016, 321). Thus far, there is little empirical work to suggest that implementation of diversity policies improves productivity or effectiveness ('Storytelling and diversity management', an unpublished paper by Mustafa Özbilgin & Ahu Tatli).

2.1 The Centralising of an International Policy

Within this huge literature indicated above, we will concentrate on the implementation of management and its relationship to the international context, where an organisation has a central head office and an international structure. We suggest that the literature illustrates how the authors of policy on the one hand and practitioners on the other have specific positions on how they, respectively, develop diversity policies or engage with diversity, and that these may not be congruent. Indeed, against this background Yang and Konrad (2011) show that diversity management policies will necessarily differ due to a complex mix of legalisation and national policies. Daya (2014) argues that there is limited research on how organisation operates in multi-contexts and especially in transitional economies. For instance, as suggested by Edwards, Marginson, and Ferner (2013), there is potential in all multinational organisations for tensions between the converging notion of technology, markets and multinational practices and the divergence of cultures and institutions. This leads to a 'country of origin' effect by the central head office on how the policies are implemented, emphasised or countered and to what degree, and this requires a study of how central policy towards diversity management is interpreted and practised in foreign subsidiaries.

To investigate these issues, Syed and Özbilgin (2009) have adopted an analysis of different realities to explore the international transfer of practices consisting of *macro*-level (laws, national cultures); *meso*-level (organisational approaches), which are often interwoven; and *micro*-level factors (identity and relationships). Within such a framework, the research indicates that the greater the legal difference between the host and the home countries, the smaller the degree of similarity between the *macro* and *meso* practices. A number of important studies have recently used this approach in multinational studies, and three are discussed briefly here: Daya's (2014) study in South Africa, Pringle and Ryan's (2015) in New Zealand and Bešić and Hirt's (2016) in Austria and Bosnia.

In the first of these studies, Daya identifies that in multinational organisations working in South Africa, the leaders of these pluralistic and multicultural organisations should focus their attention on developing inclusion areas that are weak and require more consideration. She suggests that in order to build multicultural, inclusive environments, organisations should continuously focus on achieving diverse representation on all levels through senior leadership, organisation climate, organisational belonging, communication and transparent recruitment, promotion and development.

The Pringle and Ryan research is a study of Maori culture in the profession of accounting: they argue that 'multi-level analyses of context and power have the potential to enhance theory and practice of diversity management' (2015: 479) and that an analysis of power will show multiple diversity managements, specific to country, region and organisation. Further, Bešić and Hirt (2016) reveal challenges for the transferability of such diversity management arguing that societal, legal and political factors determine the general view of diversity management and hence this influences the transferability of such practices. They also concluded that there is a need for clarity when seeking interconnectedness of local practice with central policy diversity management. They support the findings of Pringle and Ryan (2015), in that authors do not identify a significant transfer of diversity management practices from the head office to its foreign subsidiaries and attribute this to concerns relating to local cultural values and even to the trivialising of important issues including ethnicity.

The idea of realities as a dynamic field of relationships provides the framework within which the project was conducted and report our narrative study. The second part of this review discusses the narrative and interpretive approach and its relevance to the project. The approach has a strong endorsement from Greeff's (2015) study in South Africa, where he concludes that:

> it becomes clear that organisations are only in a position to wholly or utterly manage diversity once the collectively constructed experience of employees within their specific organisational context are understood, in all its diversity. (2015: 508)

2.2   Researching Diversity Management

There is a wide and varied literature on approaches and methods within the rubric of narrative inquiry. Texts explore the methodological requirements of approaches and offer detailed processes and rationales for how data should be collected and analysis. The most interesting and recent texts include Andrews, Squire, and Tamboukou (2013), De Fina (2011), Livholts and Tamboukou (2015), Underberg and Zorn (2014) and Wells (2011).

The use of narrative inquiry in the literature on equality, diversity and inclusion is extensive and beyond the scope of this paper to catalogue in detail. Sufficient, for this study, is to give an indicative outline of the extent, forms of analysis used and the topics covered. The analysis is constructed by selecting academic papers in which diversity projects which have used narrative enquiry in their research methods. This search was conducted using the Middlesex University search engine 'Summon', searching for full texts and using equity, diversity and inclusion with stories. There were over 500 for the year 2016. To give an indicative idea of the driplines and topic the final 6 months of 2016, 190 academic papers were analysed. The results reveal that management/business/human resources accounted for the largest number of papers (28%) followed by social policy/sociology (20%), education (15%) and then law (9%), communication/media studies (8%) and health care (8%). There were a number of other but smaller categories. The topics in this are varied and included studies on lesbian, gay, bisexual, transgender, queer, plus (LGBTQ+), disability, children's rights, multiculturalism and racism. The papers were written by or upon the following geographic regions: Europe, Africa, South Asia, the United States and Australia. The most explicitly philosophical stances were feminism and humanitarianism

The interrelationship of theory and ethnography (cultural description) in the building of understanding and sense-making lies at the core of the discipline of anthropology, integrating its commitment to taking seriously individual lives within the comparative dimension of an institutional existence which is both countercultural and chosen. Certainly, sociocultural anthropologists have long studied myths, legends, life histories and other stories for what they tell us about the storyteller, their audiences and the social and cultural frameworks in which the stories are told.

The ethnographic approach used here builds upon the synthesis developed by Maggio (2014), from the anthropological literature, and considers the story at three levels.

- The relational—where dynamics between the people involved in the storytelling situation are considered. These might include the 'the storyteller(s), the listener (s), but also the entities who take the role of characters in the story, who might be real persons (such as members of the storyteller or listener's social network) or representations of real persons (such as fictional versions or caricatures)' (ibid.: 92).
- The content of the story—here the focus is on the action of telling and listening to stories and the reasons why a story is particularly appealing for a particular audience which 'might be found in people's reactions to the cultural relevance of characters, plot, and/or theme of the story' (ibid.: 93).
- The type of storytelling techniques—how to obtain particular effects; how shared knowledge is negotiated with their audience and the stories formulated accordingly and 'to what extent they show their personal selves as opposed to making themselves mere medium for the telling of the story' (ibid.).

The approach is well suited to studying subjectivity and identity in context largely because of the importance given to imagination and the human involvement in constructing a story as a way to make meaning of both familiar and strange phenomena experienced in space, place and time. Ethno-narratives also reveal much about social life or culture, as culture, as a system of homogeneous and heterogeneous practices, speak through a story. Finally, following good practice, we support the view that ethnographies should be written or embodied in a way that is accessible to most of the people who provided the original information.

3   Contextualising an International Policy

There is no convincing evidence of a causal or even correlational relationship between increased equality, diversity and inclusion and their professed benefits, nor is it clear whether business models are asking the right questions (Özbilgin, Tatli, Ipek, & Sameer, 2016). More importantly, Zanoni's et al. (2010) tripartite challenge to diversity studies remains unanswered, that is, that such work is often weakened by three specific features: *a positivist ontology based on notions of a fixed identity, an inadequate theorisation of power and the minimal place given to the influences of context.* These three features will provide the structure for this section and seek to provide solutions. Setting aside the literature discussed in the paragraphs above, we will concentrate on looking at Zanoni's challenge with regard to research about the implementation of management and its relationship to the international context, where an organisation has a central head office and an international structure.

With regard to *a positivist ontology based on notions of fixed identity*, we note that sampling may reflect researchers' assumptions: Sippola and Smale interviewed a small sample of 12 Finnish staff in order to look at a company (TRANSCO) that has operations in over a hundred countries (2007). The voices of those considered to be diverse are not heard in that research and, indeed, are very seldom heard in current research.

We suggest that the literature illustrates how the authors of policy, on the one hand, and practitioners, on the other, have specific positions on how they, respectively, develop diversity policies or engage with diversity and that these may not be congruent. Marfelt and Muhr assert that it is not the actual differences among people that determine diversity practices, but the ways in which diversity 'is produced, presented and negotiated in a given context' (2016: 248). As a solution to this, Tatli and Özbilgin offer a way of thinking differently (emic) that identifies relations and processes of power instead of working with accepted types of diversity, which involves accepting the status quo (etic) (2012: 196). Emerging from the diversity management sampled in previous paragraphs is a fascinating strand that challenges the positivist thinking upon which such work is often based. This challenge is made either by critiquing management literature (Marfelt & Muhr, 2016) or by offering a new paradigm taken from beyond the business world (Tatli & Özbilgin, 2012), and this is particularly necessary in international contexts.

We need to account for the characteristics of international organisations: Yang and Konrad (2011) show that diversity management policies will necessarily differ due to a complex mix of legalisation and national policies (which is an unavoidable source of 'positivist' thinking). Indeed, Daya (2014) argues that there is limited research on how organisations operate in multi-contexts and especially in transition economics. For instance, in all multinational organisations, there is the potential, as suggested by Edwards et al. (2013), for tensions between the converging notion of technology, markets and multinational practices and the divergence of cultures and institutions. This leads to a country of origin effect of the central head office on how the policies are implemented, emphasised or countered and to what degree'. It requires a study of how central policy towards diversity management is interpreted and practised in foreign subsidiaries.

To investigate these issues, Syed and Özbilgin (2009) have adopted an analysis of different realities to explore the international transfer of practices consisting of *macro*-level (laws, national cultures); *meso*-level (organisational approaches), which are often interwoven; and *micro*-level factors (identity and relationships). Within such a framework, the research indicates that the greater the legal difference between the host and the home countries, the lower the degree of similarity between the *macro* and *meso* practices. A number of important studies have recently used this approach in multinational studies, and three are discussed briefly here: Daya's study (2014) in South Africa, Pringle and Ryan's study (2015) in New Zealand and Bešić and Hirt's study (2016) in Austria and Bosnia.

In the first of these studies, Daya identifies that in multinational organisations working in South Africa, the leaders of these pluralistic and multicultural organisations should focus their attention on developing inclusion areas that are weak and require more consideration. She suggests that in order to build multicultural, inclusive environments, organisations should continuously focus on achieving diverse representation on all levels through senior leadership, organisation climate, organisational belonging, communication and transparent recruitment, promotion and development. It is worth pausing for consideration of the issues around leadership and diversity in international settings: the literature tends to rely upon researching leaders' attitudes towards diversity, rather than their impact in increasing diversity. Moreover, these research models do not question the conventional definitions of diversity (Nielson, 2010; Ng & Sears, 2012).

With regard to Zanoni's second challenge, *the inadequate theorisation of power*, Pringle and Ryan conducted a research study of Maori culture in the profession of accounting: they argue that 'multi-level analyses of context and power have the potential to enhance theory and practice of diversity management' (2015: 479) and that an analysis of power will show multiple diversity managements specific to country, region and organisation. Further, Bešić and Hirt (2016) reveal challenges for the transferability of such diversity management, arguing that societal, legal and political factors determine the general view of diversity management; hence this influences the transferability of such practices. They also conclude that there is a need for clarity when seeking the interconnectedness of local practice with central policy diversity management. They support the findings of Pringle and Ryan (2015) in that the authors do not identify a significant transfer of diversity management practices and power from the head office to its foreign subsidiaries, attributing this to concerns relating to local cultural values and even to the trivialising of important issues, including ethnicity.

There are certain identifiable trends in the literature: when conducting literature reviews on the subject and focusing upon international human resource management as if it is a measurable phenomenon, poor consideration is given to complex issues around power, equality and inclusion (Holck, Muhr, & Villesèche, 2016; Scroggins & Benson, 2010). Even acknowledging this fact has not usually led to deeper investigations (Shen, Chanda, D'Netto, & Monga, 2009; Shin & Park, 2013), although Lauring (2013) begins to extrapolate from power to its possible impacts, arguing that headquarters and subsidiaries need to be in constant dialogue about international and local issues, their interconnectedness and their possible relationships.

Tatli and Özbilgin propose that we need to look much harder to find the sources of power. They draw on French philosopher Pierre Bourdieu to analyse diversity through identifying relations and processes of power. Their 'emic' approach looks ahead with a view of human existence as dynamic and growing and rejects the 'etic' approach in which ideas about diversity are pre-decided and thus form a pre-existent source of power through labelling. They use Bourdieu's analysis of human activity as determined by capitals (economic, social, symbolic and cultural) to show 'how privilege and disadvantage work across the lines of difference' (2012: 196). Transnational dialogue and transfunctional partnerships are advocated (Özbilgin et al., 2016).

Thirdly, in Zanoni's challenge, what can we do *to be more sensitive to context?* Some advances have been made here through research in international contexts, but must be treated with caution. Lauring and Selmer (2011), for example, consider language as part of context and analyse the use of English as the common corporate language in culturally diverse organisations. They conclude that diversity improves when English is used in this way, but their work was conducted in Denmark among university academics from many countries, so English seemed reasonable as a shared language.

If we look at the approach of Tatli and Özbilgin (2012), they look critically at the context of management literature itself and assert the need to draw on ideas from beyond management literature. In using Bourdieu to suggest an emergent approach to diversity, they take diversity to be managed in context in response to the role that it plays in generating power and in privileging advantage, disadvantage, discrimination and inequality within the workforce. They are offering us a critical view of the workplace as one framing diversity management as a contextualised dynamic construction that 'attends to temporal and geographic conceptuality of ructions of power, privilege, inequality and disadvantage' (2012: 181). Again, the voice of the person viewed as different in the workplace is not present in their research, yet they offer a different and potentially productive way of understanding.

4   Where Next?

The following chapters take this context chapter and develop it further in a comprehensive discussion of global diversity management that is followed by a more in-depth exploration of the methodological issues of narrative inquiry as a precursor to a discussion of the main topic of this section, the case study of diversity management within the British Council in more detail and its appropriateness for diversity management studies.

References

Andrews, M., Squire, C., & Tamboukou, M. (2013). *Doing narrative research*. London: Sage.

Armstrong, C., Flood, P. C., Guthrie, J. P., Liu, W., MacCurtain, S., & Mkamwa, T. (2010). The impact of diversity and equality management on firm performance: Beyond high performance work systems. *Human Resource Management, 49*(6), 977–998.

Arnold, J. (1997). *Managing careers into the 21st century*. London: Paul Chapman Publishing.

Baixauli-Soler, J. S., Belda-Ruiz, M., & Sanchez-Marin, G. (2015). Executive stock options, gender diversity in the top management team, and firm risk-taking. *Journal of Business Research, 68* (2), 451–463.

Bentham, J. (1843/2002). Rights, representation, and reform: Nonsense upon stilts and other writings on the French Revolution. In P. Schofield, C. Pease-Watkin, & C. Blamires (Eds.), *The collected works of Jeremy Bentham* (pp. 317–401). Oxford: Oxford University Press.

Bešić, A., & Hirt, C. (2016). Diversity management across borders: The role of the national context. *Equality, Diversity and Inclusion, 35*(2), 123–135.

Davis, P. J., Frolova, Y., & Callahan, W. (2016). Workplace diversity management in Australia. *Equality, Diversity and Inclusion: An International Journal, 35*(2), 81–98. https://doi.org/10. 1108/EDI-03-2015-0020.

Daya, P. (2014). Diversity and inclusion in an emerging market context. *Equality, Diversity and Inclusion: An International Journal, 33*(3), 293–308.

De Fina, A. (2011). *Analyzing narrative: Discourse and sociolinguistic perspectives*. Cambridge: Cambridge University Press.

Dick, P., & Cassell, C. (2002). Barriers to managing diversity in a UK constabulary: The role of discourse. *Journal of Management Studies, 39*(7), 953–976.

Edwards, T., Marginson, P., & Ferner, A. (2013). Multinational companies in cross-national context: Integration, differentiation, and the interactions between MNCs and nation states. *Industrial and Labor Relations Review, 66*(3), 547–587.

Evans, C. (2014). Diversity management and organizational change. *Equality, Diversity and Inclusion, 33*(6), 482–493.

Foster, C., & Harris, L. (2005). 'Easy to say difficult to do': Diversity management in retail. *Human Resource Management Journal, 15*(3), 4–17.

Gilbert, J., & Ivancevich, J. (2000). Valuing diversity: A tale of two organisations. *Academy of Management Executive, 14*(1), 93–105.

Gotsis, G., & Kortezi, Z. (2013). Ethical paradigms as potential foundations of diversity management initiatives in business organizations. *Journal of Organizational Change Management, 26* (6), 948–976.

Greeff, W. J. (2015). Organisational diversity: Making the case for contextual interpretivism. *Equality, Diversity and Inclusion: An International Journal, 34*(6), 496–509.

Greene, A., & Kirton, G. (2009). *Diversity management in the UK: Organisational and stakeholder experiences*. London: Routledge.

Holck, L., Muhr, S. l., & Villesèche, F. (2016). Identity, diversity and diversity management: On theoretical connections, assumptions and implications for practice. *Equality, Diversity and Inclusion: An International Journal, 35*(11), 48–64.

Hume, D. (1748/1998). Section V, Sceptical solution of these doubts. In A. Flew (Ed.), *David Hume. An enquiry concerning human understanding*. Illinois: Open Court Publishing.

Kant, I. (1788/1996). Critique of practical reason. In M. Gregor (Ed. & Trans.), *The Cambridge edition of the works of Immanuel Kant: Practical philosophy* (p. 5.99). Cambridge: Cambridge University Press.

Kirton, G., Robertson, M., & Avdelidou-Fischer, N. (2016). Valuing and value in diversity: The policy implementation gap in an IT firm. *Human Resource Management Journal, 26*(3), 321–336.

Kulik, C. (2014). Working below and above the line: The research-practice gap in diversity management. *Human Resource Management Journal, 24*(2), 129–144.

Lauring, J. (2013). International diversity management. *British Journal of Management, 24*, 211–224.

Lauring, J., & Selmer, J. (2011). International language management and diversity climate in multicultural organizations. *International Business Review, 21*, 156–166.

Livholts, M., & Tamboukou, M. (2015). *Discourse and narrative methods.* London: Sage.

Maggio, R. (2014). The anthropology of storytelling and the storytelling of anthropology. *Journal of comparative Research in Anthropology and Sociology, 5*, 89–106.

Marfelt, M. M., & Muhr, S. L. (2016). Managing protean diversity. *International Journal of Cross Cultural Management, 16*(2), 231–251.

Ng, E., & Sears, G. (2012). CEO leadership styles and the implementation of organizational diversity practices. *Journal of Business Ethics, 105*, 41–52.

Nielsen, S. (2010). Top management team diversity. *International Journal of Management Reviews, 12*, 301–316.

Oswick, C., & Moon, M. (2014). Discourses of diversity, equality and inclusion: Trenchant formulations or transient fashions? *British Journal of Management, 25*, 23–39.

Özbilgin, A., Tatli, A., Ipek, G., & Sameer, M. (2016). Four approaches to accounting for diversity in global organisations. *Critical Perspectives on Accounting, 35*, 88–99.

Pringle, J. K., & Ryan, I. (2015). Understanding context in diversity management: A multi-level analysis. *Equality, Diversity and Inclusion, 34*(6), 470–482.

Schneider, S., & Northcraft, G. (1999). Three social dilemmas of workforce diversity in organisations: A social identity perspective. *Human Relations, 52*(11), 1445–1467.

Scroggins, W., & Benson, P. (2010). International human resource management. *Personnel Review, 39*(4), 409–413.

Shen, J., Chanda, A., D'Netto, B., & Monga, M. (2009). Managing diversity through human resource management: An international perspective and conceptual framework. *International Journal of Human Resource Management, 20*(2), 235–251.

Shin, H. Y., & Park, H. J. (2013). *What are the key factors in managing diversity and inclusion successfully in large international organisations?* Cornell University ILR School. Available at: http://digitalcommons.ilr.cornell.edu/cgi/viewcontent.cgi?article=1044&context=student

SHRM. (2009). *Global diversity and inclusion.* Alexandria, VA: Society for Human Resource Management.

Siebers, H. (2009). Struggles for recognition: The politics of racioethnic identity among Dutch national tax administrators. *Scandinavian Journal of Management, 25*(1), 73–84.

Sippola, A., & Smale, A. (2007). The global integration of diversity management. *International Journal of Human Resource Management, 18*(11), 1895–1916.

Syed, J., & Özbilgin, M. (2009). A relational framework for international transfer of diversity management practices. *Human Resource Management, 20*(12), 2435–2453.

Tatli, A. (2011). A multi-layered exploration of the diversity management field: Diversity discourses, practices and practitioners in the UK. *British Journal of Management, 22*, 238–253.

Tatli, A., & Özbilgin, M. (2012). An emic approach to intersectional study of diversity at work: A Bourdieuan framing. *International Journal of Management Review, 14*(2), 180–200.

Underberg, N. M., & Zorn, E. (2014). *Digital ethnography: Anthropology, narrative, and new media.* Austin: University of Texas Press.

Wells, K. (2011). *Narrative inquiry.* Oxford: Oxford University Press.

Yang, Y., & Konrad, A. M. (2011). Understanding diversity management practices: Implications of institutional theory and resource-based theory. *Group & Organization Management, 36*(1), 6–38.

Zanoni, P., & Janssens, M. (2004). Deconstructing difference: The rhetoric of human resource managers' diversity discourses. *Organization Studies, 25*, 55–74.

Zanoni, P., & Janssens, M. (2008, July). *Contesting institutions across borders: The case of diversity management in a European branch of a US multinational.* Presented at EGOS Colloquium 'Upsetting Organizations', Amsterdam.

Zanoni, P., Janssens, M., Benschop, Y., & Nkomo, S. (2010). Unpacking diversity, grasping inequality: Rethinking difference through critical perspectives. *Organization, 17*(1), 9–29.

Global Diversity Management

Mustafa F. Özbilgin

Abstract

Managing diversity is an imperative for organisations of all sectors and sizes. If managed effectively, workforce diversity promises to have positive social, economic and environmental consequences by removing barriers to contributions of individuals from diverse backgrounds; by transforming ways of thinking, structures and routines of work; and by regulating work and life in unprecedented ways. As the literature on diversity management is littered with narrow rationales, it may seem as if workforce diversity does not have intrinsic merit or wider purpose (social, economic and environment) than that. This chapter brings together a wider range of rationales than just organisational longevity and sustainability alone in pursuing diversity management. It explores the practice of global diversity management (GDM) through models of change and brings evidence together from field studies and organisational case studies. The chapter discusses the three main challenges that face GDM: individualism, deregulation and financialisation. In response to these challenges, the chapter introduces three innovative approaches as contemporary remedies: intersectional solidarity, global value chain and synchronicity, respectively. Intersectional solidarity can help organisations to overcome the individualist tendency that renders diversity management practices ineffectual. The global value chain approach can help organisations to have a more robust and meaningful accounting of diversity interventions across their value chain. Finally, the synchronicity approach challenges the domination of financial decisions on business case arguments, alerting practitioners to the wider possibilities of social, economic and environmental benefits in acausal forms of togetherness and coexistence.

M. F. Özbilgin (✉)
Chair in Organisational Behaviour, Brunel Business School, Brunel University London, London, UK
e-mail: mustafa.ozbilgin@brunel.ac.uk

© Springer Nature Switzerland AG 2019
M. F. Özbilgin et al. (eds.), *Global Diversity Management*, Management for Professionals, https://doi.org/10.1007/978-3-030-19523-6_3

1   Introduction

Diversity, with its many categories including gender, ethnicity, class, sexual orientation, disability and age, is a global reality that is becoming more evident with the advent of communication and transportation technologies that bring people from different backgrounds together. Democratisation of education and social movements have pushed for equality and human rights for different groups in society (Köllen, 2016; Reilly & Williams, 2016; Syed & Özbilgin, 2015). Diversity as a social reality has been urging organisations to capture and manage the potential of workforce diversity globally (Özbilgin, Tatli, & Jonsen, 2015). For almost three decades, diversity management has been highlighted as a business imperative, the effective management of which can present organisations with competitive advantages (Barak, 2016; Jackson & Alvarez, 1992). Yet this supportive stance towards diversity management has been criticised for being instrumental, that is, reducing the case for diversity to the single bottom line, and for failing to acknowledge the moral case for diversity and the limitations of the effectiveness of diversity management interventions in delivering their promised outcomes (Romani, Holck, Holgersson, & Muhr, 2017).

What makes diversity management an imperative for organisations is widely debated and sometimes contested (Kochan et al., 2003; Wrench, 2016). There is evidence of growing cynicism and a backlash to diversity management (Dobbin & Kalev, 2018; Kidder, Lankau, Chrobot-Mason, Mollica, & Friedman, 2004). Despite the reported failings of diversity management, particularly in contexts where there is a lack of historical fit and a dearth of regulatory, political and social supports (Tatli, Vassilopoulou, Ariss, & Özbilgin, 2012; Vassilopoulou, Rocha, Seierstad, April, & Özbilgin, 2013), it remains one of the very few mechanisms to manage differences in workplaces. Therefore, it is important to identify antecedents, correlates and consequences of effective diversity management in organisations. What makes the difference between effective management of diversity and diversity management is the fact that effective management of diversity attempts to garner positive outcomes of diversity, such as positive economic, social and environmental outcomes, as well as improvements to organisational, team and individual well-being, performance, innovation and engagement, among others. Furthermore, effective management of diversity attempts to address the possible negative consequences of workforce diversity, such as problems in communication, job embeddedness, litigation based on discrimination and harassment and industrial disputes. In this chapter, we bring together insights on why and how global organisations manage diversity more effectively. In particular, we discuss the contemporary frames and challenges of managing global diversity. The chapter offers innovative solutions to the challenges facing GDM.

2   Global Diversity Management: Antecedents, Correlates and Consequences

In line with the title of this volume, global diversity management is defined as a fusion of ideas, stories and practices of managing social and demographic differences in global organisations. This definition reflects the fact that diversity management has three key sources of inspiration: ideas based on opinions and evidence, stories based on facts and fictions and practices based on actions and interventions (Nentwich, Özbilgin, & Tatli, 2015). Availability of varied sources of inspiration renders global diversity management a site rich in both activity and contested debate. There is extensive literature that has studied the antecedents, activities and consequences of diversity in a process model. Nishii and Özbilgin (2007) show that in order to accrue the positive benefits of diversity, such as knowledge sharing, staff engagement and reduced backlash in comparison to affirmative action interventions, global diversity management activities should be supported by the top management team and that they should be resourced well and there should be a preparedness for diversity and inclusion in the organisation. The authors argue that global diversity management activities should include agreed definitions of diversity, flexibility on human resource policies and practices and competency training for management staff to appreciate diversity. Authors explain that if the global diversity management is managed effectively, it serves to create a virtuous cycle by which the organisational leaders may dedicate further resources and support for diversity activities.

A process approach to global diversity management brings together the antecedents of diversity, diversity management activities and consequences into a single framework. Yet some authors argue that context is a more important process in the case of diversity, as diversity gains meaning in a relational context (Syed & Özbilgin, 2009) and there could not be a single best way or process to manage diversity, considering the variability of diversity practices across the international context, in national settings, by industry, sector and organisational ethos. Even at the level of teams and individual agency of the diversity manager there are variations. As such, in order to understand global diversity management activities, we need to understand the requirements of the specific context and the interplay between layers of macro-, meso- and micro-level influences on the generation of meanings, processes and policies of GDM.

There are a number of antecedents to effective management of diversity. For example, Ng and Sears (2018) identify that leadership commitment, discourses and actions are significant antecedents if diversity interventions are to be taken seriously within organisations. Similarly, Nishii and Özbilgin (2007) note that diversity interventions require a conducive diversity culture, resource allocation and organisational maturity that support the diversity interventions. Strong leadership support, maturity and resource allocation as antecedents and preconditions help any diversity intervention to have a strong base in the organisation.

The link between workforce diversity and positive organisational outcomes remains tenuous and complicated for a number of reasons (Özbilgin, Tatli, Ipek, &

Sameer, 2016a, 2016b; Roberson, 2018). The primary reason for absence of a strong link between workforce diversity and positive organisational outcomes is that there are many diversity categories, such as gender, ethnicity, age and sexual orientation, which yield different and complex outcomes (Galbreath, 2018). Workforce diversity does not present a monolithic and linear relationship with organisational outcomes. When one category may lead to positive outcomes under certain circumstances, other categories may require other contextual preparedness for the positive benefits of diversity to be accrued. For example, Joo, Kong and Atwater (2018) explain that in a country without a strong tradition of gender equality, gender diversity leads to negative outcomes. Therefore, the context as well as local history as antecedents matter in understanding the outcomes of any category of workforce diversity. Thus, the local context complicates diversity outcomes. Secondly, the narrow focus on organisational performance and innovation outcomes underplays the significance of the moral case for diversity and social, economic and environmental benefits of diversity. In the absence of robust scientific evidence between diversity and performance, widening the business case for effective management of diversity from a single bottom line approach, which merely focuses on profitability, to a triple bottom line approach, which includes people, profits and the planet, can be helpful for strengthening the bargaining power of diversity actors in organisations (Özbilgin et al., 2016a, 2016b).

Although the scientific relationship between workforce diversity and organisational outcomes is complicated by multiple factors, effective management of diversity reportedly leads to positive outcomes (Roberson, 2018). If the organisational climate and leadership is ready, receptive and supportive, workforce diversity, if managed effectively, may yield positive outcomes for the organisation, for wider society, the economy and environment. Effective management of workforce diversity promises to contribute to organisational performance (Özbilgin et al., 2015); increase innovation (Lorenzo & Reeves, 2018), sales, market share and longevity; and help organisations to transform the ways of thinking among workers, structures and routines of work and to regulate work and life in unprecedented ways (Herring, 2009; Roberson, Ryan, & Ragins, 2017). Such supportive arguments for the benefits of diversity management are clustered under the label of 'the business case for diversity management', which is research-based evidence that shows the contribution of workforce diversity to the organisational bottom line: profits, people and planet (from a narrow focus on profitability to a broader range of responsibility for people and the environment). Business case arguments based on single bottom line, that is, profitability, are criticised by scholars who argued that the triple bottom line with a focus on profits, people and planet can enhance the legitimacy and effectiveness of diversity management. Similarly, the legal case (Özbilgin & Slutskaya, 2017) and social justice case (Noon, 2007; Seierstad, 2016) arguments could help practitioners to frame their diversity management efforts in increasingly challenging contexts in which austerity and backlash against equalities force practitioners of diversity to defensive corners in many global organisations (Mor Barak, 2018; Chatrakul Na Ayudhya, Prouska, & Alexandra Beauregard, 2017; Vassilopoulou, Kyriakidou, Rocha, Georgiadou, & Barak, 2018).

Kyriakidou, Kyriacou, Özbilgin, and Dedoulis (2016) explain also that effective management of diversity is predicated on the North American context and it does not travel easily and without complication to other contexts. Tatli et al. (2012) compare the regulatory and historical context in three countries in Europe (Germany, France and the United Kingdom) in order to illustrate how management of diversity should be crafted to capture and address complexities of the particular local priorities, circumstances, hegemonic structures and taboo subjects. Therefore, it is important that diversity management efforts capture the local realities and that they are crafted to address local priorities, blended with universal values of equality and fairness for all. This complex formulation requires diversity actors to be insightful about the historical context in which their organisation and diversity interventions operate.

Although much is known about the benefits of managing workforce diversity effectively, possible negative consequences of not managing diversity effectively also provide motivation for organisations to take up diversity interventions. If left unattended and unmanaged, diversity may lead to industrial conflict, incidents of bullying, harassment and discrimination and resultantly harm the organisation by causing toxic employment relationships and extensive legal and reputational damage (Özbilgin et al., 2015). Violations of equality, diversity and inclusion through harassment and bullying at work could have detrimental consequences for organisations. Even when diversity management is practised, there are various challenges to its effective implementation. Ill-thought-out diversity interventions, training or change initiatives can lead to negative outcomes. For example, Noon (2018) explains how some diversity training can be meaningless. Dobbin and Kalev (2016, 2018) provide evidence of such cases where diversity interventions and training may fail if they are formulaic, pay only lip service or fail to challenge systemic and structural inequalities. Robinson and Dechant (1997) suggest that when there is lack of investment and prioritisation of diversity as a business priority, diversity initiatives do not yield the desired outcomes. The systematic review by Kalev, Dobbin, and Kelly (2006) shows that diversity management interventions generate stronger outcomes if they are connected with organisational change efforts than interventions focused on awareness-raising at the individual level. In the same vein, Özbilgin et al. (2016a) demonstrate that legal enforcement and widening of the responsibility for managing diversity across the value chains of organisations enhance the effectiveness and accountability of diversity interventions.

Most of the diversity management research is limited to single-country studies (Özbilgin & Chanlat, 2017), apart from a growing number of studies that provide international and global insights on diversity management (Gardenswartz, Rowe, Digh, & Bennett, 2003; Nishii & Özbilgin, 2007; Özbilgin et al., 2015; Sippola & Smale, 2007; Syed & Özbilgin, 2015). Needless to say, for global, international and transnational organisations, managing diversity at a global level is a business prerogative. However, global diversity management is not a practice that can be limited to global organisations alone. In a connected world (Raco, 2018), despite an upsurge in protectionism and nationalism, even locally embedded organisations are exposed to the shifts and changes in the global context.

3   Global Diversity Management: Observing, Overcoming or Transcending Context

The practice of global diversity management draws on a range of considerations. Alternative models of global diversity management have been developed in order to meet varied organisational needs such as developing strategies for observing the requirements and priorities of the local context or overcoming the local context by standardising global policies, to help processes of management and intervention and to capture the multilayered complexities of context by transcending local context (Jonsen, Tatli, Özbilgin, & Bell, 2013). Global organisations have long struggled with the dichotomous choice between localising their policies of diversity management at national level and standardising their policies across their international networks. Context is sometimes viewed as fixed, as destiny or as a challenge. Some diversity actors prefer to view context as a construct that can be challenged, changed and crafted. Similarly, the third approach to context is to accept context as dynamically and relationally changing, an ephemeral and transversal construct that should be navigated, negotiated and co-constructed.

The former strategy of localisation promises to capture local priorities and helps global diversity management to achieve local buy-in. Yet it can also expose the organisation to uneven practices of equality and reputational risk when, for example, in one country child labour is allowed and in another child labour is sanctioned by law. When an organisation standardises its global diversity management practices, it achieves consistency and demonstrates unwavering commitment to diversity principles and policies across its operations. Yet such standardisation may mean that diversity policies generated in the head office may be in breach of law or customs when transferred to another country (Lauring, 2013). A remarkable example of this is the transfer of ethnic data collection practices from English-speaking countries to countries such as France, Germany and Italy in continental Europe, which have specific laws preventing the collection of ethnic data. Tatli et al. (2012) explain that the transfer of diversity policies to Britain, France and Germany, three countries with extensive historical ties, has led to significant differences in adoption. In order to mitigate the negative consequences of localisation and standardisation, some global organisations adopt a transversal approach, which brings together a diversity council with representatives from each country and region in their network. The transversal approach (Jonsen & Özbilgin, 2013) recognises the tension between the availability of national priorities and the need to standardise diversity practices. As such, the transversal approach builds on the knowledge of members of the international diversity council (Karabacakoglu & Özbilgin, 2010).

Although much is now known about the contextual and effectiveness requirements of diversity management and the detrimental outcomes of failing to manage diversity in single national settings, there is a paucity of insights into innovative and creative ways to manage diversity in the global context. This chapter addresses this issue by outlining current knowledge on the practice of GDM, focusing on three challenges that are facing effective management of global diversity

Table 1 Challenges facing global diversity management and corresponding responses

Challenges facing GDM	Innovative responses to challenges facing GDM
Individualisation	Intersectional solidarity
Deregulation	Global value chain
Financialisation	Synchronicity

and providing three innovative corresponding approaches to combat these challenges (Table 1).

4 Global Diversity Management: Challenge of Individualism, Deregulation and Financialisation

There are three main challenges that face effective implementation of diversity management in global organisations: individualisation of GDM, deregulation of GDM and financialisation of GDM. Özbilgin and Slutskaya (2017) explain that these three conditions are a product of neoliberal marketisation that render the problems facing diversity management invisible, and yet these three fundamental turns in global diversity management present a challenge to the effectiveness of global diversity management interventions. The toxic allure of neoliberal expansion rests in its appealing promises, such as that individuals can craft their own careers, that organisations do not need legal regulation to manage diversity effectively, and that identifying a link between diversity and performance outcomes can motivate organisations to engage in diversity management. Authors demonstrate that these fundamental promises of the neoliberal approach to diversity do not materialise in desired tangible outcomes such as effective management of diversity. Conversely, they lead to deterioration of equality and diversity structures at work. We need to explore the values of individualisation, deregulation and financialisation in order to understand their negative consequences on global diversity management practices. Diversity actors in organisations need to consider these three challenges in crafting their diversity interventions, as falling into their traps may render diversity interventions ineffective.

Individualisation in the context of global diversity management is a process by which the responsibility of change rests with an individual. Individuals, rather than collectives such as trade unions or works councils, are expected to demand recognition of their difference and recognise and respect diversity in their work environments. Considering that diversity management is an organisational responsibility to change and make adjustments to make everyone feel welcome, individualisation of diversity management shifts the responsibility to the individual worker. The organisation tries to fix the individual rather than the system or the process that generates unequal or discriminatory outcomes. Individualisation can manifest in a global diversity management policy as a focus on awareness-raising activities, unconscious bias training and diversity competence training that target individuals for change. Although training and education may have useful outcomes for behavioural change towards effective management of diversity at work, when it is practised on its own individualisation of global diversity management, activities would not be sufficient to generate desired outcomes of change because effective global diversity management policies should aim not only to change the individuals but also the systems, structures and institutions that are not welcoming to difference at work. A narrow framing of global diversity management to the individual level alone can lead to significant disillusionment and cynicism about diversity management, as effective global diversity management is the responsibility of everyone and should also involve an organisational change and development plan. Dobbin and Kalev (2016) explain that diversity management programmes that focus on individual training and behavioural change without commitment to organisational development fail. Holck and Muhr (2017) demonstrate that diversity management that is based on assumptions of integration of migrants into the Danish model holds individuals responsible for integration, exposing them to unequal forms of solidarity with the majority ethnic population in the case of Denmark, where ethnic differences and pecking order are pronounced. Critiquing the use of unconscious bias training for diversity management, Noon (2007) explains that overstating the individual and agentic aspects of diversity by overemphasising awareness merely serves to keep the status quo and unequal power relations at work intact and renders an organisation's responsibility change invisible. Thus, individualisation in the context of global diversity management presents a major challenge to effective implementation of diversity interventions, which in essence should serve to change not only individual perceptions and awareness but also the systems, structures and institutions that lead to the unequal distribution of power and influence.

Deregulation is the outcome of the discourse of voluntarism, which is another significant neoliberal value, that organisations would engage in global diversity management interventions without the force of coercive legislation because diversity has a voluntary business case. Ideally, if this view holds true, we would have organisations taking up diversity interventions when such interventions may yield business benefits even in categories of diversity that are not regulated by law. However, this proves to be a naive expectation. Research shows that diversity management requires adjustments for organisations to undertake (Bell, 2018), and without social and legal coercion, organisations do not invest resources and undertake diversity activities, despite the availability of voluntary discourses (Jonsen et al., 2013; Klarsfeld, Ng, & Tatli, 2012; Özbilgin et al., 2016a, 2016b). Further, global organisations already operate in a regulatory vacuum in terms of accountability of their diversity practices across national borders. They merely operate only with normative pressure and risk to their corporate reputation from customers, trade unions and social movements (Klarsfeld, 2009). Indeed, most global organisations can shift their diversity investment from one country to another. Resultantly, global organisations may provide gender balance in the boardroom in countries where they are legally forced to do so yet exploit women in sweatshops in a less-regulated country where there are no normative or legal pressures (Özbilgin et al., 2016a, 2016b). Therefore deregulation, which appears at first sight to offer an appealing route for global organisations to voluntarily engage in diversity management, remains a major challenge in effective implementation of diversity, as moral (Köllen, Kakkuri-Knuuttila, & Bendl, 2018), social and legal pressures (McHugh & Perrault, 2018) are still important drivers for global organisations to invest resources in diversity management.

Financialisation is prioritisation of financial rationales above and beyond moral, social and economic rationales for diversity management. Financialisation means that diversity management interventions are allowed when diversity contributes to the single bottom line of organisations; that is, it contributes to the profitability of organisations. One of the recent outcomes of the financialisation of diversity management has been the expansion of the concern for financial benefits of diversity management in sectors beyond the private sector, including public and voluntary sector organisations (e.g. Opstrup & Villadsen, 2015). Financialisation is a malaise that results from international expansion of neoliberalism and global capitalist interest. Financialisation presents a Polanyian nightmare (1944) in which everything turns into a marketable resource (Gibbs, 2018) by which even human beings are framed as human resources and diversity is managed in a world where everything is commodified. The consequence of the apparently innocuous discourse of the business case for diversity is connected to financialisation, as diversity is legitimated from a single bottom line if it contributes to the profitability of organisations (Noon, 2007). Tomaskovic-Devey and Lin (2013) demonstrate that financialisation, or the spread of financial logics to sectors of work outside financial services sector, is detrimental to the negotiation power of labour and increases inequality between workers.

Effective management of diversity in global organisations faces the above three challenges, that is, individualisation, deregulation and financialisation, all of which collude and corrode the moral and social value and meaning of diversity. In the next section, we turn to some ways that global organisations may transcend these three challenges. The chapter explores intersectional solidarity to transcend individualisation, the global value chain to transcend deregulation and synchronicity to transcend financialisation.

---

5   Global Diversity Management: Towards Intersectional Solidarity, Global Value Chains and Synchronicity

In response to the above challenges that global organisations experience in managing diversity, the chapter introduces three innovative approaches as contemporary remedies, that is, intersectional solidarity, the global value chain and synchronicity. In response to the individualisation tendencies of approaches to diversity, *intersectional solidarity* can be adopted as an approach to diversity management. Intersectional solidarity is defined as the ways in which an organisation can create solidarity across actors and networks of multiple strands of diversity for organisational progress and change (Özbilgin, 2018; Özbilgin & Slutskaya, 2017). As it is outlined above, individualisation serves as an impediment to the effective practice of GDM. Each strand of diversity, such as gender, ethnicity, disability, sexual orientation, age and belief, has its own set of priorities. Individuals have intersectional identities. As each individual has a gender, ethnicity, disability status, sexual orientation and age, institutions have such intersectional identities also. The propensity to deal with each of these diversity criteria at an individual level renders diversity a rather fragmented phenomenon, reducing the bargaining power of individuals in the context of diversity claims and placing the sole responsibility for managing diversity on the individual in terms of raising their awareness. Individualisation means that diversity is considered the responsibility of the individual to change, rather than the organisation. We propose in this chapter that intersectional solidarity can be created by connecting individuals to efforts to manage multiple forms of diversity. Similarly, each internal diversity network, such as women's groups, race equality networks, disability and LGBTI+ (lesbian, gay, bisexual, transgender, queer, plus) networks and external social movements, has limited reach and resources, yet, in collaboration, they can build up their resources and gain power. Intersectional solidarity can also help diversity groups to galvanise greater support from each other in pushing for social and organisational change. In the field of political science, Tormos (2017) explains that intersectional solidarity is the way that intergroup hostilities can be overcome and strength can be supported. In progressive organisations, diversity managers use internal and external networks and build intersectional solidarity among them to pursue an intersectional diversity agenda. If left unmanaged, gender, ethnicity, religion and sexual orientation identities and networks operate in isolation and may even develop antagonistic relationships due to conflicting agendas for change. Building intersectional solidarity can help to overcome the risk of clashes in diversity claims (Özbilgin, 2018). Intersectional solidarity can be explained using the metaphor of a dinner table for a community. Each diversity network can take from the collective resources, provided that it collaborates with others and brings something to the table.

Diversity management operates in an adversarial political context today across many countries. There is a backlash against diversity and inclusion, and major attacks on structures of equality, diversity and inclusion in the political sphere (Mushaben, 2017), despite some support and progress in terms of gender representation in the boardroom (Kakabadse et al., 2015). Furthermore, there is greater awareness that global diversity management operates in a regulatory vacuum (Özbilgin et al., 2016a, 2016b): even when shareholder and stakeholder approaches are common in organisations, there is no regulatory pressure that can encourage global organisations to have diversity standards across their national networks in a consistent way. In fact, many organisations provide progressive equality approaches in some countries with strong equality laws and continue to exploit workers and ignore the equality, diversity and inclusion needs of employees in other locations with limited regulatory protections, such as equality laws.

A global value chain approach (Gibbon, Bair, & Ponte, 2008) to global diversity management stipulates that global organisations should be held accountable for their impact in terms of management of equality and diversity across their value chain, from the inception of an idea to the design of products and services to the consumption. A global chain approach has the potential for organisations to examine the impact of their diversity interventions across all of their operations. If such account-ability is achieved, more consistency across the value chain can be demanded from global organisations. Considering the dominant power and influence of global organisations in the political sphere, the power of customers, social movements and research is needed to encourage regulatory change. International organisations such the International Labour Organization (ILO), United Nations (UN) and inter-national trade union organisations could be brought together to redefine the role of corporations and organisations and their role in managing global diversity. A global value chain approach can help social movements and internal diversity structures to understand the true impact of global organisations on intergroup power relations at work and build solidarity in order to curb the corrosive impact of global capitalist interests to exploit labour. The global value chain approach can help organisations to have a more robust and truthful accounting of diversity interventions across their value chain. In turn, both social movements and consumer groups could be used to encourage organisations to be more accountable across their value chain in terms of their diversity interventions and impact. Most organisations today care about their global brand, and their efforts with diversity and inclusion serve to enhance their brand. Yet organisational efforts to account for diversity interventions remain locally based and partial at the global level. A global value chain is a way to encourage a more meaningful and value-based governance for the diversity efforts of global organisations. In the current climate, a global value chain approach rests on volun-tary initiatives by organisations. As we explained earlier, voluntarism does not work. In order to curb malpractice by global organisations in terms of equality and diversity, there is need for international regulation of value chains and possibly a redefinition of a global corporation as not responsible solely to its shareholders but as an entity that has a wider range of responsibilities to care for its social, economic and environmental impacts and to provide equity, equality and diversity across its value chain.

Financialisation is a challenge to the effective implementation of diversity in global organisations. Financialisation of diversity management has led to the prioritisation of the profitability and organisational performance outcomes of diver-sity, above and beyond the wider social, economic and environmental rationales for effective management of diversity.

Synchronicity is a concept developed by Karl Jung (1930/2010), and it can be defined as the energy and positive outcomes that can be garnered from the acausal togetherness and coexistence of people. As diversity management is often contested and diversity actors face questioning in terms of utility of diversity for the organisational profitability and financial health, synchronicity as an approach helps them to see a wider range of rationales than the financial one alone. In fact, the synchronicity approach encourages diversity actors to see merit in coexistence and togetherness of difference as a positive thing on its own, without the expectation of an immediate reward. As such, the synchronicity approach presents a challenge to not only the financialisation of diversity activities but also to the planned nature of diversity interventions, which hinders their ability to capture the real priorities of diversity. One pertinent example of synchronicity is the position of refugees in well-planned Western societies. Refugees are often treated as dirt in the well-oiled machine of developed economic systems. The synchronicity approach can provide diversity interventions with new perspectives on the inclusion of others who would be excluded if financial considerations dictated the value of difference. Synchronicity as an approach challenges the domination of financial decisions on business case arguments, alerting practitioners to the wider possibilities of acausal forms of togetherness and coexistence of people from different backgrounds. Another example of synchronicity would be the diversity interventions that create cross-functional, intersectional engagement with both internal and external stakeholders. There is scope for social responsibility initiatives and diversity initiatives to use joined-up thinking to achieve such synchronicity outcomes, bringing multiple stakeholders together in an acausal way to inculcate possible energy from such unplanned forms of coexistence and togetherness.

6   Conclusions

Global diversity management has lost some steam in global organisations since its launch as a significant management idea in North America in the early 1990s. The main setbacks for effective implementation and legitimacy of global diversity management have been the antagonistic political discourses and practices (Conley & Page, 2017) against migration, about women's and the LGBTI+ rights internationally, despite modest progress towards equality in some countries, which remain fragmented. Therefore, it is urgent for us to attend to the challenges facing global diversity management and to cultivate new and innovative ways to manage global diversity in contexts that are individualised, deregulated and financialised. In this chapter, we provided three innovative approaches that can shape the way that we regulate global diversity: intersectional solidarity to combat individualisation, the global value chain approach to combat deregulation and the synchronicity approach to combat financialisation.

The current impasse and inertia regarding global diversity management are the result of the neoliberal treatment of diversity in instrumental ways through the values of individualisation, deregulation and financialisation. Diversity actors in organisations are not passive agents who simply accept the current context as destiny. In fact, diversity actors can play significant roles in resisting, redefining and transcending neoliberal tendencies in management of diversity. The three approaches that are offered in this chapter can help diversity actors to broaden their repertoires of intervention beyond the narrow rationales offered in the neoliberal political economy in which most global organisations operate today.

References

Barak, M. E. M. (2016). *Managing diversity: Toward a globally inclusive workplace*. Thousand Oaks, CA: Sage.

Bell, M. (2018). Adapting work to the worker: The evolving EU legal framework on accommodating worker diversity. *International Journal of Discrimination and the Law, 18*(2–3), 124–143.

Chatrakul Na Ayudhya, U., Prouska, R., & Alexandra Beauregard, T. (2017). The impact of global economic crisis and austerity on quality of working life and work-life balance: A capabilities perspective. *European Management Review*.

Conley, H., & Page, M. (2017). Revisiting Jewson and Mason: The politics of gender equality in UK local government in a cold climate. *Gender, Work and Organization, 24*(1), 7–19.

Dobbin, F., & Kalev, A. (2016). Why diversity programs fail and what works better. *Harvard Business Review, 94*(7–8), 52.

Dobbin, F., & Kalev, A. (2018). Why doesn't diversity training work? The challenge for industry and academia. *Anthropology Now, 10*(2), 48–55.

Galbreath, J. (2018). Is board gender diversity linked to financial performance? The mediating mechanism of CSR. *Business & Society, 57*(5), 863–889.

Gardenswartz, L., Rowe, A., Digh, P., & Bennett, M. (2003). *The global diversity desk reference: Managing an international workforce*. San Francisco, CA: Pfeiffer.

Gibbon, P., Bair, J., & Ponte, S. (2008). Governing global value chains: An introduction. *Economy and Society, 37*(3), 315–338.

Gibbs, P. (2018). The marketingization of higher education. In M. Peters (Ed.), *Encyclopedia of educational philosophy and theory*. Singapore: Springer.

Herring, C. (2009). Does diversity pay?: Race, gender, and the business case for diversity. *American Sociological Review, 74*(2), 208–224.

Holck, L., & Muhr, S. L. (2017). Unequal solidarity? Towards a norm-critical approach to welfare logics. *Scandinavian Journal of Management, 33*(1), 1–11.

Jackson, S. E., & Alvarez, E. B. (1992). Working through diversity as a strategic imperative. In S. E. Jackson (Ed.), *The professional practice series. Diversity in the workplace: Human resources initiatives* (pp. 13–29). New York: Guilford.

Jonsen, K., & Özbilgin, M. (2013). *Models of global diversity management. Diversity at Work: The practice of inclusion* (pp. 364–390). San Francisco: Wiley.

Jonsen, K., Tatli, A., Özbilgin, M. F., & Bell, M. P. (2013). The tragedy of the uncommons: Reframing workforce diversity. *Human Relations, 66*(2), 271–294.

Joo, M. K., Kong, D., & Atwater, L. (2018, July). Workforce gender diversity, human resource practices, and organizational outcomes. In *Academy of Management Proceedings* (Vol. 1, p. 17603). Briarcliff Manor, NY: Academy of Management.

Jung, C. G. (2010). Synchronicity: An acausal connecting principle. In *The collected works of C. G. Jung* (Vol. 8). Chicago: Princeton University Press.

Kakabadse, N. K., Figueira, C., Nicolopoulou, K., Hong Yang, J., Kakabadse, A. P., & Özbilgin, M. F. (2015). Gender diversity and board performance: Women's experiences and perspectives. *Human Resource Management, 54*(2), 265–281.

Kalev, A., Dobbin, F., & Kelly, E. (2006). Best practices or best guesses? Assessing the efficacy of corporate affirmative action and diversity policies. *American Sociological Review, 71*(4), 589–617.

Karabacakoglu, F., & Özbilgin, M. (2010). Global diversity management at Ericsson: The business case. In L. Costanzo (Ed.), *Cases in strategic management* (pp. 79–91). London: McGraw-Hill.

Kidder, D. L., Lankau, M. J., Chrobot-Mason, D., Mollica, K. A., & Friedman, R. A. (2004). Backlash toward diversity initiatives: Examining the impact of diversity program justification, personal and group outcomes. *International Journal of Conflict Management, 15*(1), 77–102.

Klarsfeld, A. (2009). Managing diversity: The virtue of coercion. In M. Özbilgin (Ed.), *Equality, diversity and inclusion at work: A research companion* (p. 25, 322). Cheltenham: Edward Elgar.

Klarsfeld, A., Ng, E., & Tatli, A. (2012). Social regulation and diversity management: A comparative study of France, Canada and the United Kingdom. *European Journal of Industrial Relations, 18*(4), 309–327.

Kochan, T., Bezrukova, K., Ely, R., Jackson, S., Joshi, A., Jehn, K., et al. (2003). The effects of diversity on business performance: Report of the diversity research network. *Human Resource*

Management, in cooperation with School of Business Administration, University of Michigan, and in alliance with Society of Human Resources Management, 42(1), 3–21.

Köllen, T. (Ed.). (2016). *Sexual orientation and transgender issues in organizations: Global perspectives on LGBT workforce diversity.* Heidelberg: Springer.

Köllen, T., Kakkuri-Knuuttila, M. L., & Bendl, R. (2018). An indisputable 'holy trinity'? On the moral value of equality, diversity, and inclusion. *Equality, Diversity and Inclusion, 37*(5), 438–449.

Kyriakidou, O., Kyriacou, O., Özbilgin, M., & Dedoulis, E. (2016). Equality, diversity and inclusion in accounting. *Critical Perspectives on Accounting, 35*, 1–12.

Lauring, J. (2013). International diversity management: Global ideals and local responses. *British Journal of Management, 24*(2), 211–224.

Lorenzo, R., & Reeves, M. (2018). How and where diversity drives financial performance. *Harvard Business Review, January*, 1–5.

McHugh, P. J., & Perrault, E. (2018). Accelerating time: The effect of social pressures and regulation on board gender diversity post-IPO. *Journal of General Management, 43*(3), 95–105.

Mor Barak, M. E. (2018). Erecting walls versus tearing them down: Inclusion and the (false) paradox of diversity in times of economic upheaval. *European Management Review.*

Mushaben, J. M. (2017). Misrepresenting America's women: Trump's three-pronged attack on gender equality. *FEMINA, 2*, 147.

Nentwich, J. C., Özbilgin, M. F., & Tatli, A. (2015). Change agency as performance and embeddedness: Exploring the possibilities and limits of Butler and Bourdieu. *Culture and Organization, 21*(3), 235–250.

Ng, E. S., & Sears, G. J. (2018). Walking the talk on diversity: CEO beliefs, moral values, and the implementation of workplace diversity practices. *Journal of Business Ethics, November*, 1–14. https://doi.org/10.1007/s10551-018-4051-7.

Nishii, L. H., & Özbilgin, M. F. (2007). Global diversity management: Towards a conceptual framework. *The International Journal of Human Resource Management, 18*(11), 1883–1894.

Noon, M. (2007). The fatal flaws of diversity and the business case for ethnic minorities. *Work, Employment and Society, 21*(4), 773–784.

Noon, M. (2018). Pointless diversity training: Unconscious bias, new racism and agency. *Work, Employment and Society, 32*(1), 198–209.

Opstrup, N., & Villadsen, A. R. (2015). The right mix? Gender diversity in top management teams and financial performance. *Public Administration Review, 75*(2), 291–301.

Özbilgin, M. (2018). *What the racial equality movement can learn from the global fight for women's rights.* Retrieved from https://theconversation.com/what-the-racial-equality-move ment-can-learn-from-the-global-fight-for-womens-rights-105616

Özbilgin, M., & Chanlat, J. F. (Eds.). (2017). *Management and diversity: Perspectives from different national contexts.* Bingley: Emerald.

Özbilgin, M., & Slutskaya, N. (2017). Consequences of neoliberal politics on equality and diversity at work in Britain: Is resistance futile? *Management and Diversity: Thematic Approaches, 4*, 319–334.

Özbilgin, M., Tatli, A., Ipek, G., & Sameer, M. (2016a). Four approaches to accounting for diversity in global organisations. *Critical Perspectives on Accounting, 35*, 88–99.

Özbilgin, M., Tatli, A., Ipek, G., & Sameer, M. (2016b). *The business case for diversity management.* ACCA and ESRC-sponsored research project report. Retrieved from https://www. accaglobal.com/content/dam/acca/global/PDF-technical/human-capital/pol-tp-tbcfdm-diver sity-management.pdf

Özbilgin, M., Tatli, A., & Jonsen, K. (2015). *Global diversity management: An evidence-based approach.* New York: Palgrave Macmillan.

Polanyi, K. (1944). *The great transformation: Economic and political origins of our time.* New York: Rinehart.

Raco, M. (2018). Living with diversity: Local social imaginaries and the politics of intersectionality in a super-diverse city. *Political Geography, 62*, 149–159.

Reilly, P., & Williams, T. (2016). *Global HR: Challenges facing the function*. London: Routledge.

Roberson, Q. M. (2018). Diversity and inclusion in the workplace: A review, synthesis, and future research agenda. *Annual Review of Organizational Psychology and Organizational Behavior, 6*, 69–88.

Roberson, Q., Ryan, A. M., & Ragins, B. R. (2017). The evolution and future of diversity at work. *Journal of Applied Psychology, 102*(3), 483.

Robinson, G., & Dechant, K. (1997). Building a business case for diversity. *Academy of Management Perspectives, 11*(3), 21–31.

Romani, L., Holck, L., Holgersson, C., & Muhr, S. L. (2017). Diversity management and the Scandinavian model: Illustrations from Denmark and Sweden. In *Management and diversity: Perspectives from different national contexts* (pp. 261–280). Bingley: Emerald.

Seierstad, C. (2016). Beyond the business case: The need for both utility and justice rationales for increasing the share of women on boards. *Corporate Governance: An International Review, 24* (4), 390–405.

Sippola, A., & Smale, A. (2007). The global integration of diversity management: A longitudinal case study. *Human Resource Management, 18*(11), 1895–1916.

Syed, J., & Özbilgin, M. (2009). A relational framework for international transfer of diversity management practices. *Human Resource Management, 20*(12), 2435–2453.

Syed, J., & Özbilgin, M. (Eds.). (2015). *Managing diversity and inclusion: An international perspective*. London: Sage.

Tatli, A., Vassilopoulou, J., Ariss, A. A., & Özbilgin, M. (2012). The role of regulatory and temporal context in the construction of diversity discourses: The case of the UK, France and Germany. *European Journal of Industrial Relations, 18*(4), 293–308.

Tomaskovic-Devey, D., & Lin, K. H. (2013). Financialization: Causes, inequality consequences, and policy implications. *NC Banking Institute, 18*, 167.

Tormos, F. (2017). Intersectional solidarity. *Politics, Groups, and Identities, 5*(4), 707–720.

Vassilopoulou, J., Da Rocha, J. P., Seierstad, C., April, K., & Özbilgin, M. (2013). International diversity management: Examples from the USA, South Africa, and Norway. In B. Christiansen, E. Turkina, & N. Williams (Eds.), *Cultural and technological influences on global business* (pp. 14–28). Hershey, PA: IGI Global.

Vassilopoulou, J., Kyriakidou, O., da Rocha, J. P., Georgiadou, A., & Barak, M. E. M. (2018). International perspectives on securing human and social rights and diversity gains at work in the aftermath of the global economic crisis and in times of austerity. *European Management Review*. https://doi.org/10.1111/emre.12333.

Wrench, J. (2016). *Diversity management and discrimination: Immigrants and ethnic minorities in the EU*. London: Routledge.

Narrative Inquiry

Kate Maguire and Alison Scott-Baumann

Abstract

It is falling increasingly to international organisations and institutions to provide a coherent and workable global value system that embraces difference, internally and externally, with compliance expected from every level of the organisation. International human rights conventions and statutory regulations require compliance to human rights principles putting such organisations at the forefront of cultural relations. A global value framework gives them the opportunity to shake off colonial pasts and to strive to make a good business case for adherence to such principles. As principles are more challenging to enact than to formulate, to support this values portfolio, research is needed into how principles can be enacted in everyday matters of the organisation. Current literature highlights the use of storytelling as sense-making, and, as such, there is a growing trend in the use of the narrative approach across disciplines and professional sectors. Its contributors are from anthropology, education, linguistics, translation studies, literature, politics, psychology and sociology, organisational studies and history. This chapter surfaces the link between local and grand narratives through an ethno-narrative approach contextualised within a recent study of diversity (equality, diversity and inclusion) and specifically global diversity management.

K. Maguire (✉)
Faculty of Professional and Social Sciences, Hendon Campus Middlesex University, London, UK
e-mail: K.Maguire@mdx.ac.uk

A. Scott-Baumann
Department of Religions and Philosophies, SOAS, London, UK
e-mail: as150@soas.ac.uk

© Springer Nature Switzerland AG 2019
M. F. Özbilgin et al. (eds.), *Global Diversity Management*, Management for Professionals, https://doi.org/10.1007/978-3-030-19523-6_4

1   A Cautionary Note from History: New Lamps for Old?

Narrative, storytelling and ethnography fall into the qualitative basket of research approaches. Embracing qualitative approaches to research as being reliable took considerable time. They were, in a sense, tolerated in the fields of anthropology, geography and analytical psychology because everyone loves a story and that is what they were to many—adventurous, naughty, exotic windows into 'the other'. But to the early story gatherers, these accounts of lives, rituals and beliefs held within them the complexities of the human condition and the diversity of meanings made of the human's place in the world. Accumulated stories became accumulated knowledge and functioned, paradoxically, to both facilitate and challenge the hegemony of paradigms in the West and the political, social and economic behaviours that they generated as indicators of civilisation. As Cope (2010) points out, it was geographers who opened up large swathes of the world by gathering stories from indigenous peoples about their environments, putting them together into a narrative of geographical routes and locations and making it possible for the commercial, political and religious power zealots to exploit the other and the places they inhabited for gain:

> The history of 'writing the world' necessitates a critical look at the two Cs that underlie geography in its infancy: colonialism and capitalism. The two went hand-in-hand as powerful European states of the fifteenth century and beyond began to systematize their methods of production, consumption and exploitation, creating new demands for goods and labor and simultaneously meeting those demands by developing new supplies (furs, sugar, cotton, human slaves, etc.)... (Cope, 2010: 27)

Cope goes on to quote the geographer and historian D. N. Livingstone's observation (1993, 170) that:

> There is something to be said for the claim that geography was the science of imperialism *par excellence.*

Much like the geographers, the work of a later field, that of social anthropology, whose researchers sought to study 'primitive' society to better understand their own, was also, in many cases, expropriated by colonisers for their own purposes. Anthropology's chosen method of ethnography, a form of story collecting and telling, became, for the colonisers, a convenient form of intelligence-gathering for purposes not intended by anthropologists. Many anthropologists, changed by their lived experiences with the communities of the storytellers, became advocates of the right of these societies to continue to exist autonomously in the face of threats from the grand narratives of colonialism and capitalism. This gave rise to the term 'salvage anthropology', as anthropologists found the purpose of their work was becoming more often about preservation of traditional artefacts and practices before their inevitable annihilation by modernity. Their experiences of the other led several to advocate on issues in their own countries. Price (2004), in his exploration of FBI archives, exposes how anthropologists were treated in the United States during the

Cold War because of their stance on human rights and freedom of inquiry, for which they were labelled 'communist' or 'Marxist' and many punished for their 'un-American' attitudes:

> Today, few American anthropologists engage in activities designed to threaten the status quo of American or international patterns of inequality at the level of past anthropologists like Jacobs, Morgan, Swadesh or Weltfish. Instead the discipline is awash with postmodern reflectionists, many of whom skilfully critique the manifestations of hegemonic power in subjects both ideographic and universal but few of whom actually confront the political-economic power bases that generate and support these structural exhaust features of the contemporary world. (Price, 2004: 349)

Since Price's expose 15 years ago of a time in American history that preceded the technological revolution, the world has become interconnected and global. However, exploitation and discrimination remain. Cultural relations, cultural diplomacy, legislation on diversity and international agreements have moved into this vacant space about which Price was so worried and now with nomenclature that promises an era of more enlightened approaches. While commercial interests and political alliances in this new era remain the primary motivators, the proselytising of particular religious beliefs and their related values has now been replaced by negotiating for a global set of values that everyone can adhere to while respecting local values in communities. These may differ considerably from the global grand narrative which sees, in theory, the commercial and political advantages in diversity as it widens the pool from which excellence can be drawn. As employees in global organisations tend to work globally and live locally, this interface can produce some strategic and tactical choices.

Local and global organisations have already begun to explore how equality, diversity and inclusion can be brought to life in the workplace and how their socio/political and economic benefits can be facilitated and demonstrated. However, the world has also shrunk, population is increasing and the competition for jobs is still exacerbated by fear of the other and who that other might now be. There is also the fear of conceding values of the local—culture, belonging, tradition, safety, identity—to the global anonymity of merit in the pursuit of employment. Organisation policy-makers of diversity and its management find themselves in a delicate balancing act of redressing historical and current discrimination, respecting the local, recognising how inclusion of one can be exclusion of another and making decisions in the best interests of the economic viability of their organisations. While this may be possible to achieve at the policy level, based on a set of human rights principles that might conflict in some aspects with the pursuit of commercial success, it is on the everyday ground of practice that tensions, contradictions and individual and tribal competition are played out with different levels of intensity. This is not new. An organisation that works hard at change strategies to create a culture of belonging for everyone creates a family dynamic, and, like all families, it is vulnerable to divisions motivated by, among other things, rivalry, fear and a challenging of parental control. As the British Council has stressed, there remains the constant misunderstanding among several staff that equality, diversity and inclusion are about accepting and respecting the other, not a requirement to become the other. Getting underneath what is played out is a worthy focus for research, for without knowledge of the multiple unspoken variables, principles cannot be brought to life in everyday practice. In this chapter we present one way that has yielded significant results for a number of organisations.

2   The Commerce Paradox

Many organisations are now paying less attention to the grand narratives of the range of countries and systems where they do business and focusing on the cultures of their own organisations which are a microcosm of local and global collisions. Pinker (2011: 682) refers to value-spreading organisations as 'gentle commerce'. Drawing from Mueller's ideas on merchants (1999, 2010), he goes on to say:

> As far as I know, in the vast literature on empathy, cooperation and aggression, no one has tested whether people who have consummated a mutually profitable exchange are less likely to shock each other or to spike each other's food with three-alarm hot sauce. I suspect that among researchers, gentle commerce is just not a sexy idea. Cultural and intellectual elites have always felt superior to business people, and it doesn't occur to them to credit mere merchants with something as noble as peace. (Pinker, 2011: 684)

Such organisations that venture along this path are seedbeds for complex cultural change and, due to the nature of global business, have a better chance than nations of spreading a coherent value system, even if the sole reason why an individual might be disposed to subscribe to this new order is because it will secure them employment, even if those values conflict with local and personal ones and even if the motivations of commerce are economic power.

In order to harness this considerable potential for change, traditional research methods of surveys and questionnaires generally benchmark the issues but often replicate the limitations of the research apparatus itself. A questionnaire, for example, is a pre-prepared tool delivered online or by a human being eliciting confirmation of what is, for the most part, already visible, rather than the human agent cast as listener, the appreciative audience, whose attention stimulates increasing layers of story and hence revelation of what is hidden. There is no doubt that organisational research is needed to map out what is not only visible but what is hidden, what connects the past, the present and the future (Boje, 2008) and surfaces the tension threads between the local narrative of the employee and the grand narrative, in this case, of the organisation. Findings from such engagement can inform change strategies that do not focus on implementing change but on providing the conditions for enduring change to be possible.

A recent research project by the British Council[1] explored exactly this in a small group of local offices in five countries with diverse ethnic, religious, historical, cultural and geographical differences. The British Council uses a diversity framework tool to evaluate its diversity strategy in practice but had come to recognise from its various encounters with local staff that there was much that remained unspoken yet was significantly present as an influence on achievement, compliance, contentment and belonging. It consulted an academic research team with backgrounds in diversity matters, and together they collaborated on the development of an ethno-narrative approach to surface the underlying tensions in an atmosphere of safety achieved through three key components of the research: the engagement of an outside team, the guarantee of anonymity and confidentiality for participants and the use of an open, non-interventionist, non-judgemental approach. It was anticipated that a narrative/storytelling method would fulfil the requirements of that third component and elicit stories and illustrations of individuals and groups in their work and their lives, surfacing the resonances and contradictions that arise when diversity values come into play. The researchers initiated the individual and group conversations with one open question—*What is your experience of working with the diversity policies required by your employer?*

The findings revealed layers of tensions from a minority which were more to do with generic office politics and issues of fairness to deeper issues of compromising their own values to uphold those of the British Council, the latter only occurring in relation to two areas: sexual identity and religion. Furthermore, struggles with these seemed to trigger comments around neocolonial intentions and lack of training of executives and international staff on local history, understanding of religions in the context of community and belonging, and lack of political sensitivity in countries where religion and state are not separate. There was also the dissonance between the 'moral' values of the organisation supporting communities to practise such values and the business values that were necessary to maintain a viable presence in these countries. The reasons behind some of these views were complex, idiosyncratic and ideographic. In some cases they also chimed uncomfortably with shadows from the past which continue to exert both explicit and nuanced influences on individual and group behaviour of employees, partners and the global organisations themselves, who may never think of themselves as colonial or neocolonial but can be perceived as having patronising and paternal attitudes. However, what was evident across the five countries was a deep enjoyment of their work, freedom to explore difference in other cultures and pride in achievements of value to the local, including more elected female government representatives, women being successful in football in a traditional culture, attention to disability being 'the right thing to do', significant contributions to education and youth, and art as a way to dissolve all kinds of differences. The deeper-level findings, which are often those which lie concealed

---

[1]Equality, Diversion and Inclusion: An investigation into international contexts (January 2018), Professor Paul Gibbs, Associate Professor Kate Maguire, Dr Alex Elwick (Middlesex University) and Professor Alison Scott- Baumann (SOAS, London).

to all participants in the 'culture', further demonstrate the value of this approach to diversity management. They are shared, by courtesy of the British Council, in chapter 'Five Nations: A Diversity Study'. This chapter continues with a summary of the literature that underpins our ethno-narrative approach and a brief introduction to the method of analysis, which can be used and adapted for other types of organisations and which is also further elucidated in chapter 'Five Nations: A Diversity Study'.

3   Introduction to Narrative Inquiry

If it is true that fiction cannot be completed other than through life, and that life cannot be understood other than through stories we tell about it, then we are led to say that a life *examined*, in the sense borrowed from Socrates, is a life *narrated*. (Ricoeur, 1991)

Narrative analysis takes the story itself as the object of study. The focus is on how individuals or groups make sense of events and actions in their lives through examining the story and its linguistic and structural properties (Riessman, 1993). The approach enables the capture of social representation processes, such as feelings, images and time. It offers the potential to address the ambiguity, complexity and dynamism of individual, group and organisational phenomena.

Each culture has its own stories and metaphors that are useful for learning a new way of thinking about how to act well, understand each other and make better sense of our lives. Increasingly, narrative is being used at the organisational level to clarify goals (Yang, Kang, & Johnson, 2010), to understand cross-cultural meanings (Howard, 1991) and to improve mutual understanding in therapeutic settings (Hall & Powell, 2011).

Current literature highlights the use of storytelling as sense-making and, as such, has become a growing trend in the use of the narrative approach across disciplines and professional sectors. Its contributors are from anthropology, education, linguistics, translation studies, literature, politics, psychology and sociology, organisational studies and history. Anthropology has employed ethnographic[2] approaches and examined narratives in the form of life histories, and, in turn, anthropology has been refigured to explore business practices including diversity (Qirko, 2012). However, narrative differs from ethnography and textual analysis. Ethnography places an emphasis on exploring the nature of particular social phenomena and, increasingly in more recent times, working primarily with unstructured data, investigating small numbers of cases (maybe even a single case) in depth and detail. This may be followed by interpretation of the meanings of the data and critical reflections upon the purposes and motivations of social actions and human

---

[2]Van Maanen's (1988) publication, written from the point of view of anthropology, gives a critical introduction to the ethnography of storytelling, both as subject matter and as an ethnographer's written form.

interaction with others and with artefacts. Such engagement allows individuals to reflect and reconstruct their personal, historical and cultural experiences (Gill, 2001).

The capturing of stories and analysing them, therefore, may lead to a better organisational understanding and yield a far deeper insight into the complexity of life within the organisation, especially in terms of cultural relations both inside and outside the organisation. The organisation relies on local experiences to bring to life and disseminate its value principles yet, at the same time, function as a business that generates income. Moreover, narrative can be used to facilitate organisational change or promote learning. This is achieved through:

- Presenting stories within an organisation, as the sense-making enabled through narratives promotes understanding throughout the organisation.
- Eliciting these stories, particularly those where things go wrong.
- Applying the methodology, stories told can be actively reshaped and retold to promote the values and culture desired by the organisation.

Narrative analysis can forge connections between personal biography and social structure—the personal and the political—although there is a tendency to downplay the role of organisational and societal contexts in shaping the meaning of diversity. This is particularly true in organisational studies of intersectionality. Applied to organisations, intersectionality allows connecting multiple work identities to wider societal phenomena, leading to a more fine-grained analysis of processes of identity construction and the underlying power relations (Holvino, 2010), clarified and expressed powerfully by a participant in the British Council research:

> If we can't deal with respect for difference inside we should not be trying to spread it outside. . . we need to get better at it ourselves, not avoid the dilemmas before we can say we have a right to bring it to others. . . In our hearts we all want to live in peace and respect each other but that is not the only thing which rules us. . .
>
> If we go out and sell this image are we not hypocrites if we can't fix it here first. . .

---

4   Ethno-narrative: Helping Organisations to Learn

The structural power position of those engaging in the meaning-making largely determines the outcome of the process. Understanding the voice of the storyteller is one way to encounter the implicit in the story. Individual voices can be inhibited by peer views that can move towards a 'false' consensus emerging from the complex dynamics of group experience. The host organisational culture has a range of practices and beliefs that may come into direct or indirect conflict with the values and practices of the domestic dominant cultures. Such situations develop complex dialectics that influence the practice that the stories are telling. Boje (1995: 1002) uses the term 'multi-discursive struggle' to describe what he sees as the main characteristic of organisations and their stories when seeking to establish the power of one story over another. Over time, the same narratives conflict with each other, for example, domestic/international, male/female and local diversity principles/multinational rules. We would not accept the accuracy of the dialectic that emerges, but this is the way in which many of us think, so it serves the purpose of helping us to see how people are using stories to make sense of their workplace. How then do we understand each other?

Language, then, is viewed as a medium that reflects singular meanings. Stories do not reflect the world out there but are constructed, rhetorical and interpretive (Riessman, 1993). As Maggio states, by just 'looking at a story as the creation of a particular individual rather than intersubjective creation of experience would deprive the study of its anthropological value' (2014: 91). The ethnographic approach builds upon the synthesis developed by Maggio (2014) from the anthropological literature and considers the story at three levels: **the relational**, where dynamics between the people involved in the storytelling situation are considered; **the content of the story**, here, the focus is on the action of telling and listening to stories and the reasons why a story is particularly appealing for a particular audience; and **the type of storytelling techniques**, how to obtain particular effects, how shared knowledge is negotiated with their audience and the stories formulated accordingly and 'to what extent they show their personal selves as opposed to making themselves mere medium for the telling of the story' (ibid.). This is captured in the following comment from another participant:

> The professional and the personal are closer in me now. I have changed how I think, how I do my job, my friends think I am crazy, I got my children to watch the Paralympics, I help blind people, I am more aware of mobility issues, the British Council put in a lift and a ramp...
>
> People can see that we are a place that respects difference...
> Word gets around.

Current tools of evaluation used by organisations to 'shift culture' have limitations and are not purposely designed to capture the lived experiences of diversity at work, although this indeed comes through in various ways. An organisation's particular diversity policy embodies a set of principles and values—*its story*—in an artefact that has emerged from historical movements and responses to international and national legislation such as the United Nations Human Rights Council (OHCHR), established by the United Nations General Assembly in 2006, the European Convention on Human Rights (1950, 1953), the Human Rights Act (UK) (1998, 2000) and events in national cultures such as the civil rights movement in the United States and gay pride in British culture.

In this scenario it is constituted as holding the grand narrative. By adopting an ethno-narrative approach, the organisation is creating an opportunity for *its story* to be challenged through its internal inconsistencies, through questioning its source and coherence and through seeing it through the eyes and ears of those who did not construct that particular story (Derrida, 1977). The purpose is learning about diversity policies' potential to flourish as a medium for deepening understanding between difference in diverse cultural contexts, being the bridge between cultural diplomacy and civil society and contributing to widening and endorsing recognition that cultural relations is about what happens at the edges of difference in the local contexts:

> [Respect is] not about superficial acceptance, not about let's 'do' diversity but how one respects difference. I think diversity can be called respect. We are asking everyone to respect the difference of the other without asking them to become the other, people fear they are being asked to give something up which is part of their core beliefs. If people understand that is not what diversity is about they will be less afraid...

5   Analysing: Making Sense of Narrative

The purpose of collected stories from the field, that is, the context where the practices are situated, is to provide rich data for analyses, the findings from which can contribute to (1) deepening understanding of diversity issues, challenges and experiences and diversity policy's relationship to cultural relations, (2) enhancing the organisation's cultural relations work to create friendly knowledge and understanding between the host and guest cultures, (3) informing the future organisational direction and strategy for diversity and (4) contributing to bridging the gap between the local and the grand narratives at play where the local has something significant to offer to shifts in the grand narrative. It is the local that has contributed to paradigm shifts in global concerns such as poverty, climate change, fishing rights and conflicts.

Stories generate a significant amount of data which need to go through at least three processes of analysis: firstly an analysis that brings order to the data, an organising frame usually of dominant themes and consensus themes across different stories; secondly, an interpretation of both the dominant themes and the context-specific themes using context knowledge, existing literature relating to such issues as organisational dynamics and power structures; and, thirdly, a translation of the findings into recommendations of focus for the particular organisation. Analysing storytelling data in such a way leads to a narrative of deep-level findings of what has been hidden, giving direction to how such local narratives can be negotiated to unblock the obstacles to the purposes and implementation of diversity initiatives which usually come from the grand narrative of the organisation. The core skill in analysing storytelling data is the interpretation stage which has to be through the lens of plurality and recognition of the multilayered contexts in which all participants and the objects that they have created are located and of the influences exerted by these different forces and entities. The purpose of interpretation needs to be infused with the purpose of the research activity which in the main study is a global diversity framework with moral and ethical mandates. Global organisations are now at the forefront of positive value dissemination through 'gentle commerce' and other means. The history of the colonial period, which has left a dark heritage, is a history from which important learning can be derived. Such purposes need to go beyond good intentions and recognise that, if paid attention to, cultural shifts are possible, if uncomfortable for a time.

We hope that further interest in narrative research approaches will be stimulated not only by an introduction to the possibilities demonstrated through this chapter but by a sharing of the whole literature review below which was put together as part of the British Council-commissioned diversity report and additions made in relation to this particular chapter. Returning to the cautionary note of 'new lamps for old', stories have many functions. One of them is to take on the form of folklore or parables which are instructive reminders of the difference between awareness and acting upon it and between good intention with insight and good intention without it. The fact that so many such stories remain universally within our contemporary cultural narratives is indicative of our voluntary reminder to ourselves that they are still needed.

References

Ahonen, P., Tienari, A., Meriläinen, S., & Pullen, A. (2014). Hidden contexts and invisible power relations: A Foucauldian reading of diversity research. *Human Relations, 67*(3), 263–286.

Andrews, M., Squire, C., & Tamboukou, M. (2013). *Doing narrative research*. London: Sage.

Armstrong, C., Flood, P. C., Guthrie, J. P., Liu, W., MacCurtain, S., & Mkamwa, T. (2010). The impact of diversity and equality management on firm performance: Beyond high performance work systems. *Human Resource Management, 49*(6), 977–998.

Arnold, J. (1997). *Managing careers into the 21st century*. London: Paul Chapman Publishing.

Baixauli-Soler, J. S., Belda-Ruiz, M., & Sanchez-Marin, G. (2015). Executive stock options, gender diversity in the top management team, and firm risk taking. *Journal of Business Research, 68*(2), 451–463.

Bešić, A., & Hirt, C. (2016). Diversity management across borders: The role of the national context. *Equality, Diversity and Inclusion, 35*(2), 123–135.

Boje, D. M. (1991). The storytelling organization: A study of story performance in an office-supply firm. *Administrative Science Quarterly, 36*, 106–126.

Boje, D. M. (1995). Stories of the storytelling organization: A postmodern analysis of Disney as 'Tamara-land'. *Academy of Management Journal, 38*(4), 997–1035.

Boje, D. M. (2008). *Storytelling organizations*. London: Sage.

Boje, D. M., Haley, U. C. V., & Saylors, R. (2016). Antenarratives of organizational change: The microstoria of Burger King's storytelling in space, time and strategic context. *Human Relations, 69*(2), 391–418.

Boje, D. M., & Saylors, R. (2013). Virtuality and materiality in the ethics of storytelling. In F. Cooren, E. Vaara, A. Langley, & H. Tsoukas (Eds.), *Organizational change, leadership and ethics: Leading organizations towards sustainability* (pp. 75–96). New York: Routledge.

Bruner, J. (1990). *Acts of meaning*. Cambridge, MA: Harvard University Press.

Clandinin, D. J., & Huber, J. (2010). Narrative inquiry. In B. McGaw, E. Baker, & P. P. Peterson (Eds.), *International encyclopedia of education* (3rd ed.). New York: Elsevier.

Cope, M. (2010). A history of qualitative research in geography. In D. DeLyser (Ed.), *The Sage handbook of qualitative geography* (pp. 22–45). Thousand Oaks, CA: Sage.

Czarniawska, B. (2004). *Narratives in social science research*. London: Sage.

Davis, P. J., Frolova, Y., & Callahan, W. (2016). Workplace diversity management in Australia. *Equality, Diversity and Inclusion, 35*(2), 81–98. https://doi.org/10.1108/EDI-03-2015-0020.

Daya, P. (2014). Diversity and inclusion in an emerging market context. *Equality, Diversity and Inclusion: An International Journal, 33*(3), 293–308.

De Fina, A. (2011). *Analyzing narrative: discourse and sociolinguistic perspectives.* Cambridge: Cambridge University Press.

Derrida, J. (1977). *Of grammatology.* Baltimore: Johns Hopkins University Press.

Dick, P., & Cassell, C. (2002). Barriers to managing diversity in a UK constabulary: The role of discourse. *Journal of Management Studies, 39*(7), 953–976.

Edwards, T., Marginson, P., & Ferner, A. (2013). Multinational companies in cross-national context: Integration, differentiation, and the interactions between MNCs and Nation States. *Industrial and Labor Relations Review, 66*(3), 547–587.

Equal Rights Trust/Kenya Human Rights Commission. (2012). *In the spirit of harambee addressing discrimination and inequality in Kenya.* Country Report Series 1. London: Equal Rights Trust/Kenya Human Rights Commission.

European Convention on Human Rights. (1950, 1953). Retrieved from https://www.equalityhumanrights.com/en/what-european-convention-human-rights

Evans, C. (2014). Diversity management and organizational change. *Equality, Diversity and Inclusion: An International Journal, 33*(6), 482–493.

Ford, J. D., & Ford, L. W. (2009). Decoding resistance to change. *Harvard Business Review, 87*(4).

Foster, C., & Harris, L. (2005). Easy to say, difficult to do: Diversity management in retail. *Human Resource Management Journal, 15*(3), 4–17.

Gilbert, J., & Ivancevich, J. (2000). Valuing diversity: A tale of two organisations. *Academy of Management Executive, 14*(1), 93–105.

Gill, P. B. (2001). Narrative inquiry: Designing the processes, pathways and patterns of change. *Systems Research and Behavioral Science, 18*(4), 335–344.

Gotsis, G., & Kortezi, Z. (2013). Ethical paradigms as potential foundations of diversity management initiatives in business organizations. *Journal of Organizational Change Management, 26*(6), 948–976.

Greeff, W. J. (2015). Organisational diversity: Making the case for contextual interpretivism. *Equality, Diversity and Inclusion: An International Journal, 34*(6), 496–509.

Greene, A., & Kirton, G. (2009). *Diversity management in the UK: Organisational and stakeholder experiences.* London: Routledge.

Hall, J., & Powell, J. (2011). Understanding the person through narrative. *Nursing Research and Practice.* Article ID 293837. https://doi.org/10.1155/2011/293837

Holck, L., Muhr, S. L., & Villesèche, F. (2016). Identity, diversity and diversity management: On theoretical connections, assumptions and implications for practice. *Equality, Diversity and Inclusion: An International Journal, 35*(11), 48–64.

Holvino, E. (2010). Intersections: The simultaneity of race, gender and class in organization studies. *Gender, Work and Organization, 17*(3), 248–277.

Howard, G. (1991). Culture tales: A narrative approach to thinking, cross-cultural psychology and psychotherapy. *American Psychologist, 46*(3), 187–197.

Human Rights Act (UK). (1998, 2000). Retrieved from https://www.equalityhumanrights.com/en/human-rights/human-rights-act

Institute of Development Studies (IDS). (2017). *Country report: Empowerment of women and girls.* Retrieved from http://interactions.eldis.org/unpaid-care-work/country-profiles/kenya/social-economic-and-political-context-kenya

Katan, D. (1999). *Translating cultures. An introduction for translators, interpreters and mediators.* Manchester: St Jerome.

Kenya Human Rights Commission. Retrieved from http://www.khrc.or.ke/

Kirton, G., Robertson, M., & Avdelidou-Fischer, N. (2016). Valuing and value in diversity: The policy implementation gap in an IT firm. *Human Resource Management Journal, 26*(3), 321–336.

Knights, D., & Omanović, V. (2016). (Mis)managing diversity: Exploring the dangers of diversity management orthodoxy. *Equality, Diversity and Inclusion: An International Journal, 35*(1), 5–16.

Kulik, C. (2014). Working below and above the line: The research–practice gap in diversity management. *Human Resource Management Journal, 24*(2), 129–144.

Lauring, J. (2013). International diversity management. *British Journal of Management, 24*, 211–224.

Lauring, J., & Selmer, J. (2011). International language management and diversity climate in multicultural organizations. *International Business Review, 21*, 156–166.

Livholts, M., & Tamboukou, M. (2015). *Discourse and narrative methods*. London: Sage.

Livingstone, D. N. (1993). *The geographical tradition: Episodes in the history of a contested enterprise*. Cambridge, MA: Blackwell.

Maggio, R. (2014). The anthropology of storytelling and the storytelling of anthropology. *Journal of comparative Research in Anthropology and Sociology, 5*, 89–106.

Maguire, K. (2015). *Margaret Mead: Contributions to contemporary education*. (Springer briefs in education). Dordrecht: Springer.

Marfelt, M. M., & Muhr, S. L. (2016). Managing protean diversity. *International Journal of Cross-Cultural Management, 16*(2), 231–251.

Melissen, J. (2005). *The new public diplomacy: Between theory and practice*. New York: Palgrave Macmillan.

Mueller, J. (1999). *Capitalism, democracy and Ralph's pretty good grocery*. Princeton, NJ: Princeton University Press.

Mueller, J. (2010). Capitalism, peace and the historical movement of ideas. *International Interactions, 36*, 169–184.

Ng, E., & Sears, G. (2012). CEO leadership styles and the implementation of organizational diversity practices. *Journal of Business Ethics, 105*, 41–52.

Nielsen, S. (2010). Top management team diversity. *International Journal of Management Reviews, 12*, 301–316.

Oswick, C., & Moon, M. (2014). Discourses of diversity, equality and inclusion: Trenchant formulations or transient fashions? *British Journal of Management, 25*, 23–39.

Özbilgin, M., Tatli, A., Ipek, G., & Sameer, M. (2016). Four approaches to accounting for diversity in global organisations. *Critical Perspectives on Accounting, 35*, 88–99.

Pinker, S. (2011). *The better angels of our nature: The decline of violence in history and its causes*. London: Allen Lane, Penguin Imprint.

Price, D. H. (2004). *Threatening anthropology*. Durham: Duke University Press.

Pringle, J. K., & Ryan, I. (2015). Understanding context in diversity management: A multi-level analysis. *Equality, Diversity and Inclusion: An International Journal, 34*(6), 470–482.

Qirko, H. N. (2012). Applied anthropology and business diversity management. *International Journal of Business Anthropology, 3*(2), 97–121.

Ricoeur, P. (1991). *Oneself as another* (K. Blamey Trans.) (1992). University of Chicago Press.

Riessman, C. K. (1993). *Narrative analysis*. Qualitative Research Methods Series, No. 30. Newbury Park, CA: Sage.

Rosile, G. A., Boje, D. M., Carlon, D., Downs, A., & Saylors, R. (2013). Storytelling diamond: An antenarrative integration of the six facets of storytelling in organization research design. *Organizational Research Methods Journal, 18*, 16–30.

Schneider, S., & Northcraft, G. (1999). Three social dilemmas of workforce diversity in organisations: A social identity perspective. *Human Relations, 52*(11), 1445–1467.

Scroggins, W., & Benson, P. (2010). International human resource management. *Personnel Review, 39*(4), 409–413.

Scruton, R. (2017). *On human nature*. New York: Princeton University Press.

Shen, J., Chanda, A., D'Netto, B., & Monga, M. (2009). Managing diversity through human resource management: An international perspective and conceptual framework. *Human Resource Management, 20*(2), 235–251.

Shin, H. Y., & Park, H. J. (2013). *What are the key factors in managing diversity and Inclusion successfully in large international organisations?* Cornell University ILR School. Retrieved from http://digitalcommons.ilr.cornell.edu/cgi/viewcontent.cgi?article=1044&context=student

SHRM. (2009). *Global diversity and inclusion*. Alexandria, VA: Society for Human Resource Management.

Siebers, H. (2009). Struggles for recognition: The politics of racioethnic identity among Dutch national tax administrators. *Scandinavian Journal of Management, 25*(1), 73–84.

Sippola, A., & Smale, A. (2007). The global integration of diversity management. *International Journal of Human Resource Management, 18*(11), 1895–1916.

Smith, J. A., Jarman, M., & Osborn, M. (1999). Doing interpretative phenomenological analysis. In M. Murray & K. Chamberlain (Eds.), *Qualitative health psychology: Theories and methods* (pp. 218–240). London: Sage.

Strauss, I. (1968). *The savage mind*. Chicago: University of Chicago Press.

Syed, J., & Boje, D. M. (2007). *In praise of dialogue: Storytelling as a means of negotiated diversity management*. Retrieved from https://kar.kent.ac.uk/24891/1/Web_Version.pdf

Syed, J., & Özbilgin, M. (2009). A relational framework for international transfer of DM practices. *International Journal of Human Resource Management, 20*(12), 2435–2453.

Tatli, A. (2011). A multi-layered exploration of the diversity management field: Diversity discourses, practices and practitioners in the UK. *British Journal of Management, 22*, 238–253.

Tatli, A., & Özbilgin, M. (2012). An emic approach to intersectional study of diversity at work: A Bourdieuan framing. *International Journal of Management Reviews, 142*, 180–200.

Tobin, K., & Kincheloe, J. (Eds.). (2012). *Doing Educational Research: A handbook*. Chicago: University of Chicago Press.

Tyler, T. R. (2003). Trust within organisations. *Personnel Review, 32*(5), 556–568. https://doi.org/10.1108/00483480310488333.

Underberg, N. M., & Zorn, E. (2014). *Digital ethnography: Anthropology, narrative, and new media*. Austin: University of Texas Press.

United Nations Human Rights Council (OHCHR). Retrieved from https://www.ohchr.org/EN/HRBodies/HRC/Pages/Home.aspx

Van Maanen, J. (1988). *Tales of the field: On writing ethnography*. Chicago: University of Chicago Press.

Wells, K. (2011). *Narrative inquiry*. Oxford: Oxford University Press.

Yang, S., Kang, M., & Johnson, P. (2010). Effects of narratives, openness to dialogic communication, and credibility on engagement in crisis communication through organizational blogs. *Communication Research, 37*(4), 473–497.

Yang, Y., & Konrad, A. M. (2011). Understanding diversity management practices: Implications of institutional theory and resource-based theory. *Group & Organization Management, 36*(1), 6–38.

Zanoni, P. (2011). Diversity in the lean automobile factory: Re-doing class along socio-demographic identities. *Organization, 18*, 105–127.

Zanoni, P., & Janssens, M. (2004). Deconstructing difference: The rhetoric of human resource managers' diversity discourses. *Organization Studies, 25*, 55–74.

Zanoni, P., & Janssens, M. (2008, July). *Contesting institutions across borders: The case of diversity management in a European branch of a US multinational*. Presented at EGOS Colloquium 'Upsetting Organizations', Amsterdam.

Zanoni, P., Janssens, M., Benschop, Y., & Nkomo, S. (2010). Unpacking diversity, grasping inequality: Rethinking difference through critical perspectives. *Organization, 17*, 9–29.

Five Nations: A Diversity Study

Alex Elwick, Paul Gibbs, Kate Maguire, and Alison Scott-Baumann

Abstract

This chapter outlines some of the findings and conclusions of a project that aimed to capture and disseminate good practice in the area of equality, diversity and inclusion (diversity) within the British Council and to influence others through a study of the stories that local and international staff tell. The approach was one of co-production of the research by the British Council's Diversity Unit, the academic research team and the British Council's Education and Society commissioning team. It used the research method chosen in the previous section to better understand the nature of actual practice within two British Council regions. The two objectives informed the fieldwork undertaken in the regions of Middle East and North Africa (MENA) and in sub-Saharan Africa (SSA). The findings illustrate the difficulties of central delivery of policy implementation within diverse geographical locations and the value of storytelling as a way to reveal actual diversity practice.

A. Elwick
Centre for Education Research and Scholarship (CERS), Middlesex University, Hendon Campus, London, UK
e-mail: a.elwick@mdx.ac.uk

P. Gibbs (✉)
Centre for Education Research and Scholarship, Middlesex University, London, UK
e-mail: p.gibbs@mdx.ac.uk

K. Maguire
Faculty of Professional and Social Sciences, Hendon Campus Middlesex University, London, UK
e-mail: K.Maguire@mdx.ac.uk

A. Scott-Baumann
Department of Religions and Philosophies, SOAS, London, UK
e-mail: as150@soas.ac.uk

© Springer Nature Switzerland AG 2019   55
M. F. Özbilgin et al. (eds.), *Global Diversity Management*, Management for Professionals, https://doi.org/10.1007/978-3-030-19523-6_5

This chapter outlines some of the findings and conclusions of a project that aimed to capture and disseminate good practice in the area of equality, diversity and inclusion (diversity) within the British Council and to influence others through a study of the stories that local and international staff tell. The approach was one of co-production of the research by the research team, the British Council's Education and Society commissioning team and its Diversity Unit. It used the research method chosen in the previous section to better understand the nature of actual practice within two British Council regions. The two objectives informed the fieldwork undertaken in the regions of Middle East and North Africa (MENA) and in sub-Saharan Africa. The findings illustrate the difficulties of central delivery of policy implementation within diverse geographical locations and the value of storytelling as a way to reveal actual diversity practice.

Co-production maximises reciprocal trust to combine the expertise and creativity of all workers for an improved approach, asserting, for example, that those with seniority and formal training do not necessarily have the best ideas and practices. Its application provides a research model that has practical implementation as a core feature of its purpose.

The aims of the project were threefold:

1. To establish the validity of narrative investigation and capture its application in the field of diversity. In doing this, we highlighted its applicability to the British Council's diversity goals, engaged British Council staff digitally across the organisation to share experiences and practice and developed an in-depth field-work study in two regions—the MENA and SSA.
2. To capture staff responses to diversity-related challenges that they encountered through the use of an interactive platform and through direct approaches, such as a short questionnaire distributed to regional diversity leads.
3. To produce a report nested in the review of narrative methodology that reflected the current diversity environment in the selected countries and provided enriching stories that could be developed and shared to further the diversity goals of the British Council.

The aim of the fieldwork was to gather data in a storytelling/narrative form of the experiences of staff in using the diversity principles as embedded features in their projects, teaching and other deliverables, as well as informing ways of being with each other as colleagues, in selected British Council offices. This is a report of the outcome of this aspect of the fieldwork, which took place in Egypt, Ghana, Kenya, Jordan and Saudi Arabia, as selected by the British Council.

The researchers were tasked with exploring the experiences of using and disseminating the values and practices of the British Council in a variety of cultural contexts that may, or may not, share the same thinking, values and practices. Therefore, the research approach chosen for such a task is ethnographic, as it has at its core a non-judgemental, non-intentional interference position. It seeks, through the process of conversations with individual members (or groups of members) of a 'culture' (work culture, ethnic culture, belief culture), to establish how those members understand the cultural phenomena and the artefacts produced by the culture of which they are a member while at the same time being members of contiguous cultures.[1] 'Understanding' is also necessarily influenced by the prior experiences of the researcher. An ethnographic process or experience of deepening understanding can also, in turn, illuminate the researcher's understanding of their own culture or the culture that they represent by bringing into awareness that which has been habituated and is therefore out of awareness. The narrative research approach necessarily produced artefacts, as in the stories, that emerged from the encounter between the researcher and the storyteller and were subsequently interpreted by the researcher in the context in which the stories were told. This accounts for the variation in the interpretation of the stories by the individual researchers.

In recognition of this as the outcome of narrative enquiry, initial common questions were built into the research design at the pre-fieldwork stage to ensure a broad range of pertinent literature-informed areas of enquiry common to all researchers, and these were agreed. However, the responses to these questions and others that emerged within the fieldwork could not be predicted for the actual engagement with the storytellers. In the post-fieldwork write-ups, the research team members shared experiences of their fieldwork and broad themes emerged, but these had different strengths and importance in each of the research strings. These broad thematic areas are used to structure the fieldwork reports yet were not used to standardise them, for this would have lost aspects of the integrity of the research.

1   Research Approach: An Ethno-narrative Analysis

The interrelationship of theory and ethnography (cultural description) in the building of understanding and sense making lies at the core of the discipline of anthropology, integrating its commitment to taking seriously individual lives within the comparative dimension of an institutional existence, which is both counter-cultural and chosen. Certainly, sociocultural anthropologists have long studied myths, legends, life histories and other stories for what they tell us about the storyteller, their audiences and the social and cultural frameworks in which the stories are told.

Language, then, is viewed as a medium that reflects singular meanings. Under the narrative movement and criticisms of positivism, language is seen more as deeply constitutive of reality, not merely a device for establishing meaning. Stories do not reflect the world out there but are constructed, rhetorical and interpretive (Riessman, 1993). As Maggio (2014: 91) states, just 'looking at a story as the creation of a particular individual rather than intersubjective creation of experience would deprive the study of its anthropological value'. Clandinin and Huber (2010) also suggest,

---

[1]British Council staff come from a variety of local and regional traditions in terms of ethnicity and beliefs that may not subscribe to all of the diversity principles.

'Narrative inquirers create research texts that show the complex and multi-layered storied nature of experience. In this way, they create research texts that represent the complexity of people's lives and experiences'.

The ethnographic approach used here builds upon the synthesis developed by Maggio (2014) from the anthropological literature and considers the story at three levels:

- The relational—where dynamics between the people involved in the storytelling situation are considered. These might include the 'the storyteller(s), the listener (s), but also the entities who take the role of characters in the story, who might be real persons (such as members of the storyteller or listener's social network) or representations of real persons (such as fictional versions or caricatures)' (ibid.: 92).
- The content of the story—here, the focus is on the action of telling and listening to stories and the reasons why a story is particularly appealing for a particular audience, which 'might be found in people's reactions to the cultural relevance of characters, plot and/or theme of the story' (ibid.: 93).
- The type of storytelling techniques—how to obtain particular effects; how shared knowledge is negotiated with their audience and the stories formulated accordingly and 'to what extent they show their personal selves as opposed to making themselves a mere medium for the telling of the story' (ibid.).

The approach is well suited to studying subjectivity and identity in context, largely because of the importance given to imagination and the human involvement in constructing a story as a way to make meaning of both familiar and strange phenomena experienced in space, place and time. Ethno-narratives also reveal much about how social life or culture, as culture, as a system of homogeneous and heterogeneous practices, speaks through a story. Finally, following good practice, we support the view that storied ethnographies should be written or embodied in a way that is accessible to most of the people who provided the original information.

The research was undertaken by a team of four field researchers: three from Middlesex University, London, and one from SOAS (School of Oriental and African Studies), London. We come from a range of disciplines and work with issues of diversity, conducting multidisciplinary research in a variety of countries. We decided on a consistent approach that would frame and facilitate the emergence of stories and also hold the range of narratives that was anticipated. Individual and group experiences of working with the diversity artefact would be shaped by contextual factors, personal and cultural histories, and intra- and intersubjectivities, the last to include the interaction between the researcher and the storyteller.

The British Council had embodied a set of principles and values—its story—in an artefact called diversity, which had emerged from powerful movements and events in British culture. The British Council had asked its staff from diverse cultures and backgrounds in its national and international offices to adopt it and, as necessary and in consultation, to adapt it to their local work cultures. The Diversity Unit then created a measurement tool called DAF, based on extensive and ongoing consultation and interaction, to track its progress. However, it recognised that richer learning could be gained through an expanded approach.

This commissioned research has been shaped by a process of collaboration between the research team and the British Council, harnessing existing expertise to arrive at an ethno-narrative approach. This approach is about the British Council giving the opportunity for its story, embodied in the diversity artefact, to be challenged 'through its internal inconsistencies, through questioning its source and coherence, and seeing it through the eyes and ears of those who did not construct that particular story', with the purpose of learning about the artefact's potential to flourish as a medium for deepening understanding between difference in diverse cultural contexts.

2   Preparation

In consultation with the British Council, five countries were chosen for the fieldwork that would represent a range of social, political, cultural, economic and linguistic field conditions: Egypt, Jordan and Saudi Arabia (from the British Council's MENA region) and Kenya and Ghana (from the organisation's SSA region). In addition, a website was set up for all British Council staff members worldwide to access, containing (1) a survey for members of its diversity global leadership community, (2) an invitation to share their stories with other members through the site and (3) an easy 'barometer' tool to input where they believed their office was in terms of embedding diversity into its practice. It was the intention of the research team to ensure that there was easy access by staff members across the world to contribute to the research.

Information sheets and introductions to the field research and to the research team were disseminated by the British Council to the offices where the fieldwork would be located. The fieldwork took place between March and June 2017. It was recognised that British Council staff would have busy daily routines and, to minimise disruption, the decision was made, in consultation with the head of the Diversity Unit, to limit the visits to 3 days, with an average target of ten individual conversations to elicit individual narratives and one group meeting to invite a group narrative that may, or may not, resonate with individual narratives.

3   Structure of the Research Design

The participants were selected by diversity leads in the country offices on the basis of (1) voluntary and informed consent, (2) roles to ensure a range of experiences and (3) availability. The group meeting, held on the last day, was open to anyone who could come.

Conversations were recorded with permission, and handwritten notes were made if a person elected not to be recorded. A person could withdraw, change their mind or ask for their contribution to be erased without being disadvantaged in any way.

Confidentiality was assured: (1) everything would be anonymised; (2) transcripts would be read only by the research team; (3) transcripts and recordings would be password protected, with only the research team having access; (4) permission would be sought from the individual if the team thought a particular example or story would help others, if shared; (5) individuals could have a copy of their transcript if requested; and (6) all primary data would be destroyed after the project was completed.

Overall, the team gathered 5 group narratives and 62 individual narratives, reflecting the experiences of diversity in five locations in a range of jobs within administration, human resources, management, teaching and exams, projects, media and communications, ancillary staff and a small number of external partners.

All recordings were transcribed by a reliable transcription service used by university researchers. An interpretative phenomenological analysis (IPA) was used by each member of the team to extract themes in a hierarchy of both occurrence and weighting supported by ante-narrative, which helps to approximate phrases in narratives into meanings to thematise. A simple example might be 'hearing that news was the last straw' approximates to 'stress', and, depending on what has come before and after that phrase, this will either be 'personal stress' or 'work stress' or 'conflation/catastrophising' and so on. Researchers shared and compared their findings to each other, and a meta-analysis of this data set was undertaken to reveal the dominant themes of resonance and dissonance that emerged in engaging with the diversity story and the possibilities for connecting stories that came to life to become 'our stories'.

4   Analysis Details

The purpose of the collected stories from the field was to provide rich data for analyses, the findings from which would contribute to:

1. Deepening understanding of diversity issues, challenges and experiences
2. Enhancing the organisation's cultural relations work to create friendly knowledge and understanding between the United Kingdom and other countries
3. Informing the future organisational direction and strategy for diversity

The analysis was conducted in two stages. In both stages, the following emergent variables were considered:

- Context place/time/space: cultural, social, economic and geopolitical conditions
- Internal cultural diversity, ethnic/religious/cultural, form of contracts for staff and language
- Roles within the British Council: teaching, project work exams, media and communications, administration, leadership and ancillary
- Personal contexts: gender, disability, identity, marital status, age and professional status

Stage 1—Individual researcher analyses of each location data, using:

- Interpretative phenomenological analysis coding of superordinate and subordinate themes to produce a distillation of the main themes that emerged from each of the five locations, indicating commonalities and the particularities. This is an approach that recognises that the experience of interactions with anything in socially constructed reality is phenomenological. IPA, employed to explore in detail the participant's perspective of the topic under investigation (Smith, Jarman, & Osborn, 1999: 218), was developed from phenomenological analysis to include the researcher's experience as an interpretative frame. This is not dissimilar to an anthropologist's field notes being used to contextualise the interpretations of data of phenomena in relation to other factors, including dissonance, both within a culture and between other cultures including their own.

The reference given above sets out clear examples of how the analyses can be carried out from scanning the text for initial summarising/preliminary interpretations to making connections to a table of superordinate and ordinate themes and then returning to check each story for 'weighting' against the themes. This captures both the particularity issues (specific, ideographic, contextual) and the broader range of what is common or similar.

Stage 2—Meta-analysis of all the location data that had been individually analysed:

- IPA for common themes to emerge from an examination of the five initial analyses.
- Interpretation through reference to (1) Boje's notion of a storytelling organisation, which aligns to the motivation and purpose of the British Council's commissioning of the research; (2) Tatli and Özbilgin's work on diversity at work using an emic approach, which may succeed in capturing issues of power and gender; (3) Syed and Boje (2007) *In Praise of Dialogue: Storytelling as a Means of Negotiated Diversity Management*; and (4) Rosile, Boje, Carlon, Downs, and Saylors (2013) *Storytelling Diamond: An antenarrative integration of the six facets of storytelling in organization research design.*

5   Boundaries

The wider contextual factors in which the research takes place are considered when examining narrative data. First-level interpretation consists of description/reporting, frequency, identification and thematic organisation. Themes are patterns in data that help to give thicker description to the phenomenon being explored, in this case the lived experiences of diversity. The second level is to thematise according to interpretative frames that are informed by political, social and cultural discourses of power.

This piece of narrative research took place within five intentional boundaries: commission, focus, location, participants (staff) and timescale. Additional boundaries to the research were the availability and willingness of staff to participate, the time allotted for each visit and the researchers' knowledge of diversity.

6 First-Level Analysis: Interpretative Phenomenological Analysis

The IPA exploration across the countries produced the following table of superordinate themes and a consensus on the issues. In this case, consensus refers to an agreement that these issues were to the foreground, but for different reasons such as context. A weighting of less than 5 indicates that it was not a superordinate theme in all the countries. The country narratives reveal the explicit and implicit articulation of these issues. The fieldwork data were produced by those who were voluntary participants. However, due to the considerable internal consistency between participants in a single site and across participants in all the sites, we can accept the stories as having a reliable level of representation of the wider community. However, the range of activities is likely to be more than was storied. What was storied was what was important to the individuals who participated in the research. Therefore, Table 1 indicates a broad brushstroke.

Apart from age, relating to the elderly—and this in reference to tensions about respectful treatment of the elderly shifting with changes in practice or expectations of imported social manners (Ghana)—most of the content in the narratives can be subsumed under superordinate themes.

7 Second-Level Analysis: Emergent Themes

The following themes were surfaced through this second-layer process. The exploration goes beyond describing and organising the data to making meaning of the data in a wider knowledge context. Using an interpretative frame of organisational power dynamics, it reveals inherent dilemmas and contradictions that support a deeper understanding of the phenomenon in order for it to be grounded, acted upon and shaped. The following categories that emerged are not intended to resolve the dilemmas, contradictions and dissonance but to provide a lens through which they can be identified and alleviated through a process of orchestrating the plurality of voices. They are the counternarrative to the positive and appreciative aspects of diversity, as highlighted frequently in the first-level analysis. Second-level analysis is where effective learning usually resides and emerges because of the power of storytelling. It gives not statements of fact but emergent themes for consideration.

Table 1 Superordinate themes derived from the research

Superordinate theme	Detail/examples	Consensus
Prioritisation of areas of diversity in terms of projects and activities	**All locations prioritised the areas according to the cultural context**	**5 All locations prioritised the areas according to the cultural context**
Scale of priority 1–7, in terms of achieving what could be done within certain constraints such as cultural constraints or availability and type of partnerships	1. Disability and gender (gender is viewed as attending to women's issues)	5 Consensus on which areas were most engaged with and the order
	2. Age/youth	
	3. Race/ethnicity	
	4. Work–life balance	
	5. Religion	
	6. Sexual orientation	
	7. Age/elderly	
Challenges in practice		
Diversity raises awareness	Diversity raises awareness, which also raises expectations	5
	Trust is central to the implementation of diversity	5
Diversity and teaching	More support for teachers at the frontline in how to resolve diversity-related dilemmas in the classroom	3
Accompanying gains		
Women's projects and initiatives	Were considered to hit a number of diversity targets at the same time, women's emancipation and political engagement at this level can have impact on society's attitudes to diversity. Women were seen almost as a test case	5
Youth projects	Helping young people be better prepared for employment	5
	Helping young people to debate and have a political voice was seen as countering the radical narrative and helping them establish confident identities	
	Youth projects were also a way of bringing young females into sports	4
Arts/creative projects	Had considerable collateral benefits, from raising awareness of diversity issues to living the	3

(continued)

Table 1 (continued)

Superordinate theme	Detail/examples	Consensus
	principles, to helping to separate tradition from religion	
Diversity areas most challenging to work with		
Sexual orientation	Conflated with religion and the most challenging in cultural contexts.	5
Religion	Mostly relating to traditions and practices such as dress code, praying and adhering to religious practices. Religion is very much embedded in culture. It is not something that can be 'fixed', like a management system Religious practices also have value principles.	5
Race/ethnicity	Discrimination within the British Council and against British Council employees outside— South Asian, Black, Eastern European	3
	Discrimination relating to internal and external sociopolitical situation	3
Not as important as other areas in priority		
Work–life balance	However, 'no time to do extra work/volunteering' was a common theme, which indicates that it is an implicit priority for staff	5
Practice dissonance		
Internal dissonance in living diversity values at work	Not understanding other cultures; behaviours that are not respectful of another's beliefs	5 Some incidents were more frequent in some locations than others
Dissonance between living values and disseminating values	We need to practise the principles if we are to bring them and their benefits to others	5
Contextual factors inhibiting living values at work and disseminating values outside	Religion, traditions, law, sociopolitical situation	5 All had contextual factors but they varied in type and intensity
Inequality/issues of fairness	Different pay scales and benefits between UK-contracted and local staff, favouritism, management not trained to handle certain issues The British Council sometimes	5

(continued)

Table 1 (continued)

Superordinate theme	Detail/examples	Consensus
	not living up to its own diversity expectations	
Effectiveness and efficiency	The tension between values focused and business focused The need to make more of diversity as a positive contribution to businesses	4
Practice resonance		
Disability, gender (women's issues)	Energy in projects, practices and gains are evident and impressive	5
Age: youth	Projects to help young people have a voice; to have access to sport, for example, and teaching, not just being about English	5
Pride in British Council	Staff are proud to work for an organisation that has values, even if there are internal tensions	5
Creative projects like arts projects, creative teaching, staff gatherings; projects like Springboard	Arts projects are seen as achieving several diversity targets at once, depending on the activities: accelerated change for the staff involved; positive attitudes to disability; increasing attention to women's issues and making practical gains; raising cultural awareness; increasing understanding through art as metaphor on women and youth issues; increasing understanding between difference in a respectful way; easing tensions	4
Internal cohesion		
	Trust was brought up frequently in the stories as being 'necessary', 'present' and 'absent'. There was a clear link between safety and trust, particularly in relation to trusting others to be able to accept difference and trusting leadership to keep everyone safe	5
	Staff involved in art projects; meals together; gatherings and events were important opportunities to promote understanding and respect for each other's ways of being in the world. This was particularly	4

(continued)

Table 1 (continued)

Superordinate theme	Detail/examples	Consensus
	important for the offices that had a high diversity of staff	
Personal change		
	All staff in their narratives spoke of personal change, with a number giving examples influencing friends and family to be more aware	5
Systemic challenges		
Cascading of information downwards and across	Would like better channels of communication	5
	More shared learning	
	Support for the barometer tool	3
Distance between London and country offices	Staff coming in from London for quick visits, helpline not knowing local conditions, UK staff not having cultural or religious literacy	4
Not enough resources	To support diversity	5
Not enough time	For extra activities like volunteering and DAF	5
Diversity Assessment *Framework* (DAF)	General consensus that this was a necessary exercise, but not enough resources behind it and it did not capture the energy, the variety and the advances being made adequately	5
	Could be prepared with more planning, rather than a rush at the last minute	5
	Positive references to DAF and to feedback	5
	Could be pared down, and other forms of progress monitoring used	4
	The league table is a great idea	1
Enjoyment in successes		
	Even if not directly involved in each other's work, there was a sense of enjoyment of achievements of others	5
Language translating terms and concepts and use of diversity acronym		
	Diversity acronym in conversations replaced by trust, respect, fairness	5
	Mainstreaming is hard to translate into Arabic. For	

(continued)

Table 1 (continued)

Superordinate theme	Detail/examples	Consensus
	example, *There are just some things you can't say in our languages, because language, religion and tradition are woven together*	
	Staff tended to use 'respect' and other terms for diversity, rather than the acronym	5
	Diversity was spoken about in terms of a British Council initiative, and not in terms of Universal Human Rights	4
	Attached to this issue was to always ensure all staff are included in the 'family'; reference made to ancillary staff, kitchen workers, drivers, those whose English was perhaps not at the level of other members of staff and allowances could be made for how to include them more, such as translating diversity materials	3
	There was a call for more materials to be translated for businesses, many of which have staff that did not speak English	3
Good practices		
	Arts projects; disability awareness and practical solutions to mobility and changes in attitudes; women and youth projects; partnerships; positive attitudes; constructive questioning; disseminating the values of British Council; showing organisations how they work; practising values inside and outside	5

They have been in part generated by assumptions, misperceptions and misunderstandings of diversity as an imported value system that can conflict with beliefs and practices of the host culture, rather than as an awareness-raising strategy that seeks an outcome of respect for difference, rather than one which seeks conversion.

8   Thematic Analysis: Themes from the Field

8.1   Effectiveness and Efficiency

Tension arises from a fundamental contradiction between a dissemination of a values system of caring alongside a business model of income generation in contexts where the values are dissonant with the prevailing cultural norms, thereby setting up conditions for compromising on the values. An organisation disseminating a set of values may, in some circumstances, find that they are not good for business if there is no advantage to be gained from adopting them. Values need to be tempered to evidence effectiveness and efficiency for businesses.

8.2   Structural Ambiguity

Through our conversations with staff across the country offices in which we conducted our research, there emerged a clear 'inside–outside' dissonance between what was expected of internal staff (in terms of their behaviour and practices) and what was considered appropriate in their external cultural context. Employees may subscribe to the values of the organisation while inside the safe space of the work environment, yet may be required to behave differently according to cultural expectations once outside. An interviewee in Ghana remarked that:

> It must be very, very difficult, and I don't use this term in a derogatory way, but it is like bi-polar lives. They come here and they are expected to act in a certain manner and then they go out and are expected to act in a different way. (Ghana)

The aspiration of a set of values to be adhered to in recruitment, for example, in order to demonstrate fairness, presents both logistical problems and perceived unfairness. Such adherence becomes embedded as an order, which begins to reduce the organisation's ability to adapt to changing environments and to recruit on the basis of the skills, capabilities and aptitudes required for the success of the organisation:

> I often think that diversity can also be a weapon. 'You're discriminating against me, how come you only selected men? How come you only selected girls? How come you do this, that's not diversity, you're discriminating.' You hear these things. (Egypt)

8.3   Colonising Values

Perceived inequality between local and UK-contracted staff can be conflated with the past, emerging as a new form of, or a modified version of, colonialism:

> People have felt, say, White people were taking local posts, so somebody, a local person, occupying a particular post and the person leaves and it's not filled. Before long you find a White person coming in to replace that person. (Ghana)

People need good jobs, and the organisation, because of its values and its influence locally and internationally, was often perceived as a good employer in the countries we visited, giving status to its employees. Pride was expressed among the interviewees for having been chosen to work for such a well-known organisation and being able to contribute to its work even when staff find it challenging to 'live' all the values.

> Every time I do tell people I work for the British Council, if I'm asked what do you do, I say I work in the British Council, their face lights up. (Kenya)

> I feel more proud as a professional, as a human being. (Jordan)

> I think actually on the whole our assessment framework which has improved... is slightly more challenging... it's asking us to mainstream our activity more, so it's not just making sure our paperwork is okay, but actually demonstrates evidence that we're putting this into life day to day in the operation. (Egypt)

There was a sense of conflict between desire, aspiration and need, on the one hand, and accepting values that one might not be fully committed to, on the other hand: of not subscribing completely to values that have arrived, fully formed, into their contexts. This conflict can give rise to inner tension, frustration and fear. Knowledge of the existing value systems in countries was often cited as an important first step, and building on such systems may help to reduce levels of dissonance:

> Ghanaians are very religious, so you get somebody from the UK, or that is not a Ghanaian, who is not very religious; I expect them to respect the fact that the people are religious, rather than trying to make them feel, because you are religious you are not diversity compliant, so that is really the challenge. (Ghana)

8.4   Adaptation and Temporality

Traditional cultures, or conformity-focused societies, due to an acceleration of time perception and driven by technology and globalisation, are in a transitional stage of change before there has been sufficient time and circumstances to adapt. Rapid change often stimulates passive and active resistance. As one interviewee in Jordan noted, time and practice are required for change to take hold:

> Respect is not promoting or enforcing beliefs on someone else, it is accepting that there are good reasons why people hold certain beliefs and it is not easy to change. It takes time and practice. (Jordan)

Yet there is an awareness that if a cultural ecology does not adapt it will become resistant and decay. Identity formation is shaped by cultural DNA, transmitted through family. Values from a prefigurative culture such as the United Kingdom can separate the individual from their cultures unless sufficient time is given to adapt. An interviewee in Kenya noted that time brings the confidence to tailor approaches:

But with time—because we've worked with them over a period of two years—the coaches are now confident, they can question us and say, 'No, that wouldn't work in my community. It may have worked in yours, but here it won't work.' And it's a confidence that comes with time. (Kenya)

Katan suggests that:

Culture consists of patterns, explicit and implicit of and for behaviour acquired and trans-mitted by symbols, constituting the distinctive element of human groups, including their embodiment in artefacts; the essential core of culture consists of traditional (i.e. historically derived and selected) ideas and especially their attached values. Culture systems may, on the one hand, be considered as products of action, on the other hand, as conditioning elements of future action. (Katan, 1999: 16)

8.5   Gained in Translation

Language is a transmitter of cultural memes. Language is also what challenges them. History literally means story of the wise man, though it is often that of the victor. Language is power. In translating the world's most powerful language, English, we need to be clear of the purpose—'a wish-to-know and a wish-to-understand, rather than a wish-to-control perspective' (Toury, 1995: 57).

We use too many words that only mean something to the organisation like diversity, say it simply, we are the bridges to understanding, we help the disabled etc… (Jordan)

The value set of diversity is a cultural artefact; therefore its story and terms within the story such as mainstreaming and sexual orientation are either linguistically difficult to translate or culturally fraught with problems. In response, the stories from the frontline translated the imported, cultural artefact into a story of respect, fairness and acceptance. Art and metaphor were used to facilitate understanding for themselves, as well as 'translating' the imported artefact to others:

Art can help people in other countries to understand each other's cultures through exchange of art. We have done this through exhibitions. There was the role of art in helping people to separate religion and tradition. (Saudi Arabia)

Respect—I think that is the word that is missing, respect for diversity more than mainstreaming diversity because that is the first step, mainstreaming is very difficult to translate into Arabic… (Jordan)

8.6   Collusion, Compliance, Compromise, Loyalty and Alienation

There were stories of compliance without internal belief and stories of compromise, among our interviewees. Compromise is contextually judged as positive, as in reaching a point of coexistence between oppositional or polarised positions, or negative, which is more closely akin to a negation of power for short-term gain, a situation that renders little satisfaction to the players, being rarely more than a diluted accommodation. The latter does not remove inherent tensions but can increase them, as compromise in itself does not resolve differences between positions. At best it is pragmatic in the short term, but more often it gives the illusion of resolution without attention to the underlying emotions and behaviours of difference, which then persist. An interviewee from Ghana talked about the necessity of compromise while hinting at the underlying remaining tensions:

> Because it's the work we do, it has to be behind everything we do, and if it is behind everything we do that means that if it's in your deliverables then as an individual you need to have something whether you like it or not. (Ghana)

There were also stories of conversion and of alienation among our interviewees. Some people were genuinely changed through working with diversity:

> Actually, I consider diversity as being about respect. We are respecting people who are different from us whatever their gender, capability. For example, some people have the idea that a woman cannot do as a man. They can't drive, they cannot do a lot of things. But after I took a course, I see that you can do whatever you want as a woman. So it changes you here inside and outside the British Council. (Saudi Arabia)

> I do have that passion about how we can bring diversity closer in our lives like we bring everything else closer. It is something that we live. (Jordan)

Others, however, felt that aspects of diversity required something of them, which felt like collusion with another culture and betrayal of their own. Cultural shifts are, for the most part, slow processes of adaptation. The most successful are those which build on beliefs and practices that already exist in the culture that is being influenced, to shift by internal or external influences:

> We wanted to bring diversity closer together, we wanted to share our values with each other and get to know each other's culture better so we had a community meal, people dressed up in their traditional clothes and those who didn't went back and changed, we had stalls with our own food and symbols of our culture, we had our own music, we encouraged our Saudi colleague and hers was the best, really… that gathering was great and we should do it more often. (Saudi Arabia)

One of the most positive external influences is the Universal Declaration of Human Rights (UDHR), which was adopted by the United Nations General Assembly in 1948. Human rights projects through the United Nations (UN) and through non-governmental organisations (NGOs) and educational bodies like the British Council subscribe to these human rights, values which inform and guide all their activities. The link between diversity and the UDHR and its subsequent amendments can be made more explicit in the everyday working lives of staff, which can mitigate perceptions of imported or neocolonial values.

There were many stories of loyalty to the British Council but also the need to keep secure employment. There was a vicarious enjoyment of the freedom that the British

Council space offered for part of the day, and, for others, it was the realisation of the disabling aspect of cultural traditions and freedom from them:

> It's good, it's an open office which—I came from a corporate before that and you had to have an appointment, there is a room before you see the actual manager in another room and you have to ask permission. (Kenya)

The British Council's prioritisation of diversity areas of action reflected choices to adopt or adapt to that which most resonated with the cultural norms or rising local trends, the options that required the least amount of compromise and were a visible and impactful outcome of effort. Compromise needs to be seen as temporary. While compromise may not be a satisfactory resolution to any party in the dynamic, it should be acknowledged that it can shift over time if it is recognised as a step in a process and not a resolution in and of itself. In contrast, alienation in the context of being separated or separating from traditional identity through knowledge and awareness can be equated to migration and the hazards that accompany this form of movement that is forced or brought about by a complex series of factors and events. An interviewee from Kenya summarised the contextual cause of alienation in one instance:

> Tribe is a very, very, very emotive issue in Kenya, it's a big deal and especially in an election year it is a big deal. People fight, people kill each other, people don't talk to each other because the two main political parties are owned by the two main tribes, so it is a big, big issue in Kenya and in terms of diversity I feel like, diversity probably being a concept that comes from the UK, I feel like the tribe, it is not really addressed properly. (Kenya)

8.7   Projection and Perception

Perceptions and assumptions misdirect feelings about what is and is not and are informed by a complex range of factors, from the personal to the professional, from tradition to modernity, from a sense of self in the world to fear of loss of identity and support and from righteousness to doing what is right.

There were examples of projection onto the organisation: for it to be what staff cannot yet be. It was held up to higher scrutiny to live the values that it seeks to disseminate and to do more to raise awareness through more creative and resourced activities. Like all projections, it lays responsibility on another for what cannot yet be achieved or tolerated in oneself. Through the organisation living its values, others are encouraged to try:

> Because every programme we do here, we take it as our programme and it must project our values... And then when it's outside we always try to push that to them, because that is our British Council policy where there's always the equality, diversity, inclusion. (Ghana)

The worthiness of the diversity areas focused on by the British Council was not what was in doubt, but contention arrived around how such values could be lived outside the British Council as well as inside. There was a powerful role expressed for the values, in terms of raising awareness by something just being there, visible as a principle, a human right, rather than having immediate expectations of them having to be acted upon and lived. They can contribute to creating the conditions for understanding to take place at some point.

8.8   Trust

Trust was considered essential to the implementation of diversity: trust in oneself, trust between colleagues, trust in leadership, trust in the motives of the organisation and trust that the organisation will look after them:

> The increasing importance of internally motivated behaviour to organisations makes clear why issues of trust and procedural justice are becoming more central to organisational studies. Both trust and procedural justice are social motives, i.e. motives that are internal or socially generated. They flow from within the person, rather than being linked to incentives or sanctions. (Tyler, 2003)

An interviewee from Egypt expressed this level of trust in terms of the support that they had been provided with by their employers:

> I'm doing a Masters in Cairo University, in Gender and Development and I can say the amount of support I am given from the office is amazing. So this is another thing. Because sometimes you would never really be able to be a student and an employee who is holding a high position as well, so the amount of support I am given to be a student is really above [what] I've ever expected from my manager and from the management. (Egypt)

Trust was both manifest in and absent from the narratives of our interviewees. Trust is a necessary condition for any contractual or voluntary agreement to take place. It involves elements of risk. Without it, safety in others is compromised; its absence can have the effect of silencing others. This raises the question of the role of trust in the implementation of diversity values: what are the indicators of trustworthiness; how can trustworthiness be increased; what undermines trust; is dissonance the absence of trust; and is resonance the presence of trust? An interviewee from Ghana discussed their perception of trust deficits in their context:

> Right now in the office we have a problem of trust, there is no trust because they feel management is making the decisions based on whether you are UK, or you're Black or you're White, so right now we need to communicate more. (Ghana)

Trust is intricately linked to reliability and accountability. If a person is reliable consistently over time and accountable for their actions and views, they are likely to be trusted, regardless of their professional, cultural or social identity.

9   Discussion and Conclusions

Across the five nations in which our research was conducted, the thematic analysis above identifies some of the common perceptions and understandings of staff at British Council offices in relation to the diversity values that they were expected to adhere to and uphold. While there were tensions between the differing cultural contexts within and outside of the offices themselves and the work that the British Council led, there were also stories of transformation and stories that emphasised the powerful role such values could play.

Inevitably, given that the British Council is a UK organisation operating in diverse country and cultural contexts outside of Britain, the values of the organisation could be viewed as colonising and as an imposition upon local customs—which emphasises the need to engage with such contexts when implementing diversity values that may not, initially, be aligned.

Our research emphasised the power of time to ease transition and to allow for change to be managed. Adaptation is not a straightforward process, and only by both allowing people to take the time needed for change and taking time, as an organisation, to understand local contexts and unique challenges can values be embedded in diverse contexts.

The stance of staff towards the diversity values was often varied, including approaches that we have characterised as colluding, complying, compromising and so on. Some of those whom we spoke to felt loyalty to the organisation's values, others felt alienated—but, for the vast majority, there was a recognition that compromise was often possible and desirable, so long as eventually underlying tensions were addressed in one way or another. Implicit, and explicit in some cases, in such an approach was the role of trust—from the organisation to its employees, but also vice versa, from the employees towards the organisation. Both parties gain from greater trust: from senior managers embedding the values in their own work and placing faith and responsibility in their staff and from staff recognising the power and value inherent in the diversity values, even when these differ from those values adhered to locally.

It could be questioned whether one set of values is appropriate for all contexts and countries in which an organisation operates, especially given the unique challenges that different contexts often present. However, we saw no reason why a single set of coherent diversity values, such as those held by the British Council, should not be shared across borders—so long as time and space are taken to understand how those values might work in location and with staff, many of whom will be local and will hold their own sets of values. The power and role of compromise should not be underestimated and ignored—as long as such an approach does not simply mask or ignore underlying tensions.

As authors of this chapter, we hope that by demonstrating the challenges and successes of implementing a single set of diversity values across these five nations (and much more broadly), other organisations might recognise the difficulties yet also opportunities that present themselves. The ability to be culturally reflexive and to embrace compromise is paramount, but need not distract from the ultimate ambition of implementing a shared set of values.

10 General Recommendation for Organisations Undertaking Global Diversity Management

Based upon the fieldwork and including our analysis of the material contributed online, we have made nine recommendations to organisations engaged in diversity management to improve their practice, going forward.

1. *Senior managers across country offices should fully embody the organisation's diversity values in all that they do, both internally and externally.*

   Some interviewees from different country offices expressed concern that senior managers did not always fully buy in to the diversity approach, particularly when it came to internal matters relating to diversity. Staff suggested that they themselves would find it easier to adopt diversity values if they saw their managers doing so too. Managers must lead by example in order to make the, at times, 'hard sell' to their staff and to ensure that the diversity strategy is fully embedded. Part of such an approach should ensure that managers fully understand the importance of implementing diversity within their own areas. This recommendation is not based on just a deficit model, but on the good practice reported for all countries.

2. *Organisations need to have open and honest discussion internally around the balance between effectiveness and efficiency: acknowledging compromises that are made, or need to be made, between embedding the diversity areas in all that they do and ensuring that the organisation's activities are sustainable and achievable.*

   In contrast to much of the literature around organisational diversity areas, conversations with staff often suggested that there were compromises to be made when adopting an approach that fully embodies diversity values. When making decisions from a purely moral standpoint, sacrifices may have to be made from an economic standpoint or in terms of efficiency. In circumstances when taking a moral position might undermine a business case, the British Council needs to be explicit in its decision-making and communicate it to/discuss this with all staff involved. At times when certain diversity areas are not given equal weight (such as in the area of sexual orientation) in specific contexts, organisations need to have internal, open discussion about why this may be the case and whether it can be justified.

3. *More attention needs to be given to both the values and the skills of local staff—identifying where there might be dissonance, as well as fully understanding the richness of staff experiences and the skills that they can contribute.*

   We recommend fully acknowledging the different skill sets, experiences and values of staff and highlighting potential areas of personal conflict within the mission of an international organisation and a local context. Such an approach counters the critique in the literature of a diminished focus on individual identity when implementing diversity, and it was clear that there were instances when the organisation's values or priorities clashed with those of individuals working across the country offices. Such dissonance is not necessarily avoidable, but it should be openly acknowledged in moving forward.

4. *Organisations should consider how to best integrate and work with those who are not able to speak English fluently, particularly supporting low-income staff and associates (e.g. by providing free English teaching) and partner organisations in host countries (e.g. by providing material and resources in a variety of languages).*

   Organisations should consider the intersectionality of those in low-status or low-income positions and those who have poor English language skills. Very often these two groups overlap, and organisations should question whether more can be done to integrate such groups within the organisation and whether there are opportunities to engage further that are being missed, particularly with external partners whose staff may not speak English. We recommend that the British Council considers how resources, in both hard and soft copy, are provided and how information is made available (in the office, online, in person).

5. *Good diversity practices should be shared horizontally across the organisation, both within and between country offices, so that colleagues can learn from each other directly.*

   We recommend that organisations should expand out from a potentially formulaic approach of reporting diversity issues and practices that largely take place in an upwards direction only. Instead, there should be further, regular opportunities for staff to share their experiences with each other across country offices. This recommendation refers particularly to good practice, but also includes challenges that staff have faced and overcome. We identified numerous positive stories and activities relating to diversity in this research and hope that this work goes some way to addressing this recommendation, but it was clear that staff would welcome an ongoing forum or facility for such sharing, and we recommend that they are encouraged to do so.

6. *Organisations should consider whether its diversity approach is applicable to all countries in the current form or whether it should reflect the different cultural contexts in which it is implemented.*

   We make this recommendation cautiously, as there was no widespread evidence that change in approach would bring tangible gains or be appropriate to the principles of diversity. However, it was clear that in certain countries the cultural and legal context has a significant effect on staff's practical approach to the implementation of diversity.

References

Clandinin, D. J., & Huber, J. (2010). Narrative inquiry. In B. McGaw, E. Baker, & P. P. Peterson (Eds.), *International encyclopedia of education* (3rd ed.). New York: Elsevier.

Katan, D. (1999). *Translating cultures. An introduction for translators, interpreters and mediators.* Manchester: St Jerome.

Maggio, R. (2014). The anthropology of storytelling and the storytelling of anthropology. *Journal of Comparative Research in Anthropology and Sociology, 5,* 89–106.

Riessman, C. K. (1993). *Narrative analysis.* Qualitative Research Methods Series, No. 30. Newbury Park, CA: Sage.

Rosile, G. A., Boje, D. M., Carlon, D., Downs, A., & Saylors, R. (2013). Storytelling diamond: An antenarrative integration of the six facets of storytelling in organization research design. *Organizational Research Methods Journal, 18,* 16–30.

Smith, J. A., Jarman, M., & Osborn, M. (1999). Doing interpretative phenomenological analysis. In M. Murray & K. Chamberlain (Eds.), *Qualitative health psychology: Theories and methods* (pp. 218–240).

Syed, J., & Boje, D. M. (2007). *In praise of dialogue: Storytelling as a means of negotiated diversity management.* https://kar.kent.ac.uk/24891/1/Web_Version.pdf

Toury, G. (1995). *Descriptive translation studies and beyond.* Amsterdam: Benjamin.

Tyler, T. (2003). Trust within organisations. *Personnel Review, 32*(5), 556–568.

Part II

Practitioners Reflecting on Practice

The following nine case stories are told by organisations and by individuals who are practitioners involved in diversity and global diversity management. Their messages are compelling and have an underlying compatibility. Each is personal, and often tells a story of practice in ways that deal with insight into the author's practice from personal histories that have shaped not just practice but the way in which they live their lives. These chapters are rich in experience, offering the reader opportunities to empathically join their process of diversity management in international and national contexts. They are from a number of fields; large organisations and small, from school education to university and to the entertainment industry, on topics such as personal leadership training, teaching and self-awareness. In common they share diversity management in international context but in different forms.

Each of the chapters speaks with the personal voice of the author and shows the compassion with which each addresses their own histories and engages with them to build an approach to diversity management that is inspiring. Very much in the style of the main project in first part of the book, many of the chapters use storytelling to help us to understand, and they are more powerful for that. In the final chapter, the hard work done in these chapters is used in a meta-narrative of the emergent power of compassion, with its contributory attributes of respect, care, belonging and empathy, to offer a theme that is implicitly referred to in all studies offered in the book. The following very brief summary of the next chapters shows where to find it.

Ágota Bíró's chapter allows us to consider that things are hardly ever perfect and that, once this is recognised, then a culture can be built that has at its core empathy and compassion, and upon them more innovation and creativity can emerge.

Patti Boulaye's harrowing tale of warfare and barbaric behaviour is tempered by kindness and compassion to strangers, and eventually finding diversity in the entertainment industry.

David Crabtree's is a discussion of exclusion reshaped by awareness through the Theatre of the Classroom, in which common concern, competency and compassion for others leads to more inclusivity, in which students are more valued and in which teachers seek to better understand their students' needs.

Simon Minty's chapter speaks to us about his professional experiences of disability training working in large multinational companies and being a disabled person himself. He uses professional knowledge combined with personal. He is not someone who advocates on behalf of another, he lives what he says. He recognises the differences and sensitivities of disability in different cultures and by pushing towards change, by including disabled people, longer lasting change can be achieved.

Wayne Mullen's chapter considers situations where differences provide opportunity to learn and develop more nuanced approaches to diversity and leadership development interventions. As he points out, this requires empathy and, where truths are being confronted, there is an underlying need for an underlying culture of trust and compassion, where hurt might be predicted and support offered.

Asif Sadiq's chapter looks at the issues that large global organisations face. He advocates a sense of belonging as central to a common cultural experience, available and implicit wherever a global organisation might locate its offices. He recognises, however, that local external environments might influence the actuality of how diversity management can be enacted.

Kathrin Tietze asks for time: time to reflect, to reframe and to change in her approach to diversity management. From her work and advocacy to dig deep into oneself for the sake of humanity, to reach people's hearts to reach them, she hopes that you find a sense of empathy and compassion.

Abid Hussain reflects on his experiences as he engages with, embraces then promotes disability in the arts. His story is one of determination, satisfaction and joy.

Doirean Wilson draws on her work on the cultural meanings of respect and how these manifest themselves. She argues that lack of awareness is at the core of these misreadings. This is true where empathy is missing, because compassion is absent.

What Makes You Successful at Diversity Management? A Personal Journey

Ágota Bíró

Abstract

In this chapter, Agota shares her personal learning journey to diversity management and the various formal and non-formal learning experiences that widened her horizons in this area. In her opinion and because the measurement of personal development is often vague, it is important to rely on personal stories that outline the various influences on a person that contributed to their becoming more empowered to be change makers in this field. In her case, one of the British Council's programmes (Intercultural Navigators) was a very important point, which was later supplemented by her work within the organisation as a diversity lead. As a diversity lead, she has had to understand the organisation's diversity strategy and framework, and this enabled her to think about mainstreaming. All these experiences contributed to who she has become and how she works now, on the individual, team and organisational levels, with diversity and inclusion.

1   I Am Who I Am

Even from the title of this chapter it is easy to recognise the danger of ambiguity and misinterpretation. Who knows what success is? And what is the definition of diversity management exactly? Also, I am sure there is more than one. Still, for some reason, I feel empowered to tell you the very personal story of my professional journey to this arena, which cannot be separated from who I am as a human being: a woman, a mother, a friend, a partner, a daughter, a human rights activist, a lover and an ex-wife. (And this is one of the miracles of working with professionals passionate

Á. Bíró (✉)

Human Resources, Emarsys, Budapest, Hungary

about diversity—their professional identity brings a lot from the personal, hence the passion, but more about it later.)

I was born in Communist Hungary and started primary school at the beginning of the 1980s, the time of the so-called Goulash Communism or 'Soft Communism'. At school, we had to wear an *iskolaköpeny*, which was dark blue upper clothing with the main objective of disguising your real clothes, thus pretending that there was no difference between us.

We hated that something, which was not really a uniform to represent belonging to the same community but was designed to hide the fact that we were all unique. However, the intention was good: to create equality between the poor and the rich, the ones with better clothes than the others.

And this little anecdote from my primary school years brings me to some of the learning points around managing diversity and inclusion, which I was unaware of in those days.

There were other influences that clarified these for me, and, as I have supported some leaders and organisations in becoming more inclusive since then, I know that similar experiences were important for other individuals and groups as well. Therefore, I will centre my chapter around the learning points illustrated by this little story from my childhood:

1. The good intention trap
2. The power of community
3. Bringing your whole self

I intend to bring these experiences to you in order to give you an insight into the complicated nature of when and how learning happens when it comes to education around managing diversity, working in diverse teams or leading in global settings. We often run and design equality-, diversity- or inclusion-related programmes, but it is hard to measure their impact. The impact on the individual is hard to grasp and is unpredictable, and it does not help us to decide whether to invest in the next programme or not. That is true in many ways; unless we are ready to listen to the individual or the groups telling their stories.

2   The Good Intention Trap

Enforcing students to cover their clothes had the intention of creating equality. When in 2009 I was invited to the British Council's Intercultural Navigators programme, to be trained as a facilitator of a leadership programme for young people, one of the stories we worked with was that of the giraffe and the elephant.[1] It is a well-known introductory activity to diversity management, because it nicely illustrates a lot of aspects of discrimination and its institutional nature. And at the beginning of my

---

[1]https://www.bacchus-env.eu/pdfs/The_Giraffe_andthe_Elephant_fable.pdf

reflections on the nature of assumptions, prejudices, diversity, identities and so on, it was more than striking to me to reflect on the fact that discrimination also happens when there is no bad intent. In my simple little world at that time, I thought there are bad people who discriminate and there are good people on top of the moral ladder looking around, spotting all the bad people who do not get it.

Why am I ready to admit to this fairly embarrassing realisation? Firstly, because this is one of the most important elements of success in working with diversity. You need to leave the idea of ladders behind and forget about being better than anyone else, simply, because you are not. You have biases, you are part of a system that discriminates, and your moral distance disables you to get to the core of the problem. Secondly, because I often see people in the field losing their credibility and integrity, specifically because they do not understand that good intent is not enough. Organisations and leaders often claim that they are on the road to inclusivity. But in reality, they have sent the elephant to the gym to make sure that they fit well into the giraffe house, or they opened the door to the basement without letting certain groups climb the stairs to the top. This happens, for example, when organisations pride themselves on increasing the number of female professionals in the company, yet you see that none of them make it to top management.

All in all, this one story, and its creative educational usage in the Intercultural Navigators programme, reminds me constantly to avoid the good intention trap.

3   The Power of Community

There is nothing revolutionary about claiming that belonging to a group with a shared goal can be empowering, and this empowerment can have a positive impact on working towards organisational or social change. In my career there have been a few moments of empowerment, rooted in the power of community (or power of sisterhood, even). In my opinion, the most important element of those experiences was the recognition that I am not alone in my intention to stop discrimination from happening or to improve the level of cooperation in diverse teams or even to make a company more inclusive. Moreover, I am not the only one inspired and satisfied when working with diversity. The first time I realised this was on a teacher training programme in which I participated as a freshly graduated teacher. It was a set of workshops improving intercultural skills organised by an independent (or, as it was called in Hungary, 'alternative') teacher training NGO. Every session we visited representatives, events or buildings of a different ethnic or religious group or subculture. It was nothing else but actively engaging with people, events and circumstances that were different from things that I had experienced before. For example, I knew something about Jewish culture but had never entered a synagogue before (mind you, I went to school at a time where religion was evil, and it was only secretly practised). But it also allowed me to have real conversations with Roma artists and so on. These visits and discussions opened my horizons; they opened the door to a world as colourful as a Persian carpet of the best kind. I somehow became addicted to difference, but not as a culture junkie—more as a person who never settles for a single perspective.

In the following years, I was lucky to work internationally in cultural diplomacy: I stayed hungry and foolish, and my hunger for all these interactions was satisfied by amazing encounters such as visiting Robben Island and meeting one of the people who stayed in the same prison as Nelson Mandela, a special guided walk in the Jewish quarter of Vienna, visiting a special needs school in Cape Town, engaging with disabled artists, developing Roma university students' leadership skills and a lot more.

What I realised on the way was that the experience, in itself, did not empower me: these interactions were shared and reflected upon by a group of engaged individuals with whom I shared goals. The sharing brought empowerment. They enabled me not to be scared, even when I stayed alone with an argument in an organisation or in a different team. Knowing that I am not alone was a special driver and supportive force. It made me understand that there is no success in managing diversity in any teams or organisations where there are lonely promoters of the agenda. We need to build the communities that learn together, work together and support one another in the moments of hardships and disappointment. Working on inclusion is a deep dive into your identity, and, when you do it together with others, usually those relationships are transformed into something much stronger. In my opinion, the transformational nature of inclusion-related work has an unprecedented impact on working culture. My theory, and it would be interesting to do some research into it, is that the intensive work around identity makes people open up in a different way. It creates a sense of shared vulnerability that builds trust. However, it is fairly indirect, so is sometimes underestimated. I passionately believe in the transformations happening alongside our work around diversity and inclusion.

However, it is also important to be aware of the risks created by the power of community. I have often seen—not surprisingly—the us and them dichotomy appearing in organisations, with us, the ones promoting inclusion and diversity, and them, the ones who do not get it. I want to be honest here, so, obviously, for a long time I have been thinking this way. But actually, there was one expression that echoed in my head for a long time: we are preaching to the converted. When I was delivering training, working with leaders and spending time with people enthusiastic about diversity management, I had this sentence coming up: 'Preaching to the converted'. And my learning was that when you have enough comfort in your community of us and you start thinking about the them, that is the right moment to stand up and walk to them, mingle with them and understand them. I used to work at the British Council. I still think that it is an organisation with an amazing diversity team and a diversity strategy and lots of learning opportunities, and I will never be able to express the gratitude I have for all the things I learned there. But there was this point of safety, when I felt it was time to get out and work in a sector that is not so good at it, namely, the tech sector. I love to work on this agenda here, because I do not feel I am preaching to the converted.

The Power of the Community enables me to ask myself:
Am I talking to the right people?
Am I sharing my knowledge and skills with the people who really need it?
Am I making a change?
Do I have an impact?

4   Bringing Your Whole Self

Remember my primary school story and the act of hiding our clothes? Well, it keeps striking me how much people are hiding about their whole selves at work. Obviously, we do not need to bring everything to work, and it depends a lot on our age, culture, interests, national identity, positions and loads of other factors what we want to bring. But as a person working a lot on leadership development and as an executive coach, my conclusion is that most people—and not only those brought up in Communist Hungary—enter their workplace in well-designed masks and armour to ensure that their flaws and hidden traits are not revealed. And people do not hide only their sexual orientation, disability, religion, marital status, number of children, mental illness and so on. They hide their real feelings, their sadness, anger, frustration, curiosity, love, happiness and so on. I am sure that you will say now, well, this is a place of work, we are supposed to perform and deliver, so obviously, it is not at all about our frustrations, love and happiness or sadness. Well, I need to disagree with you. It is all about that; I can tell you. At the moment I am responsible for HR, or as we call it there 'happiness', in a research and development centre in Budapest. People tell their stories to me and I feel privileged that they do. And I know almost all of them come to work with baggage that is not so easy to leave at the door: I have heard of many stories—good and bad—that are hard to forget in meetings, team lunches, during coding sessions and so on. These stories have an impact on performance, for sure.

This summer I lost a childhood friend and an amazing colleague to cancer. His death turned my world around in so many ways. And it had a huge impact on the work of a lot of people in our organisation. People saw me crying, and I saw people crying; people experienced my numbness, and I have experienced silence in the way I never had before. But we brought our whole self to work. This extreme situation removed masks, because in the face of death, masks do not make any sense and because the very person we lost was the symbol of bringing his whole self to work, even with his illness.

What did I learn from that? I have learned that policies do not encourage people to be themselves; people do. Amazing people, who have the courage to peel off their masks and be themselves, the way they are. With all their weaknesses, flaws and mistakes. People, who are not perfect, because perfection does not exist.

This magic of imperfection has become more and more important to me recently, because I have recognised that the assumption that things and situations that are not perfect can foster a lot of positive change in organisations: these are the ability to forgive, the ability to make mistakes and the openness to learning. All these can contribute to things that are important to me: more innovation and creativity, spiced with better teamwork.

So there is a lot at stake! Stopping our people from bringing their whole selves to work can stop the innovative power of our organisation. This inspires me, and this makes me wake up in the morning, and this makes me passionate about work around diversity and inclusion. A life where you need to hide has great dangers for me: boredom and dishonesty. I am scared by both. Obviously, there is a simplicity in uniforms and *iskolaköpeny*. On the surface, things look much simpler and predictable. But there is no evidence that they are, actually.

And this sentence brings me to a recent realisation that contributes to the success of diversity management. I think that people in this professional scene have spent too long gathering and presenting evidence that inclusion and diversity are good things that make individuals, teams, organisations and societies more successful. I more and more want to ask a different question:

Where is the evidence that homogenous teams, organisations and societies perform better?

I think the answer is simple: nowhere. For some reason, they do not even exist, really. So I stopped focusing on making the case. I live with the assumption that the case is made, and, if someone does not believe it, I give them a challenge to prove it. This whole realisation started at the Open Conference in Budapest in November 2017, when one of the speakers talked about the need for shifting the burden of proof. There were so many important things at that conference, but at that moment this was my key 'takeaway'. And I have got back to the point of evaluating, assessing the value of diversity programmes, conferences, talks and so on. It is impossible, because all the people involved enter these spaces with a unique perspective and whatever speaks to one of them may not speak to someone else: the sentence echoing in one head will be lost in another.

All in all, bringing your whole self to the world is about integrity. And integrity is one of the traits of successful leaders: those leaders who walk the talk, who are successful, because they have the courage to be themselves even in all those moments when they are lost and have no idea how to do things, who face their own mistakes in order to become better and who walk the talk and do not let their team members get away with decisions driven by bias, prejudice, fast thinking, group pressure and a lack of emotional intelligence.

Spending all those years thinking about diversity mainstreaming equipped me to become a leader who asks a lot of questions about diversity, inclusion and relationships. It developed me into a leader who focuses more on upward feedback when things do not work well and who is actively engaged in facilitating learning around inclusion and diversity, not only as part of an HR function but more as part of values-based leadership.

We do believe in different things. I believe in integrity. And I believe that diversity and inclusion-related activity in any organisation foster innovation. I do hope that my story gave a clear explanation why. If it did not, just take it as my story, my explanation and my reality. And I am always happy to listen to yours, for a new perspective.

Diversity in Global Management

Patti Boulaye

Abstract

Patti shares narratives based on reflections on her personal and career life-course journey of diversity from two cultural standpoints. These experiences had a significant impact on her understanding of people differences and how these can be harnessed so that others can benefit. She offers a critical review of her early learning, born of her Nigerian upbringing, that helped to shape her beliefs. She compares this experience with the reality of finding herself in a culture different from her own, due to the horrors of the Biafran War, before her journey to Britain.

I was born in Nigeria, an Igbo and the seventh of nine children, and attended a Catholic boarding school in Lagos. My fellow students included children of ambassadors from many countries. Inevitably, we learned about each other's food, fashion, dances, music and cultural differences. We accepted, celebrated, respected, enjoyed, understood and appreciated the beauty of our varied cultures. For me, this was the perfect training needed to travel the world as an entertainer.

I am keen to promote and encourage diversity. Diversity is a serious and vital matter, not just something nice that we should have. If you do not have acceptance of other cultures, colours and races, war and death are the results. My personal experience of the Biafran War confirms to me that the absence of the acceptance of diversity always leads to horrors like the Holocaust, terrorism and war.

P. Boulaye (✉)
Faculty of Professional and Social Sciences, Middlesex University Business School, Middlesex University, London, UK

Bipada Academy, London, UK
e-mail: patti@pattiboulaye.com

© Springer Nature Switzerland AG 2019
M. F. Özbilgin et al. (eds.), *Global Diversity Management*, Management for Professionals, https://doi.org/10.1007/978-3-030-19523-6_7

As I have written in my autobiography, 'The Faith of a Child', when I was 12 in 1966, our neighbouring tribes killed tens of thousands of Igbos. The Eastern Region declared independence under the name Biafra, as one million Igbo refugees had fled into Biafra. The new state was formed because the Central Military Federal Republic had not protected the Igbos. Personally, I feel as though I spent the most impressionable part of my childhood stepping over dead bodies, learning not to look at the faces in case I recognised them.

When the war ended, two million people had died. The head of state, General Gowon, declared 'no victor and no vanquished' and issued an amnesty for those who participated in the Biafra uprising to defend themselves. This enabled the hugely diverse population of Nigeria to live with itself once again after the bloodletting. My childhood experiences have convinced me that the pursuit of diversity and the acceptance of the differences of our fellow humans are vital to our very survival.

In 1967 I was just 13 when the Biafran War broke out. My sister Rosie and I were on a rare visit to our birth father (Papa) in Asaba, which was in Biafra. However, our visit to Asaba was cut short. Papa arrived very early one morning, and we were told to gather our belongings. A car was waiting to take us back to our mother and home in Lagos. Papa thought we should risk the journey home as the enemy was approaching Asaba fast and we would certainly be safer away from the war zone, even though we would be behind enemy lines.

Defeated Biafran soldiers had crossed the Niger Bridge into Asaba. Igbo civilians fled across the river to the rest of Biafra. Others went into the bush. Word came of atrocities and killings of Igbos by Hausa soldiers. Igbo families were beaten, killed and left in the streets. Women were raped, and fanatical Hausas killed young Christian men from non-Igbo tribes.

Papa arranged for us to travel with Mrs Johnson (Mama), a Yoruba lady from the Western Region, whom he trusted. Her family had already left for Lagos. She had crossed the river to Asaba with Papa's help. She spoke both Igbo and Yoruba, and she would pretend that we were her children on the journey. We said our farewells to Papa and our host Mama Ngozi. She stressed that we must not admit to anyone that we were Igbos.

We got into the car with bags of drinks and other provisions. Soon we were on the main road travelling away from Asaba, heading west with the non-Igbo refugees. The road was also crowded with Igbo people heading east to Asaba, men, women and children carrying their belongings piled up on their heads. Women had babies on their backs, children carried their younger siblings, and some just pulled the little ones along. Many were on bicycles, while the lucky ones crammed onto cars, buses and lorries, some on the outside hanging on.

Our driver tooted his horn to clear people off the road. Red dust filled the air. We inched away from Asaba towards the frontlines, which we would have to cross to get home. It was difficult to make much headway, so we pulled off the main road onto the small roads through the bush. I fell asleep, as we had been rushed from our sleeping mats very early in the morning.

I was forced awake by shouts of 'Take cover! Take cover!' Someone grabbed my hand. Confused and disoriented, I allowed myself to be dragged out of the car into the bush and pushed face down onto the ground, still drowsy but with my heart pounding at the incoming whine and shock of shells smashing to earth all around us. There was confusion everywhere; people were running and shouting. Then there was an explosion that shook the ground right under me, making me deaf and setting my ears ringing. Everything was in surreal slow motion; a man's head dropped from his shoulders; the body seemed to continue running. The headless body tripped and fell forward on the uneven ground. I looked around me; I could hear no sound, but there were lips moving. Someone had spilt blood on me. I looked for Rosie; she was safe lying a few feet from me. People now lay flat on the ground, wide-eyed and petrified. One explosion followed another, although I could hardly hear them; I saw shell bursts lifting the earth and smashing the trees, hurling earth, stones, dust and splinted wood high into the air. The wrenching ground kicked the breath from my body. It seemed endless. I closed my eyes and kept still, even though I could feel something crawling on me. I was afraid to brush it away as any movement might attract the shells. The shell bursts finally ended, but we did not move until the driver spoke. I heard him as though he was a long way away and down a tunnel:

Madam, I think they've stopped.

'We will drive to Agbor, I know people there', replied Mrs Johnson.

My deafness eased a little. People began to come out of the bush. I got up and frantically brushed the insects off me. I avoided looking in the direction of the headless body. A young woman, screaming, ran out of the bush past us, towards a young child lying in the open; the child was covered in white ash and blood. She swept the child into her arms making strange deep noises as she cradled the lifeless body. Mama and other women did their best to console her. We could hear shouting and wailing in the forest. A young man sat on the ground bleeding from the head, looking straight ahead, smiling in shock. All around us men, women and children wandered about, seemingly in a trance, picking up scattered belongings. Some had tears running down their cheeks, a trail of brown skin through the dust. Many were wounded. We opened our cases and shredded our clothes, which we used as bandages. There were bodies scattered everywhere; some charred and some man-gled, lying oddly twisted like rag dolls. I tried not to dwell too long on the bodies and told myself that I was in a bad dream. But I knew the dream was reality.

Our car was damaged and would not start, and our driver said he could not fix it. Agbor was less than 10 miles away; walking, we should be able to make it before dark. Those who were going to Agbor joined us and we set off on foot. We walked along the bush path within a short distance of the main road, carrying some things we would need from the car on our heads just as we had seen the refugees doing earlier.

After a while we heard gunshots ahead of us. We all rushed into the bush, and the driver motioned that we should keep our heads down but keep moving deeper into the bush. We all followed him, crouching and hugging whatever we were carrying, and he put his finger to his mouth and motioned to us to lie down. Then we heard voices not far away. Five or six Federal soldiers came running past our hiding place towards the main road. We were frightened and unable to move, even after they had gone.

We heard rustling in the bush, and two young girls, about my age, emerged crying, leaning on each other, unable to walk properly. Both of them had blood on their legs, their dresses were torn and bloody and their faces were bruised and swollen around the mouth and eyes. They had been beaten. It wasn't until later that I realised that the soldiers had raped them. Our driver checked that they were not being followed before he attracted their attention.

The two girls froze and then slowly turned around, wide-eyed with fear. When they saw our group, tears of relief ran down their faces, and I found I was crying with them. They rushed noisily across the clearing towards us. One was shivering, though the heat was stifling. Then the driver signalled all of us, including the frightened girls, to be quiet and go back into the bush to hide. Soldiers, trucks, and armoured vehicles approached along the main road. Some soldiers were on lookout and made forays into the bush. We prayed that they could not see us.

We stayed where we were, about 50 yards from the main road. We were afraid to move for what seemed like an eternity before the adults whispered that we should go quietly further into the thick bush. We walked slowly in single file. One of the girls needed to lean on someone to walk a little faster, and they led the way. The path reached a village with some of its huts in ruins. Some had been set on fire and shells had hit one or two. They had been raided by Federal troops looking for Biafran soldiers. As we reached the clearing of the village, a few people started coming out of the bush. One woman, the girls' mother, shouted and ran to embrace them. Strangely, the girls were rigid in their mother's embrace and could not bring themselves to respond. They were bewildered and ashamed. She led them to a container of water, stripped them down and started frantically washing them. As they stood there shivering, I realised that they were much younger than I had thought. Their mother cried and washed the blood from their bodies in the clear water that sparkled in the fading sun. In the middle distance, we heard the sound of more shelling, and everyone fell to the ground. However, the sound of the exploding shells, though loud, was not getting closer. We sat where we were, not wanting to be far from the ground, until the shelling stopped.

The villagers spoke Ika, a language I had not heard before, but one or two of the words sounded like Igbo. The driver and Mrs Johnson were led a short distance to where some bodies lay. Rosie and I were told to stay where we were. I could see from where I was, a dead woman lying on her back, her stomach ripped open and her intestines exposed. Not far from her was a tiny baby with a big gash to the side of its face. Just for a second, before the adults stood in front of the body, I noticed the umbilical cord still attached to the baby. I looked away and tried to distance my thoughts from the sight and closed my mind to it all. I heard enough in Igbo to know the Federal troops killed many of the villagers. Most of the people looked dazed and many were crying, men as well. The Federal troops were not discerning as to who was, or was not, an Igbo.

By the time the villagers had dug a shallow grave and the bodies were buried, it was dusk. As the sun was already going down, it was felt that it was unsafe for us to continue on our journey, and it was suggested that we spend the night in the village and travel through the bush to Agbor the following morning.

We were taken to a large rectangular mud building with a thatched roof. The shells had hardly touched it. Inside the building was an elderly man and his wife, and he was an important man in the village. They said we could stay until morning.

We entered the shelter of the large hut, exhausted and thirsty. Both Rosie and I began to cry, one setting off the other. My stomach collapsed, even though I had not eaten for some hours, and I got no further than a few feet from the hut, unable to make it to the latrine a few feet further. I embarrassed myself, asking for water to clean up.

Boiled yam with dried fish and onions stew cooked in palm oil tasted so good. It seemed that some normality had returned, but we all ate in silence. I was afraid of the darkness that was fast approaching. Two kerosene lamps were lit, and the wooden doors to the entrance and the back of the hut were shut. We slept.

We got up early and washed our faces and chewed the *atu* (chewing stick) that our hosts provided to clean our teeth. We had some *akamu* (porridge). We offered some of the provisions we had brought with us from the car to the old man. He accepted some tins of sardines, saying that we would need the rest of the food on our journey. Such courtesy in such adversity. We said our goodbyes before setting off with farmers from the village who would lead us through the bush to Agbor. There was a smell of rotting flesh as we made our way. Flies became a nuisance.

Exhausted, we finally got to Agbor and the Benin-Agbor Road, where we were lucky to hitch a ride. Rosie had cut herself tramping through the bush, and Mama was able to get a dressing for her at a roadside stall. On the way we encountered Federal troop roadblocks. Mama passed us off as her children. She spoke Yoruba to the soldiers and the driver was Yoruba, so we were waved on. At Benin we got a car provided by a friend of Mama's to Shagamu, where we parted company with her. We clung to her when it came to saying goodbye. We got on a minibus heading for Ikeja in Lagos, where we lived. Mama asked a few passengers to keep an eye on us. I slept through the journey. I never saw Mama again. Rosie and I often spoke about her in loving terms.

Thank God, we finally got home to Ikeja before nightfall on the second day. Mummy was beside herself with worry, as she had no way of contacting us or Papa, as Asaba had fallen and was cut off. We told Mummy all that had happened. She sighed deeply and told us how kind God had been to protect us, to put everything we had been through and seen out of our minds and to forgive and leave everything in God's hands.

The war ended on Monday 12 January 1970. Over two million people had died. We learned that Papa had been pulled out of his house and lined up with others to be shot. Fortunately, one of the officers recognised him after Papa spoke to him in Hausa. Papa had become fluent, being postmaster in some northern cities. Papa was saved from the firing squad, but he was unable to save the other men.

I arrived in the United Kingdom as a tourist in the early 1970s. During my first year, I was struck by the negative stereotyping and the lack of education and knowledge of other cultures. There were still signs saying 'No dogs, No Blacks,

No Irish'. Flat-hunting was dehumanising, and even going to church on Sunday challenged my Christian faith, as no one would sit on my row unless they had nowhere else to sit. This made me very angry at times, but not bitter. I realised that my different colour was the problem, because we are all threatened by the unfamiliar.

My journey into the entertainment industry started accidentally. I had joined a queue at The Shaftesbury Theatre, which I had mistaken for Madam Tussaud's, only to be told after queuing for a long time that the queue was for an audition for *Hair*. As it happened, the show pioneered diversity. In the show I replaced a Black actress, Marsha Hunt, who was openly dating Mick Jagger, and this, like HRH Prince Harry's marriage to Meghan Markle today, was influencing opinion in a positive way and helping to break down barriers.

Though there are still some racist people today in the United Kingdom, as some reactions to Brexit have revealed, in the 1970s it was much worse, and so progress has been made. One of the actresses in *Hair* told me that, as a child, her mother would threaten to lock her up in the broom cupboard with a Black man when she was naughty! In the 1970s most auditions clearly stated, 'Whites only', but in the early 1990s, a director cast me, a Black girl, as Judy Garland for a musical at the Shaw Theatre in London. She said that the way I sang her songs did justice to them, and that was what mattered. So, in 20 years, the United Kingdom has gone from 'Whites only' auditions to a Black girl playing Judy Garland! That is diversity.

The entertainment industry is often a perfect example of diversity, with a hiring practice, in many cases, that is race-, age-, gender-, minority-, colour- and even species-neutral. Other businesses could learn from this. Show business thrives on diversity, employing people of all races, realising that money can be made and it matters not what race, gender, age or colour you are.

In conclusion, I do not believe that diversity can be enforced, and I believe that the application of diversity in society should never compromise ability. Integration and tolerance can only be encouraged and are a slow but important process of education. One good aspect of the Internet is that it has opened up the richness of diverse cultures to the world. However, if the language used to promote diversity is not simple and the benefits are not made clear to business and society, then the message will be rejected. It is clear to me that change in the United Kingdom has largely come about through education, enabling the understanding and appreciation of what we are and can be together as humans.

Nelson Mandela said: 'Education is the most powerful tool you can use to change the world.' I agree! But the most important education is how to walk the earth as civilized beings.

The Theatre of the Classroom: A Work in Progress. How Can I Meet the Needs of Everyone in the Class When I Also Have to Deal with the Pupils with Problems?

David Crabtree

Abstract

The focus of David's case study is the Theatre of the Classroom, and, by this, he means everything that happens between teachers and pupils during lessons. He uses this concept alongside reflective practice to help educators plan and prepare to meet the needs of all pupils especially those who learn differently. His work has taken him to Africa, Asia, the Middle East and Europe. The question that sparks most discussion is 'How can I meet the needs of everyone in the class when I also have to deal with the pupils with problems?' The content of the case study will spotlight the key characteristics for educators to focus their attention upon in order to create inclusive teaching and learning. David declares that, 'In this theatre, let us create stars'.

When I am delivering training, it often surprises people when I tell them that I have a disability. Many are surprised and some express disbelief. In conversation, normally over coffee, the same people will explore a little further. It would seem that I don't quite fit their expectations of a disabled person. Maybe this is because, at first glance, there is nothing obvious. When I explain a little more that it's not physical, it's cognitive, they will say, 'but you seem so intelligent and learned'.

My area of specialism is inclusive education and special educational needs (SEN), and my work has taken me to Africa, Asia, Latin America, the Middle East and Europe. I am a teacher trainer. Nearly always, there is one question that comes up more often and powerfully than any other, 'How can I meet the needs of everyone in the class when I also have to deal with the pupils with problems?'

D. Crabtree (✉)
British Council UK, Hertford, UK

© Springer Nature Switzerland AG 2019
M. F. Özbilgin et al. (eds.), *Global Diversity Management*, Management for
Professionals, https://doi.org/10.1007/978-3-030-19523-6_8

1   Where Are You in the Line?

In my work, after I have introduced myself, I suggest that there is a distinction between inclusive learning and SEN, also between SEN and SEND (special educational needs and disability). All seek to remove barriers to achievement and generally advocate a child-centred approach. The difference is that, with SEN(D), there is a tendency towards interventions and most likely around a particular child. It tends to offer 'support', 'help to bring them up to standard' or 'adjustments to accommodate the child'. This way of responding to the needs of the child tends towards a 'deficit' model. That is, it tends to focus on what a child cannot do in relation to other children. Much of what happens in schools that have a SEN(D) approach is provision of support to remove barriers so that the child is 'included'. However, very often this means that the existing structures, processes, procedures and methods of the school and teachers continue.

By contrast, inclusive learning places the greatest importance on the quality of all pupils' learning and, as such, not to be confused with 'integration' or 'including' pupils. An inclusive classroom is one that values the contributions of all pupils, their families and communities. It recognises that every learner is unique. Learning builds on the languages, cultures and interests of all the children. Underpinning this approach is a desire for every child to develop their uniqueness and strengths. Inclusive learning is about the whole child and requires an understanding about how the child learns and who they are. Inclusive learning requires a comprehensive audit of structures, processes, procedures, methods, pedagogy and attitudes across the whole institution.

I find that by offering this way to distinguish between SEN(D) and inclusion allows participants in my training sessions to locate their own practice on an 'inclusion continuum'. They do this by placing themselves in or on a line. At one end is the totally inclusive school and at the other is the totally noninclusive school. Along this line there is also a spot to mark the place where a SEN(D) approach has been adopted with some success, to the extent of putting into place reasonable adjustments for pupils. At this spot, a school will be not quite there with a full SEN(D) approach. For instance, it might not yet be sufficiently developed to put into place reasonable adjustments for all the pupils who require it. This line and the 'SEN (D) spot' can be a physical line where people place themselves by standing in a line, or it can simply be a line on a piece of paper.

Totally non-inclusive   *SEN(D) approach*   *Totally inclusive*
End of image)

Where are you on the inclusion continuum?

Participants then place themselves along this line. Where they position themselves is totally their decision. Whether they represent themselves in their professional role, their school or their educational system is also up to them. Once the line has been formed, I ask people to discuss and compare their reasons for placing themselves where they have.

2   SEN and SEN(D)

The inclusion continuum activity throws up all sorts of outcomes. For instance, when doing this in The Gambia with science secondary teachers, they tended to group around a what they called a 'pre-SEN(D) spot'. Their reason for doing so was that they felt that there was an awareness of the need to do something but only for those children with a physical disability. They also explained that there was no SEN (D) provision in their local community schools, only a specialist provision with limited places and some distance away from the pupils' homes.

In another example, in Macedonia, secondary vocational school teachers located themselves almost as a whole group on the SEN spot. Their reason for doing so was that the schools had on site both an educational psychologist and someone to provide pedagogical advice. However, the general feeling among all of the participants was that 'such children would be better off in specialist schools'.

3   Each Child Experiences Their Own Personal Education System Within This Theatre

Much of what I do in my day-to-day professional life is to look with educators at what they can do so that the classroom is a better place for all the participants. To do this, I use the idea of the 'Theatre of the Classroom', linked to a methodology known as a group relations conference.

Whether I am working with individual teachers, whole groups or school leaders, policy-makers and/or educational specialists, the focus is upon the classroom, that microscopic part of the whole education system. The Theatre of the Classroom is where education is enacted. This is where the drama of education is played out. In conjunction with this analogy, I use the methodology of a 'group relations conference' to create a focus on this drama and, in so doing, allow participants to plan ways of creating a more inclusive Theatre of the Classroom.

After the inclusion continuum line activity with the science teachers in The Gambia, we began a group relations conference.

4   Group Relations Conference

A group relations conference offers opportunities to learn about group, organisational and social dynamics; the exercise of authority and power; the interplay between tradition, innovation and change; and the relationship of organisations to their social, political and economic environments. Such a methodology has long been developed in work environments by the Tavistock Institute in the United Kingdom. I have adapted this and use some of the process in education.

In their efforts to create inclusive classrooms, the necessary institutional, organisational and pedagogical changes are not always obvious to educators. The change to create most leverage is not often easy to see, especially when steeped in one's own system and/or acting things out in one's own theatre. Examples from outside one's own context are often seductive in that they seem to work and may seem easy to simply import. However, things transferred from another place do not always take root when transplanted.

It is critical to explore one's own situation first. Solutions, if they are to take hold, need to be 'owned' by the people engaged in the change. Also, if we are going to bring about change in order to create inclusive classrooms, the methodology must also be inclusive.

My aim is to during the workshop seek agreements about how to develop a more inclusive classroom by exploration of the case study. A group relations conference provides a structure for that very purpose. The process begins with a story.

5   Gambia Science Teachers' Story Pt1

The story was of a teacher trying to convince a child and their parents that the child's needs would be better met in a specialist school for the visually impaired rather than the local community school. The teacher felt that this child's needs were unmet and also this child's behaviour disturbed other children 'who wanted to learn'.

6   The Next Phase of the Group Relations Conference Is a Questioning Phase

In the next phase, following the story drawn from the classroom, one of the questions related to the difference between SEN, SEND and SEN(D). In The Gambia, only sensory and/or physical impairment was seen as specifically a special educational need. Anything else was considered to be a 'behaviour' problem within the child. The maxim was quoted, 'spare the rod and spoil the child'.

7   Behaviour

Whether working with teachers in the United Kingdom or wherever in the world, behaviour is often a point of discussion. A group relations conference places an equal value on all the inputs, and behaviour is integral to the concept of the Theatre of the Classroom. It is very apposite. The analogy of a drama played out before us requires us to look at behaviours. Behaviour is the way in which we act or conduct ourselves, especially towards others. When teachers talk of behaviour, they are often talking about things that happen in the classroom that they do not agree with. Often this is located within particular pupils.

But, how often do we look at our own behaviour?

8   Inclusive Methodologies as Solutions to Classroom Problems

Rather than ideas of 'good' teachers and 'bad' teachers, 'good' pupils and 'bad' pupils and 'good' schools and 'bad' schools, exploring classroom interactions as a theatre proposes that we see events in the classroom as creations of the environment. Participants are able to explore creative actions that may result in better outcomes for some or all of the players. The process in the workshop enables participants to look to see how realities are constructed by the actions and/or dialogues of the players, both pupils and teachers.

Put simply, the Theatre of the Classroom is an analogy to view these interactions. It is a facilitated workshop that uses real examples from the work situation. Practitioners discuss and reflect on example/s and try, through sharing, to fully understand what happened in the situation presented before them and why. Once a 'drama' has been fully explored in the facilitated discussion, ways of improving the situation are suggested by the participants themselves. From these, action plans are developed.

The reason that it is so powerful is that it enables participants to see their way forward. In turn, inclusive methodologies become solutions to classroom problems. Inclusive learning becomes something that the participants want to adopt themselves, because it offers them a better way of working.

What happens during the group relations conference?

Essentially, the workshop is a reflective exercise that uses group discussion to look more closely at the different levels of complexity in workplace interactions. It begins by one person offering a story of an interaction in the classroom. Members of the workshop are then free to ask questions. The facilitator's role is to ensure that no one person dominates the ensuing discussion and to move the workshop through the three stages. The first stage is for one member to recount a narrative about an interaction in their work setting. The second stage is a questioning and discussing stage to explore meanings. The final stage is to seek a resolution and development.

When applied to classrooms, members of the workshop are educators following a 'story' from the classroom. The discussion about the work situation inevitably begins to connect to ideas and beliefs within their professional practice. It is important in stage two that the questions and discussion sufficiently examine the particular story offered by one person from their classroom so that each member of the group is allowed space to explore it and develop an understanding of what happened and even possibly why. When everyone feels that they have fully grasped what happened, the facilitators ask participants how they feel the situation could be reconstructed to be more inclusive.

It is really helpful in a group relations conference if the story is prepared beforehand and includes as much of the dialogue as possible. It should only be short, three paragraphs maximum, and written and prepared to be handed out to the group while they also listen.

9 Gambia Science Teachers' Story Pt2

At the science teachers' group relations conference, the view had been expressed that poor behaviour required correction. Subsequent discussion also included a consideration of the organisation of special educational needs and the fact that, in The Gambia, SEN focused almost completely on physical impairment.

The group felt the need to consider and question the view that a SEN child' needs would be better met in a specialist school. The group was offered the statement that 'schools should accommodate all children, regardless of their physical, intellectual, social, emotional, linguistic or other conditions. This should include disabled and gifted children, street and working children, children from remote or nomadic populations, children from linguistic, ethnic or cultural minorities and children from other disadvantaged or marginalized areas or groups'.

Participants felt that this was too aspirational and that it would be impossible to progress from where they were at present to where they might like to be later on. In The Gambia, as in many other West African countries, social inclusion is a significant challenge.

This group relations conference contained only teachers. The Theatre of the Classroom approach becomes even more powerful when senior educators and policy-makers can also be part of the workshop. This is because there are actions outside the ambit of teachers that also need to be taken if inclusive classrooms are to become a reality.

10 How Can We Find Answers?

In terms of this particular workshop, it is critical that the facilitation focuses the group discussion on things within the control and/or on common concern of participants. Often, a position is arrived at where members feel that the necessary change relies upon the actions of others. Inclusive classrooms require things to be different from what they are, and this is more than policy statements. However, going from policy to practice is not easy. Answers are required.

The questioning and subsequent discussion in the second part of the science teachers' group relations conference had focused on a common concern: pupil behaviour as a barrier to learning. This was seen as not only an issue for the individual child but for other children in the class as well. Essentially, the question now tabled was 'How can I meet the needs of everyone in the class when I also have to deal with the pupils with these problems?'

Another point of discussion was that the group needed to look more closely at the different levels of complexity in the workplace, particularly in relation to the understanding of SEN(D). Finally, there was an acceptance that a fully inclusive classroom in their context was some way off.

11   Ways Forward

The discussion had led the teachers to the realisation that one thing that was required was for them to reframe their thinking about behaviour.

The teachers began to put together an action plan. One action was to look at their teaching methodology and identify and try out strategies for pupil engagement in the class. They also decided to support each other to redefine behavioural difficulties by looking at the underlying reasons. They decided to take an inclusive learning perspective and adopt a focus on learning. They resolved to consider ways that they could identify patterns in individual pupil behaviour that would enable them to work out whether a pupil was experiencing communication issues, such as an expressive or receptive language difficulty, and whether such things were creating the barrier to learning. With this in mind, they decided to review their lessons to see if there were opportunities to identify where pupils required some additional support in the class as well as adapt their materials accordingly.

The teachers also decided to increase opportunities for classroom interaction between pupils and for peer learning by facilitating more group work in class. While doing this, they also recognised the need to notice behaviour more in the class but in a different way from how they had done previously. They now wanted to spend a little more time in class assessing pupils' effectiveness in the various interactions and to look at ways of encouraging and supporting students to work together more successfully.

Future information sessions and training were planned on cognition and learning. Teachers wanted to know more about learning differences and how to support children in their class who learn differently. They also recognised that they had very little awareness about social, mental and emotional health. However, at this point they considered that they had a sufficient action plan to begin to make a start. They had begun to find answers.

12   Unseen Forces

The science teachers now had an action plan to develop the situation in which they worked and to make it more responsive to a wider range of pupil needs. They had also begun to develop a critical framework in which to review their practice. However, even after the action plan and the development of a methodology, were they to return to the inclusion continuum how much further along the line might they be?

There are excluded groups in The Gambia, as in most societies. Marginalisation and exclusion, high drop-out rates, low take-up and lack of achievement all these are symptomatic of classrooms that are not inclusive.

There are unseen forces outside the classroom that have an impact upon what is being played out inside. The classroom is not only a microscopic part of the whole system. What happens within it is also affected by what has gone before or what is going on at present in society. Various forms of oppression, discrimination, domination and other social processes intersect in the classroom and influence each other. For example, pupils can belong to more than one marginalised group. A pupil may identify as being culturally different from his or her classmates, may belong to a different socio-economic group and may also identify as gay. This pupil's experience would be different from someone who is of a similar cultural and socio-economic group to the majority of the class yet who also identifies as gay. Though these two students have an identity in common, their experiences in and around the classroom would likely be quite different because of their unique outlooks, as well as their unique social and cultural circumstances.

The Theatre of the Classroom, linked to the group relations conference, offers a methodology towards inclusive learning but to do so needs to adopt within its structure an intersectional perspective. Such an approach takes notice of the various social, historical and political processes that operate as unseen forces on the Theatre of the Classroom. How can we do this?

13   Moving from a SEN Approach to a More Inclusive Classroom

As a child, my relationship to the education system was different from most other pupils. Most probably, every child's relationship to schooling is different even though it is made up of shared experiences. I first noticed my different relationship when I was 6 years old in primary school in the United Kingdom during a particular lesson. In this lesson, on this one day, every pupil was asked to take a turn, to 'continue the story out loud to rest of the class'. From my perspective, I did exactly the same as everyone else. Like the others, I best described what the people in the pictures in my class storybook were doing. The teacher was not happy with my contribution. To be frank, I had not noticed her being displeased with anyone else and I was a little upset. She came around and stood over my shoulder with what I now recognise as a strategy to observe me closely and possibly stop any hilarity from other pupils. In close proximity, she asked me to do the same again. By the way that she stood and the way that she pointed to things on the page, I was surprised. Rather than the interesting and colourful pictures, she wanted me to focus on the black squiggles. How strange. Before this lesson, I had not even noticed those strange patterns.

If we were to apply a more intersectional approach to this classroom drama, what might we look at? Also consider how powerful a child's perspective could be within the theatre workshop.

14   The Importance of Facilitation in Stage Two of the Group Relations Conference

Stage two of the group relations conference is where all the participants explore using questions to find meanings within the case study. The facilitator has a role to ensure that all participants have an equal opportunity to fully explore. It is important that no one person or no one view dominates the discussion. It is also important to provide signposts for a deeper exploration.

The 'identity' of the players in the story is a useful tool for signposting. A question about identity can reveal quite a lot. Not identity in terms of the given name but identity in the context.

In my childhood school, I was different. Not me alone: I was different along with the other children who constituted a particular group. We were 'Force's children'. We attended this school because our parents lived in the Armed Forces quarters nearby. Children from this part of town, who attended the school but in relatively small numbers, were considered to be 'rough'. I was one of those. The other local children were more 'genteel'. These other children had parents who owned their own houses, lived permanently in the area and were not in the Armed and Uniformed Services. If the school had also known that my grandmother had been a Romany gipsy, then I think that this would have even more contributed to my 'difference'. Roma children tend to be considered 'outsiders' throughout Europe.

The unseen force of different expectations for different children, based upon views of identity, may be considered as one reason why things went the way that they did.

In the Theatre of the Classroom, identity is a critical concept. It enables discussion to also look at the broader social processes at play, these unseen forces.

15   In Conclusion

To create classrooms in which all feel equally valued requires teachers to be actively responsive to student needs. The analogy of the Theatre of the Classroom provides a conceptual tool with which to explore what happens in the various interactions that take place in a typical teaching day. Approaches to inclusive learning need to offer possible solutions to problems in the classroom. A beginning point is to recognise where we would place our own practice on the inclusion continuum and then to consider it in detail and look at all the unseen forces operating to cause the players to act in the way they do.

Then, we need to consider what is required for things to be different, to move us along the continuum.

Why must we do things differently? Essentially, because different pupils may not benefit from the same types of support and they need educators and administration in schools to support and nurture their needs differently. When teachers make the necessary adjustments to how they teach, they are reconstructing the Theatre of the Classroom to make each learner feel that they are 'the star' and that this is 'their classroom'.

Training on and Exploring Cultural Approaches to Disability

Simon Minty

Abstract

This chapter discusses the field of disability rather than broader diversity, not always a bad thing, as disability is often seen as the more awkward of the strands. It is written by Simon who is a visibly disabled person himself, so he claims a natural fit. He has worked internationally for 15 years, visiting over 20 countries from Albania to Ukraine and China to Oman. Some trips have been with British Council, but he also works with international corporations such as Google, Goldman Sachs, HSBC and McDonalds.

I'm a consultant and trainer who generally works with larger companies, a number of which are international. The services I provide help them improve how they manage disability in the workplace and their interaction with disabled customers or service users.

The international aspect of my work started in 2002. Roughly a third of these projects have been with the British Council, involving travelling to countries around the world to talk about disability. The remaining two-thirds is made up of project work for a range of organisations and companies. My clients have included the Bank of America, Google, Goldman Sachs, HSBC and McDonalds. I also have a long-term relationship with Community Business in Asia, which asks me to help out from time to time. I regularly attend and occasionally chair international conferences on disability matters and am an Associate to the Business Disability Forum and Business Disability International.

S. Minty (✉)
SMinty Ltd, London, UK
e-mail: simonminty@sminty.net; https://www.sminty.net

M. F. Özbilgin et al. (eds.), *Global Diversity Management*, Management for Professionals, https://doi.org/10.1007/978-3-030-19523-6_9

Much of my work is based on oral communication, though the context in which my 'message' is delivered varies considerably. Experience has taught me that adopting a creative approach to disability often pays off; Dining with a Difference is a good example of this. In the United Kingdom, it involves myself and (usually) two colleagues hosting a dinner and talking with senior leaders, often hard to reach, about disability and business. It's a content-rich but relaxed event that has proved to be a very successful format. When going abroad, budgetary and logistical constraints unexpectedly transformed Dining with a Difference into something rather special. The participation of local disabled people—either local disability advocates or employees of the companies involved—in the event was initially necessitated by the impossibility of bringing along my colleagues. Their involvement has added an additional element of unpredictability and emotional force. Briefed in advance, they are invited to take the lead in the discussions on their respective tables. The result has been amazingly powerful and, I hope, the trigger for meaningful changes to be implemented.

My interest in the arts led to the creation of Acting on Disability. It's a training programme that uses the vehicle of theatrical performance to educate and inform audiences ranging in size from 10 to 500. Actors enact a range of scenarios that depict managers interacting with disabled employees. As host, I cut in at specific moments to ask the audience for their thoughts, what they think of the manager's behaviour and what could be done better.

Every member of my company's acting team has a disability or impairment. That means that if a character in a sketch has sight loss or a mental health issue, so does the actor playing them. The insights that they bring to their role add authenticity and depth to the scene and often generate some impactful moments when they step out of role and talk about their real-life experiences with audience members.

Performing dramatically charged but relatable situations can be very effective in developing a manager's ability to navigate their way through what might feel like an impasse. Sometimes, making the right adjustment ('accommodation', in the United States) is simple, but you don't generally need training for that. What my work concentrates on is the grey areas in which personalities and assumptions can override need and impairment. Making an adjustment can impact on other people and can be complicated and awkward to talk about; the question of what is 'reasonable' is part of managing disability at work. In modern parlance, 'managing expectations' might be a better phrase. Individuals may be very forthcoming about their disability but, equally, can be highly secretive. That's the stuff we like to talk about.

It's worth pointing out that in no country that I've visited has disability been free of complications relating to perception and understanding. Sensitivity around disability issues is truly universal.

On a recent trip to the United States, our team comprised of myself, a short person (3' 11" or 120 cm); someone with cerebral palsy; someone with sight loss; someone with mental health issues; and someone with Aspergers and dyspraxia. This means that we are also living what we're training. One moment that stood out was when all five of us decided to walk the ten blocks from our hotel to our first event in downtown Manhattan. It was a bit of a self-conscious reference to the group-shot in *Reservoir Dogs*, though in our case we were two men on mobility scooters, two women with hidden disabilities and a man who has Asperger's.

As we were walking, I remember talking to my colleagues about how polite New Yorkers were, how they move out of the way for wheelchair and scooter users and often say hello or smile. At exactly that point, an older lady stopped as we passed her, pointed at me and yelled 'Now that is not normal!' My fellow scooter user waited a moment and then asked me, 'Well, how do you feel about that?' I paused to process it and then answered, 'I feel I should be angry or upset, but actually I am rather pleased. I now have an opening line for the event we're about to do'. And so it proved.

As well as such training, I'm engaged on consultancy projects from time to time. This has included everything from writing a disability and employment guide for the Bulgarian government to setting up a disability and media organisation in Berkeley, California. The latter project was to show US news media how they could be more accurate and inclusive when reporting disability stories. All too often disability-related stories are either about inspirational disabled people overcoming barriers or the costs to the public by pesky disabled people requesting that barriers be removed.

1   How Did This Career Come About?

After school I worked in banking at Barclays plc for 7 years. During my time at Barclays, I learned a few things that were to prove useful for my future work.

Firstly, and this might seem strange to say now, I had a strong resistance to being seen as a disabled person. There are a lot of disabled people who don't want to be labelled. My main reason at the time was a fear that it would stall my career. I wasn't happy when my manager nervously asked if I wanted to go to head office in London to help the bank to develop their plans around disability. I pushed back: Why are you asking me? The fact that I am especially short, have limited mobility, a disabled parking permit, am in receipt of disability benefit and have spent a small fortune getting around the barriers that the world had put up seemed to be of no relevance. I kidded myself. I might self-identify as having a disability when it's to my advantage, but don't you dare label me!

I did go to the meeting at head office. I decided to, not because of my disability but because I am a natural networker. How often was I going to get the chance to visit our head office? I might meet someone important who could advance my career.

Although I am more comfortable in my skin now, I can recognise the resistance and feelings some people might have about sharing that they have a disability, impairment or long-term health condition. My work encompasses showing people the benefits of sharing necessary information, rather than fighting to hide something and having to work twice as hard just to keep up. Hiding a disability can be a job in itself.

The second learning I had from my banking career was some understanding of how large multinational companies operate. Hugely resourced, with an excess of talented people, they can nevertheless be incredibly complex in terms of processes and systems. And almost whimsical. They have a tendency to jump on the latest trends, be wholeheartedly involved in something genuinely revolutionary or incredibly important, but then suddenly change their mind a few months later and strike out in a different direction. Similarly, a charismatic, influential individual can revolutionise a company's culture or approach. When they move on, though, are the policies and processes strong enough to stay? Will a new person sweep all that away and start again with something new?

A third benefit of my banking days was being trained up to be a professional trainer. During my induction days, I'd seen the trainers and realised that I wanted to do what they were doing. After badgering Barclays for a while, I was sent away on a residential course to develop my training techniques—tips and techniques that remain with me today.

Finally, perhaps most critically, another manager told me about a company that she'd come across that provided disability training and consultancy. Although I was still resistant to being labelled, my curiosity was piqued, and I was bowled over by the revelation that it was possible to earn a living from disability workplace training.

But I didn't simply leave Barclays and start working as a disability trainer and consultant. After 7 years at the bank, I took a 12-month sabbatical, splitting my time equally between backpacking and working for a disability advice centre in Manchester, United Kingdom.

During my travels I visited Australia, New Zealand, Singapore and Hong Kong. Those countries made me truly realise that I was a disabled person. I hadn't changed, but my environment had. I was no longer in the comfort zone of where I grew up, my home, car, friends and family, without the strategies that I'd developed to lessen the impact of my difference. Backpacking in unfamiliar places with new people made me realise that people like me are rarely considered in terms of planning, design and transport. Combined with the attitudes that I was encountering, it was having a major impact on my ability to function. I was still me, but I felt disabled in these situations. The experience has always informed and fed into my training. It strengthened my desire to work abroad more. I'm sure there's a fridge magnet that says 'Life begins at the end of your comfort zone', and that was the point at which I crossed that threshold. This fear, this exposure—this was a chance to make a difference not only for myself but for others, too.

2   What Have Been My Observations?

A different country often means a different set of cultural assumptions about disability and disabled people. I try to understand those differences to see how, if possible, they could be used to support the independence and inclusion of disabled people. Of course, I also look at the ways in which ingrained perceptions can be a serious obstacle to disabled people in the workplace and broader society. Disabled people are often not involved in implementing disability policy, disappointingly.

Cultural differences still surprise me and can be frustrating. I can't ignore them nor can I assume that I have all the answers. I know that if I expect things to be the same as the United Kingdom and don't adapt my thinking, I will miss a trick. There's diversity in disability.

Some of the most eye-opening conversations have concerned the ways in which religious beliefs in a country have informed perceptions of disabled people. Certain cultures see disability as the result of bad karma, payment for sins in a past life. Perhaps the biggest hurdle, which isn't unique to any particular culture, is what US disability campaigner Susan Daniels referred to as 'the soft bigotry of low expectations'. It's not limited to the thoughts and behaviour of non-disabled people; it can arise from disabled people themselves. After all, you may think that you can't do much if you've had a limited education, been excluded from activities and society or not spent time with independent-minded disabled people. Families and institutions may also conceal disabled people from the public eye because of shame or a misguided belief that this is caring, also known as 'the oppression of kindness'.

In every country there are the trailblazers. My people! I feel a sense of pride and kinship when I connect with another disabled person in a very different country and realise that they 'get it'. They've learned to how to achieve change, often in extremely trying and isolating circumstances. Their aim is to remove barriers, physical and attitudinal, to enable them and others to participate. They know how to educate people using their abilities. Medical professionals, religious groups, academics, charities, NGOs and the state often try to help, too, but some end up being part of the problem if they don't listen but decide they know best.

The trailblazers are self-empowered: they want to take the bus, go to university, do some shopping, eat in a restaurant, participate in politics, earn a living and have a relationship. They want to be included and to be productive and engaged with society. They want to be able to make decisions for themselves. I don't normally subscribe to hollow, inspirational platitudes, but I've met half a dozen accidental role models who—in incredibly difficult circumstances—are leading the march of social and cultural change towards disability in their country. Their brilliance, skill and resilience impress me no end.

In the United Kingdom, we can be a little complacent, or rather our expectations are high. Access has genuinely improved, we have funding for adjustments in work, an enviable car scheme to keep us mobile, accessible buses and taxis and, for some, welfare support. Disability is recognised as something that needs legal protection, and there is now anti-discrimination legislation. There are a multitude of schemes aimed at increasing employment and service provision for disabled people, with varying effectiveness. We have funding for our Paralympians and for creative disability art. I suspect that having these laws and programmes has made United Nations efforts, such as the Convention on the Rights of Persons with a Disability and the International Day of Persons with Disabilities, less able to gain traction in the United Kingdom, although that is changing. However, if you travel abroad, particularly to the countries that don't have anti-discrimination legislation or positive action programmes, the UN efforts become a big deal. They are solid, internationally recognised symbols that can help to focus minds and help individuals to effect change.

In the United Kingdom, while we are far from perfect, we can and do talk about disability. At a dinner event in Paris, one (non-disabled) person said to me, 'Ah, but we're different here. We don't like talking about this stuff, it's awkward. Not like you British people'. Another French person has told me that such personal information cannot be measured or monitored. My worry is that if we never speak of it, will anything change? I quoted a gay Italian friend who spoke about the development of gay rights and who suggested to me that 'Sometimes you have to make it an issue, and only then can it become a non-issue'.

3   Some Practical Advice

When meeting with a new international client to discuss a strategy, despite the different cultural, legal and business approaches, a few elements can be seen as a guide:

1. Involve disabled people: colleagues, a staff network, local disabled people or international consultants like me. Speak with them to see where you're at now and what needs to be done. Explain why you need help. It will save time, provide useful information and avoid misplaced, ineffective initiatives.
2. Top-level support. Someone high in the organisation will want to improve the organisation's approach to disability. Sometimes this senior person has a direct link; that is, they have a relative or friend with a disability. They are the figurehead, a non-executive champion if you like, a person whom people respond to and who can open doors, get people in the room and access budgets.
3. Have a budget. Even if you do everything internally, it will still take resources, time and money to do it properly. If you use external expertise, expect to pay for that and value it.
4. Develop a process for making adjustments. You need a process that everyone can access and understand. The right adjustment enables the disabled employee; it's an investment in your people, and it will make them more effective. It is not a 'perk', as I heard one multinational comment!
5. Think broadly. Yes, wheelchair access to buildings and to bathrooms is critical. But don't get stuck: disability is cognitive, sensory, mental and physical. You might not be able to widen the narrow door today, but 90% of other disabled people can get in, so are you ready for them?
6. Think broadly in terms of the company. Disability isn't just about training the human resources or facilities teams. It's procurement and your suppliers, it's your technology, it's your advertising and public affairs, it's recruitment, etc.; the list goes on.
7. Think long term. Individual innovators can get things moving, but, if this all depends on a single person, it will fall apart when they leave. How can you embed this in the culture of the organisation? Ensure that those who join the company know your approach from the outset.

8. Be confident and be honest. Much of getting it right about disability involves a level of confidence and openness. It might be the disabled person being confident enough to talk about ways to meet specific needs that might not be in place or confident managers seeking advice when they don't know what to do. It is confidence for the organisation to develop disability strategies and address areas where they're not getting it right: confidence to tell people, be public and proud.

9. Don't let perfect be the enemy of the good. Organisations often start then freeze, becoming overwhelmed, seeing difficulties they can't resolve. They worry that an initiative will appear as tokenism. They worry that they might make a mistake, offend someone and be criticised, so they stop. And so nothing happens. It's better to make a start, try to make positive changes and adjust the plan as you go. If you're involving disabled people, you stand a better chance of getting it right, and you'll have a greater understanding when you get it wrong. Pragmatism reigns while we aim for perfection.

A small but notable victory happened when I visited Oman. I met with a facilities manager of an international bank. He arrived and sat down with a weary sigh, immediately explaining to me that I didn't understand the country. Specifically, he told me that the system worked differently there, that there were bank branches in remote, mountainous regions and that wheelchair access wasn't at the top of his priority list. He was resistant, reluctant, to be there and obviously couldn't wait for our meeting to be over so he could get back to his real work.

To be absolutely honest, these are the people I quite like. They tell me exactly what they're thinking and what's important to them. I can work with them. It's the ones that nod, weakly smile and say a few platitudes who are harder. I can't quite remember what I said to him, but I remember acknowledging his position and local differences. However, within 30 minutes, he had completely changed and became an evangelist, wanting to change things. I like to think that somewhere on a hilltop in Oman, there's a remote, lonely branch of a bank that now has good wheelchair access. I may not have changed the world, but such small changes could well mean the world to someone.

Tales from the Front

Wayne Mullen

Abstract

This chapter contains a series of vignettes based on Wayne's experience of leadership development and diversity work globally. Examples include launching a 360-degree feedback process globally with great results—apart from in Asia, where participation was low and scores lacked differentiation. How do you encourage upward feedback in cultures where 'losing face' is to be avoided? Wayne also discusses the challenges of positive action work, the incorporate of gender issues in leadership development, and ways in which organisations can help LGBTQ+ employee to be themselves at work.

I have seen significant shifts in the thinking and practice of diversity management over the last two decades (or so) since I started working in the field. In those early days, we talked about 'equal opportunity' and focused very much on policy and training to support compliance. Fast-forward to 2015 and I find myself with colleagues from around Europe on a float sponsored by our company, throwing swag (company-branded merchandise) to thousands of cheering people lining the streets celebrating Pride.

It has been something of a journey in the field. In the past, the imperatives for equality work were a combination of concern for fairness and for organisations to show they had dispensed with their vicarious liability under the various pieces of equality legislation—and therefore protected (at least in part) from litigation. Today, smart organisations recognise the value of diversity in relation to both team effectiveness and to servicing customers. In particular, these organisations recognise the need to reflect the demographic reality of their customers and that those known to

W. Mullen (✉)
Global Head of Human Resources at The Workshop, London, UK

© Springer Nature Switzerland AG 2019
M. F. Özbilgin et al. (eds.), *Global Diversity Management*, Management for Professionals, https://doi.org/10.1007/978-3-030-19523-6_10

have diverse workforces may actually appeal to a wider customer demographic, thus increasing their customer base. Black, Asian and Minority Ethnic (BAME) brand and marketing managers, for example, may have insights that are helpful in developing better products and propositions with appeal to a more diverse customer base. Companies recognising the purchasing power of the Lesbian, Gay, Bisexual, Transgender, Queer, Plus (LGBTQ+) community have made efforts not just to target the LGBTQ+ community in products and advertising but also to ensure that they were seen as LGBTQ+-friendly employers. Certainly, those of us who belong to one or more minority groups may be more likely to respond to brands that either cater for us or are known to be supportive of our communities. Companies that are working harder to appeal to minorities and women recognise that employment and progression of minorities are critical. Brands that have attempted to appeal to minorities without fully understanding their needs or interests have found themselves criticised or ridiculed for being 'tone deaf'.

This chapter does not intend to make the case for diversity or indeed serve as a 'how to'. My more modest aim is simply to share some examples of my own experiences of diversity work and situations where differences have provided an opportunity to learn and develop more nuanced approaches to diversity and leadership development interventions.

1   Learning Our Histories

The UK equality legislation provides a facility to take 'positive action' where certain groups are underrepresented. Appointments or promotion are always on merit, but organisations can undertake targeted advertising or specific training for underrepresented groups. The intention of positive action work is to address the legacy of discrimination; it recognises that there is not a level playing field and provides support and encouragement for under-represented groups. It is perhaps underused, particularly in the private sector.

One government department had significant vertical segregation of Black Asian and Minority Ethnic (BAME) employees: good representation in non-managerial roles but significantly less in management roles. Initial thoughts were that we might provide some training around career management, management competencies and being successful at interviews. However, the diagnostic phase revealed an interesting finding: BAME employees did not know enough about their own histories to be able to respond appropriately when the legitimacy of their presence in the United Kingdom was questioned by clumsy or racist comments. British history had been written and taught from a White perspective, at considerable cost, leaving BAME employees without the same educational capital as Whites. Aspects of their history had been omitted, leaving them unable defend themselves.

The programme to be designed had to address two critical needs. The first was to address gaps in knowledge about British history so that participants learned about the long and legitimate presence of BAME people in the United Kingdom (put simply, 'we are here because you were there'). Second, it had to identify the challenges that BAME face, develop strategies to address them and support the development of competencies that make up management.

The first half of the programme focused on the former, covering the history of Black and Asian people in Britain from Roman times, the slave-related stimulus of the industrial revolution that led to Britain's technological dominance and subsequent colonisation of so many parts of the world, including Asia.

The second part of the programme focused on leadership development by helping participants to be strategic about the development of leadership skills by breaking down 'leadership' into its constituent parts—competencies. Participants then self-assessed against those competencies, basing their ratings on evidence before identifying the actions, resources and people to support their development against each of the individual competencies. At the end of the programme, each participant left with their own individual development plan.

Research (Rosette et al., 2008) shows that being White is a central characteristic of leadership, and, consequently, White leaders are more prototypical business leaders than BAME leaders. This results in BAME employees being less likely to be promoted into leadership positions, and, even if/when they are, they are evaluated less favourably. There is effectively a White standard against which racial minorities are compared for selection and evaluation. This clearly has significant implications for the progression of BAME employees throughout their careers. A positive action training programme alone cannot support the progression of minority employees and must be part of a broader programme of work including diverse interview panels, mentoring and diversity training. However, a well-designed programme can provide the tools for participants to become more self-directed in their development and to build more confidence in addressing the very real challenges to progress that minority employees face.

2   The Breakfast of Champions

Much has been written about the importance of emotional intelligence in leadership, an important component of which is self-awareness. The 360-degree or multi-rater feedback can be invaluable in this regard—not least because, as leaders progress upwards in organisations, the quality and frequency of candid feedback diminish. Typically, leaders choose to receive feedback from their staff, their manager, peers and other stakeholders. Many 360-degree feedback processes are run as online surveys to preserve anonymity, and they assess leaders against competencies with additional facility for verbatim feedback.

At a global investment bank, we ran 360-degree feedback for all people managers globally. Communication about the purpose of the exercise was prepared and distributed, with clear instructions about how the process would work. The initiative was largely successful, providing valuable feedback to individual leaders and useful aggregate feedback for the organisation. However, the Asian offices stood out due to low participation and a clear lack of differentiation in the scoring. A trip to the office in Asia to meet with employees and their managers uncovered cultural barriers hindering the process. Employees talked about difficulties that they had with their managers, but they struggled to give them feedback even through a confidential 360-degree feedback process. They described the experience of having to provide 360-degree feedback as 'painful'. Managers acknowledged the difficulties that they and their employees had experienced in giving feedback, recognising the cultural challenges yet also the value that the feedback could bring.

How do you make upward feedback in cultures where 'losing face' is to be avoided and where there is significant power distance between managers and their employees? The following year, this was addressed by delivering both training in advance of the process and a leadership development programme once the process had been completed. The training addressed anxieties when giving and receiving feedback by positioning the process as developmental, not as a performance evaluation. Employees were asked to focus on providing feedback in a way that would support their managers' development, even if that feedback might be, at least initially, hard to receive. We also took the opportunity to help employees to give feedback to managers in the moment, using simple techniques such as 'When you … I feel … I would prefer if you …'. They found these techniques helpful. Managers were provided with training in how to read, interpret and use their feedback. They were also given a template email to send to respondents, thanking them for the feedback, summarising their key development areas and asking respondents to provide ongoing feedback when they were able, thus encouraging feedback to be more regular and informal.

The results of this second round of 360-degree feedback were significantly different. In Asia, the feedback provided to managers during this second round was more specific, helpful and, in some cases, brutally honest. Despite concerns about how it might be received, managers responded that it was the feedback that they needed to hear and at the right time. We were able to see a better differentiation of scores, more in line with global results, and we were able to design the following leadership development programme to more successfully address development areas.

The challenges experienced with 360-degree feedback are not specific to Asia, even if they may have been more pronounced in this region. There can be a degree of anxiety around feedback for both those providing it and those receiving it, irrespective of location or culture. There were certainly some lessons learned; not least that our very Western assumption that feedback was always a good thing was not necessarily correct, that 360-degree feedback would be well understood, and that it would have a positive impact. Perhaps the most important lesson learned was that the value and effectiveness of 360-degree feedback can be improved with the right framing, training and follow-up for all participants.

3   Men Are from Mars—Women Are from Mars

I recall a leadership forum that I convened in Moscow for the executive committee of a bank. During the discussions, I noticed that every time a woman in the room spoke, either she was interrupted or men broke into side conversations. I pointed this out to the team; the men were surprised and apologetic, but the women did not react at all. The women had become accustomed to that behaviour in the executive committee. It is a phenomenon that I have witnessed time and again, all over the world. One female leader in an Asian bank described an incident when one of her subordinates told her not to speak at meetings and that he would do the talking. It was assumed that it was more appropriate for him to be heard.

Some women leaders I have worked with have talked about how they have had to modify their speaking behaviour in order to be heard—slowing down, or continuing to talk when they are interrupted, for example. Some have said that it can be harder to maintain their confidence when they are not heard and when they cannot speak as much; they have to think more carefully about what they say and how they say it. Men's speaking behaviour may reflect hierarchical relationships and dominance, whereas women's speaking behaviour may be driven by their concerns with establishing rapport with others and because of concerns about the potential backlash if they talk too much. For men, their deeper voices may provide authority, and they may unconsciously recognise this. Perhaps this is something that can provide insights into the experiences of other minorities, who may also have different speaking behaviour.

Our speaking behaviour is one of the ways in which we carry identity. This may be true not just of the way that voice carries gender identity but other identities such as class, race and nationality, as examples. One leader I coached spoke gently and deferred to more senior colleagues when he spoke. He recognised that his respectful behaviour, appropriate in his (Asian) home setting, was viewed as passive and low impact in an investment bank. Another female leader, concerned that Black women were often stereotyped as aggressive, had consciously modified her behaviour to appear less so—also letting others speak first. The result was feedback that she lacked assertiveness. I recall a meeting in South Africa where people spoke throughout the meetings, and I waited for a break in the discussion that never came in order to speak. Over lunch, when asked why I had not spoken in a meeting where I was considered the expert, I explained that, as a Brit, I struggled with interrupting. My hosts were embarrassed, but I recognised that perhaps I could have adapted more to the local context.

In my work with teams, I have encouraged discussion of potential differences in speaking behaviours and recommended the introduction of 'no interrupting' rule for meetings. Certainly, bringing awareness of men's tendency to speak over women can be enough to make a difference for everybody. If someone does dominate the meeting, then simple statements like 'Can I just pause you?' can be helpful in interrupting respectfully. In addition, going around the table at the end of meetings, checking that everyone has been able to say what they wanted to, can also provide some space for people to speak, who might have been unable.

Challenges when speaking are not the only challenges that women face. Research shows that women who are successful in work that is typically male gender-typed may experience negative reactions and opposition (Heilman, 2001). Leadership is gender-typed as male (Schein, 1975), and those qualities generally believed to be necessary for leadership success, such as assertiveness and ambition, are more commonly associated with men. Sex stereotypes are highly prescriptive for women and dictate that they should exhibit nurturing, sympathetic and understanding behaviours, while competitiveness and achievement orientation are considered incompatible with prescribed feminine behaviours. French sociologist Pierre Bourdieu summed it up thus: 'If they behave like men, they risk losing the obligatory attributes of "femininity" and call into question the natural right of men to the positions of power; if they behave like women, they appear incapable and unfit for the job' (Bourdieu, 2001: 67).

As part of my work in leadership development, I encourage discussion about the role of gender in leadership. I ask how women who display agentic, directive and assertive behaviours are perceived. I am sure the reader can guess the responses. How, I ask, can women reconcile and overcome the incongruity between expected gender roles and the more communal behaviours that are more commonly associated with female managers? How do men, for example, respond to the new legitimacy in which women occupy senior positions, and what help do we need in order to adapt? How can we extend the range of leadership behaviours or styles in order to enhance the effectiveness of both male and female leaders?

I introduce in Table 1 a leadership model, the Hay McBer model (Goleman, 2000). This model uses six leadership styles: authoritative (now relabelled as 'visionary'), affiliative, coaching, democratic, pacesetting and coercive.

When working with this model, I ask groups to consider the pros and cons of each style, the situations in which they are most useful and how best to develop the style.

The model was not developed specifically to reference gender, race or sexuality, but it does extend the leadership behavioural repertoire to include styles more commonly associated with men's leadership behaviours, such as pacesetting and coercive, and those more commonly associated with women's leadership behaviours, such as affiliative and democratic. This model facilitates the integration of both the masculine and the feminine components of self, potentially changing some of the dynamics that limit male leaders' leadership styles and that hinder women's careers.

There may be comparisons with the experience of BAME leaders, since Whiteness may also be considered a central characteristic of leadership. It has been interesting for me to note, for example, the capital that White ex-patriot managers have, no matter which part of the world they are working in or, indeed, their effectiveness. Organisations may wish to consider that clearly defined leadership expectations and the application of leadership models that extend leadership repertoires may benefit all leaders.

Table 1 Hay McBer leadership styles

	Coercive	Authoritative (visionary)	Affiliative	Democratic	Pacesetting	Coaching
Leader's modus operandi	Demands immediate compliance	Mobilizes people towards a vision	Creates harmony and builds emotional bonds	Forges consensus through participation	Sets high standards for performance	Develops people for the future
The style in a phrase	'Do what I tell you'	'Come with me'	'People come first'	'What do you think?'	'Do as I do now'	'Try this'
Underlying emotional intelligence competence	Drive to achieve, initiative, self-control	Self-confidence, empathy, change catalyst	Empathy, building relationships, communication	Collaboration, team leadership, communication	Conscientiousness, drive to achieve, initiative	Developing others, empathy, self-awareness
When the style works best	In a crisis, to kick start a turnaround, or with problem employees	When changes require a new vision or when a clear direction is needed	To heal rifts in a team or to motivate people during stressful circumstances	To build buy-in or consensus or to get input from valuable employees	To get quick results from a highly motivated and competent team	To help an employee to improve performance or to develop long-term performance
Overall impact on climate	Negative	Most strongly positive	Positive	Positive	Negative	Positive

From *Harvard Business Review*, 'Leadership that gets results' (2000: 82)

4   Leading with Pride

Contemporary discourses on leadership emphasise authenticity. Possessing self-knowledge and leading in a way that is consistent with one's values may be a necessity in times of challenge and turbulence. Avolio and Gardner (2005: 316) argue that 'through increased self-awareness, self-regulation, and positive modelling, authentic leaders foster the development of authenticity in followers'. What, though, are the implications for authenticity if a LGBTQ+ leader is not out, at work?

Fear may be a significant part of the experience of LGBTQ+ employees. There may be fear of repercussions or negative consequences to coming out, such as lack of career progression or even loss of employment (or worse) in countries where LGBTQ+ people have no employment protection. While communicating information about partners or relationship status is typically low risk for heterosexuals, this is not necessarily the case for LGBTQ+ employees. As such, LGBTQ+ employers may have to weigh up the risks of disclosing potentially stigmatising information with the need for authenticity.

LGBTQ+ discrimination is the last bastion of equality, and so public support for LGBTQ+ rights may suggest that organisations have a broader concern for equality. Employment protection for LGBTQ+ people in the United Kingdom is relatively recent, compared to other groups, and is non-existent in many parts of the world. This may be particularly problematic for LGBTQ+ employees moving to other parts of the world for work, especially if the host country has no provision for the employee to be accompanied by a same-sex partner. There is no easy answer. My research (Mullen, 2011) into the factors that influence the disclosure strategies of Lesbian, Gay and Bisexual employees found that the following may be helpful:

1. Equal opportunities policies should be in place, and they should make explicit their support for Lesbian, Gay and Bisexual employees.
2. Managers should make visible commitment to those policies and tackle homophobic behaviour (or banter), irrespective of whether out Lesbian, Gay and Bisexual people are present when it occurs.
3. Management and human resources practices should emphasise diversity and inclusion.
4. Where possible, networking opportunities should be available for Lesbian, Gay and Bisexual employees.
5. Organisations must understand that the need for authenticity is compelling and that all employees are likely to perform better and be engaged if they can achieve congruence in their public and private identities.
6. A heteronormative ideology can be difficult for Lesbian, Gay and Bisexual employees, and assumptions about sexuality based on, for example, whether one has children should be challenged.

If an employee is considering an international assignment, organisations should consider issues of support and safety. They may also need to consider how they can support partners—for example, funding travel for the partner to visit.

5   Some Final Thoughts

Reflexivity, innovation and adaptability are now seen as leadership imperatives if organisations are to thrive in volatile, uncertain, complex and ambiguous environments—sometimes referred to VUCA. Minorities have often learned to adapt to prevailing circumstances that do not necessarily support them, and organisations that increase their responsive capacity by employing a diverse work-force can offer a much greater variety of solutions to problems. Diversity may well be testament to organisational agility, and, indeed, through their experiences of marginalisation, minority employees may have an advantage in contemporary contexts.

Practitioners must recognise the need for deeper and more nuanced approaches to diversity. We can no longer assume that equality can be achieved for all groups through blanket approaches to diversity—especially in a global context. As practitioners, we must take a macro and systemic view but also understand that the forces that create and sustain inequality reside in the everyday, the practices and the micro. We must also look outside, organisations are inevitably influenced by what is happening in the society more broadly. Social class, gender, ethnicity and sexuality and cognitive, learning and physical disabilities play a significant role in access to opportunities and options in society and in employment and in determining the fates of employees at work.

Some organisations are seeing the benefits not just of eliminating discrimination but of actually utilising diversity as brand capital. While diversity has been viewed in more recent years as a critical differentiator, it has been at the margins of organisations. Employee networks and industry networks such as Interbank, Intertech (both LGBT networking groups), Women in Gaming and BME in Gaming are proving to be not only a great source of support but a powerful resource for recruitment and brand capital. And they are globally accessible through their social media presence.

More companies are willing to sacrifice business in favour of their reputations in response to consumer concerns about the activities and values of the companies that they spend with. PayPal and Deutsche Bank pulled or froze hundreds of jobs in North Carolina when the state passed the HB2 Bill (Public Facilities Privacy & Security Act), which prevented trans people from using a restroom consistent with their gender identity. Starbucks CEO Howard Schulz responded to criticism that the company's support of same-sex marriage by explaining that the decision was not based on economic reasons but was out of respect for diversity. He advised the shareholders to sell their shares if they felt that they could get a better return than the 38% that Starbucks had delivered.

Twitter, Facebook and Google publish their diversity statistics, acknowledging the challenges that they face and publicly committing to do something about it, effectively merging their diversity management and corporate social responsibility agendas. These are global businesses. Whereas in the past businesses had to comply with local equality legislation (if indeed it existed), now we see global businesses applying their highest standards of compliance to equality, across the globe.

As practitioners, we have an opportunity to look at issues of equality, diversity and inclusion with a fresh pair of eyes. New approaches such as 'inclusion nudges' (Neilsen and Kepinski, 2016: 24) help organisations to make better, more objective and inclusive decisions by altering the system and elements in organisational processes, such as recruitment, promotions, performance management, succession and so on, by steering 'the brain's unconscious system towards inclusiveness by changing the system default (such as opt out instead of opt in)' (Neilsen and Kepinski, 2016: 29). Our task is to be able to understand the macro context and the micro practice; to use local knowledge to develop global practice. When addressing diversity and inclusion challenges, we need a broad perspective. As Steve Jobs once said: 'The broader one's understanding of the human experience, the better design we will have'.

References

Avolio, B. J., & Gardner, W. L. (2005). Authentic leadership development: Getting to the root of positive forms of leadership. *Leadership Quarterly, 16*(3), 315–338.

Bourdieu, P. (2001). *Masculine domination*. Cambridge: Polity Press.

Goleman, D. (2000). Leadership that get results. *Harvard Business Review, March–April*, 78–90.

Heilman, M. E. (2001). Description and prescription: How gender stereotypes prevent women's ascent up the organisational ladder. *Journal of Social Issues, 57*(4), 657–674.

Mullen, W. (2011). *Now you see me, now you don't: A study of the situational factors which influence the sexual identity management strategies of lesbians, gay and bisexual employees.* MSc thesis, Birkbeck College, University of London.

Neilsen, T., & Kepinski, L. (2016). *Inclusion nudges handbook*. North Charleston: Create Space Independent Publishing Platform.

Rosette, A., Leonardelli, G., & Phillips, K. (2008). The White standard: Racial bias in leader categorization. *Journal of Applied Psychology, 93*(4), 758–777.

Schein, V. E. (1975). The relationship between sex role stereotypes and requisite management characteristics among female managers. *Journal of Applied Psychology, 60*(3), 340–344.

Diversity in a Global Financial Organisation

Asif Sadiq MBE

Abstract

This chapter will discuss diversity and inclusion (D&I) from an international business perspective, looking at how large organisations work in various international settings, and explore how organisations embed their diversity and inclusion principles in international settings and countries where local views on certain elements of diversity can be different from those of the organisation. He will explore how managing an international workforce works in practical terms and how this raises both challenges and opportunities for a business, with a view to see how we can work towards creating truly diverse and inclusive international workplaces of the future and manage the challenges and opportunities this brings.

When we look at diversity in a global organisation, what do we think? Do we assume that we are talking about certain countries or even about first-world countries? The truth is that global financial firms are rapidly expanding to meet the business opportunities that growing markets have to offer, with many organisations establishing offices in the Middle East, Asia, Africa and beyond. This not only presents great opportunities to diversify an organisation but also brings with it challenges for how global organisations establish their D&I (diversity and inclusion) strategies internationally.

So let's start with the definition of diversity. To me, diversity is about differences. Each one of us is different. As organisations, we should value and respect individual differences, not just as they relate to gender or ethnicity but also, for example,

A. Sadiq MBE (✉)
The Telegraph, London, UK
e-mail: asif.sadiq@telegraph.co.uk

© Springer Nature Switzerland AG 2019   121
M. F. Özbilgin et al. (eds.), *Global Diversity Management*, Management for
Professionals, https://doi.org/10.1007/978-3-030-19523-6_11

background, education, nationality, generation, age, working style, religious background, sexual orientation, ability, technical skills and diversity of thought.

After diversity follows inclusiveness, which is about leveraging these differences that diversity brings to achieve better business results, more innovation and a better working world. Inclusiveness is about creating an environment where all people feel, and are, valued—where they are able to bring their differences to work each day and contribute their personal best in every encounter. In this way, each person can do their part to deliver exceptional client service, through high-performance teams (HPTs), to help their organisations grow.

Once you have the right mix of diversity and inclusion and have embedded this within your organisation, you then get 'belonging'. Belonging is about feeling that we are part of something and that we are seen and valued for all aspects of our unique identities. A diverse and inclusive organisation values the differences of each of its people, and this leads to better collaboration, retention and business performance.

Therefore, in order to achieve true success, any global firm must embed diversity and inclusion and create a sense of belonging for all its people globally. This can only be achieved through creating a universal experience for all your staff. Whether they work in China, India or Kenya, their experiences within the firm should be the same, regardless of which office they work out of.

So the million-dollar question is, how do you achieve this? Well, there are some things we can do to ensure that we are creating those experiences for our staff globally. Firstly, we need to have a truly global D&I strategy that outlines the overall D&I objectives of the organisation, the vision and key drivers that are needed to embed this strategy.

Any strategy that is global must have the flexibility to allow different regions, countries and cities to adapt the delivery of the strategy to its local market. This allows for not only ownership of the strategy by the local market but the opportunity to have a localised approach that meets the needs of the local staff while aligning to the overall goals of the strategy.

This can only be done by ensuring that all of our D&I policies globally are aligned and that the global D&I strategy has the flexibility to be adapted locally, taking into consideration local differences that might impact the delivery of the strategy in the global context. In reality, this means that we need to ensure that we take into consideration local differences that might impact certain elements of the D&I strategy and put in place local delivery plans that capture this diversity.

Let's look at this from a practical perspective and break it down by the main different diversity characteristics and see what it means for each of them.

1   Gender

Gender equality is a universal term that is being championed across the world and is one of the areas of D&I that is more than likely to appear on any global D&I strategy. Gender equality is being defended by numerous external organisations and NGOs, which raise awareness of the importance of this area of work, even in the remotest regions and countries. This also puts pressure on organisations to ensure that they have adequate D&I policies in place to support gender equality in the workplace.

However, consideration has to be given to cultural differences and policies in different countries that can impact this. Let's look at Saudi Arabia where, until recently, women could not drive; this would of course impact the access that staff would have to transport and, in some instances, limit their flexibility to travel across the country or even to certain destinations to which public transport may not be available.

As a global firm, I would say that even though the above would erect a barrier to gender equality, more can be done within the organisation to create a space where all genders are equal, and, if we take the above example, then to address the challenge, things can be put into place to ensure that the impact is minimised. For example, flexible working and the use of technology can help to reduce the need for travel and can ensure that women can service certain accounts that might be more difficult to reach.

Another example would be that of cultural differences that could have an impact on gender equality. I remember a colleague from Bangladesh, a senior accountant, who once explained to me that she had difficulty in working late evenings due to some of her commitments at home and the expectations of her family. Of course, there are other examples of why someone would not be able to work late, including caring responsibilities.

Having a good flexible working policy that empowers people to have greater choice in how, when and where they work can address the above challenges. Supporting both informal and formal flexible working is key to allowing individuals across the world to take advantage of flexible working. Giving people the opportunity (wherever feasible) to work the hours and location that help them to maximise their and the firm's performance, while considering their teams and ensuring that the client remains at the top of the value chain, is crucial.

Creating a sustainable, high-performing culture of flexible working is essential for the attraction and retention of high-quality staff and profitable growth. Future proofing a firm, supported by a compelling business case with new investment in infrastructure (as appropriate) to enable people to work flexibly, is the key to driving diversity across the globe.

2   Ethnicity

Ethnicity is becoming a global concept in the D&I space and is now becoming more and more prevalent in global D&I strategies. However, it is worth noting that what people refer to as ethnicity varies from country to country. In the United Kingdom, it is referred to as BAME (Black, Asian and Minority Ethnic) or BME (Black Minority Ethnic); in America, the term 'people of colour' is used more often; in many European countries, they use the phrase 'ethnic minority'. What is interesting is that we refer to people as minorities, yet people who are non-White actually form the majority, globally.

When addressing or looking at the challenges that people from different backgrounds face within a global business, we have to dig deeper into what ethnicity means within different countries and what other factors of diversity play a part around ethnicity in the local market and what considerations we should give to ensure that we address the challenges.

An example of this is the market in India. Although India has a rich element of cultural diversity and has people of many faiths, there is not much ethnic diversity as per the normal definition. However, one of the key challenges within the local market is the caste system, which has implications for the workplace and therefore results in barriers for some, who are perceived to be from a lower caste.

If we also take a look at South Africa, there is a policy of favouring members of a disadvantaged group who suffer or have suffered from discrimination within a culture. There are challenges in the local market that are associated with the history of the country, creating specific local challenges around addressing fairness for all the staff. The Employment Equality Act in South Africa states: 'An employer must create an action plan which makes sure it has the right proportion of designated people—Black, coloured, Indian, female and disabled people, working in all levels of the organisation'. This includes the very top levels of management. For example, if you have 50 members on your board of directors, then you must aim to have approximately 35 Black, 5 coloured, 4 Indian and 5 White directors. Of these, 25 should be female and 2 should be disabled.

This causes challenges for global D&I policies that might not want to go as far as affirmative action to support underrepresented groups in their organisations. However, the key consideration for any policy around ethnicity is that it ensures that overarching principles are set with the view of allowing flexibility in the local delivery to adhere to local cultures, laws and challenges through using local knowledge of the staff to develop local delivery plans.

3   Disability

Disability—or ability, as I like to refer to it—is an ever-evolving agenda in D&I. Over the years, the perception of what a disability is how we talk about it and how we see it have changed globally, and, despite the fact that certain countries might not fully be harnessing the power of different abilities, there is a strong sense that some change has been achieved in the area and that there is a greater understanding of what disability means.

However, when we think of global diversity and inclusion strategies, our focus is still on supporting the accessibility needs of people with disabilities, whether that be wheelchair access, software for dyslexia or other reasonable adjustments that we can make within the workplace to ensure that everyone can do their best and is able to work to the best of their ability without being disadvantaged due to their disability. It must be noted that, although this is the focus largely, a lot of organisations still have a long way to go in addressing some of the challenges that people with disability face when at work.

There is, however, a new way of thinking around abilities, and this is around harnessing the power that neuro diversity brings, as well as people with other visible and non-visible abilities. This is a concept that is making its way onto many global D&I strategies; several pieces of research have highlighted how an organisation can benefit from this. So the key question is, what does this mean? In essence, it's all about seeing ability as a positive thing and then seeing how you can utilise it to improve your business.

Organisations need to maximise their human resources by enabling their most highly skilled workers to focus on the highest value activities. Leading companies such as SAP, Microsoft, HPE and professional services firm Ernst & Young LLP are addressing strategic business issues by leveraging an often-overlooked pool of talent—people on the autism spectrum. Neurodiverse individuals are often technologically inclined and detail-oriented, with strong skills in analytics, mathematics, pattern recognition and information processing—among the very skills that businesses most urgently need.

They thrive on predictability and can be especially tenacious; loyal workers who prefer to stay with one organisation rather than move from opportunity to opportunity. Companies are finding that people with autism approach problems differently and that their logical, straightforward thinking can spur process improvements that greatly increase productivity.

4   LGBTQ+

LGBTQ+ rights and equality at work are an important element of global D&I strategies, and in recent years, there has been some real progress made in the area globally, which has had a positive impact not only on the LGBTQ+ community, has really created a positive culture of equality and inclusion for all at work, has the backing of the masses and is championing equality in the workplace.

Despite this, there are still difficulties in implementing LGBTQ+ equality in certain countries. In many countries, it is still illegal to be gay, and therefore, any global strategy implementation has to ensure that the work that the organisation is doing to advance the rights of the LGBT+ community doesn't end up actually putting them in danger or even getting them prosecuted. However, it is important to ensure that all employees can be themselves, and this involves organisations creating safe spaces for all their LGBTQ+ staff and ensuring that they have full equality in the workplace.

As mentioned, in recent years, the LGBT+ community has been met with criticism globally. In Turkey, the attendees of the 2015 Pride Parade were dispersed with tear gas and rubber bullets. In the United States, since being in power, President Trump has banned trans people from serving in the US military, and in the United Kingdom, the hate crimes against LGBT+ that have been reported have increased to 78% since 2013, with 80% not being reported. However, many global firms have signed up globally to the United Nations standards on LGBT+ inclusion, and this both supports their commitment to LGBTQ+ inclusion in the workplace and sends a clear message on its importance.

5   Faith

I mention faith, not because it is currently appearing on global D&I strategies but more to highlight the importance of faith inclusion, and an area of diversity I see taking precedence over others in the years to come. Global firms will invest their efforts in growing markets, which consist predominately of people of faith, and the rise in the Western world of a generation that sees faith as being integral to who they are. Therefore, if we are going to be truly inclusive and diverse global organisations, we need to start considering the importance of faith at work.

There is a growing trend towards recognising and embracing the importance of diversity and inclusion in both the national and global business environments. This agenda has been recognised by the UK Treasury and EY, together with many of its competitors, with its reports on gender and BAME issues. 'Making Faith Work' addresses what is still a relative gap in understanding the full range of inclusion and diversity, namely, faith and belief.

The role and impact of faith at work are becoming an increasingly important issue in the global business environment. This is not only for the benefits and assets they bring to the workplace but because of the rapidly growing policy and governance agenda that is developing around religion and belief as part of a wider commitment to inclusion and diversity and which is being pioneered by many global organisations. In business and society, faith is now being discussed more openly. In emerging markets in those parts of the world where religion is growing fastest, the use of religious ideology by global terror groups and the inclusion of religion and belief as a protected category in equalities and human rights legislation have all put the understanding of and working with religion and belief at centre stage.

So what are the benefits of faith at work? At an individual level, it helps to create a confident and empowered person, one able to undertake their duties to the highest ethical and professional standards and to reflect on who they are, why they do what they do and how they can improve as human beings. At a team level, it helps to foster a pragmatic yet creative attitude towards team-building and problem-solving. This stems from a commitment to listening, supporting and also challenging that comes from a position of greater personal knowledge and awareness of not only 'who I am', but 'who you are', as well. At a strategic level, a pro-faith, pro-belief business environment helps to foster more creative and 'out of the box' thinking.

Another area that is important for any global strategy is the consideration that we give to the many challenges that arise by working globally between staff who work in different countries. I believe that the challenges that we need to be aware of are things like language barriers, understanding protocol, time zones and distances, problem-solving and decision-making, motivating and creating a sense of urgency, building relationships across cultural differences, communicating virtually and resolving conflict. All these areas can be addressed if we embed the true concepts of diversity and inclusion and provide our staff with training and understanding around not only how to operate in their own environment but how to work in a global context. I cannot emphasise the importance of this enough. As technology advances and we are better connected globally, as we reduce costs and outsource certain functions to other parts of the world, we will find ourselves working days that will involve us in engaging with colleagues from around the world, and, unless we adapt and learn how to work best with our global teams, we will fail as businesses.

In conclusion, it is essential for any global organisation to ensure that it has a clear and adaptable D&I strategy that allows all its staff across the world to feel a sense of belonging to the organisation and also that staff member's experiences working for the company are replicated across the organisation, regardless of where they work in the organisation. That is true inclusion, and it will result in the most benefit from diversity for the organisation.

Global D&I strategies are essential if businesses are to operate across borders, and the only way in which they can develop a global culture is through understanding the diversity of their staff and how they can best utilise this to create an inclusive working environment for all, which of course results in better output and more innovation. Saying that, as we have explored, there are challenges to this, but no D&I strategy is without its challenges.

How to Start an Emotion-Reflective Journey

Kathrin Tietze

Abstract

This chapter deals with case studies in relation to human relationships, personal feelings, reflection and development in the area of diversity implementation. Through examples drawn from her experience as a professional in international diversity management implementation, lecturer of diversity management and process worker/Deep Democracy practitioner, she highlights the importance of empowering people to recognise and deal with their feelings, privileges and the ever-changing power structures they partake in.

When I was a student at Lancaster University in the 1990s, I undertook research for my final thesis. I interviewed children by means of a hand puppet play on the subject of being different. The children played, and I recorded, transcribed and analysed the play. I interviewed girls and boys. They were about 10 years old. When observing their play and re-listening to the recordings, I noticed that there was a striking difference in the children's play.[1] The girls were very caring, nurturing and trying very hard to find a good solution for all. The boys were much more physical, running around the room and very violent, shockingly violent to the point that in one version of the play, they actually killed the hedgehog. You could say that the children

---

[1]The children were presented with a dilemma, and I wanted to see their solutions to this. Two beavers were happily living in their cave when a hedgehog came along asking for shelter for the winter, as he didn't have a cave of his own. In the beginning, they get along fine until the hedgehog's prickles are too much for the beavers and they ask him to leave. This is where the narrative ended, on my side, and I asked the children to continue the play with hand puppets.

K. Tietze (✉)
be diversity—Consultancy, Projects, Training, Bremen, Germany
e-mail: mail@be-diversity.com; http://www.be-diversity.com

© Springer Nature Switzerland AG 2019
M. F. Özbilgin et al. (eds.), *Global Diversity Management*, Management for Professionals, https://doi.org/10.1007/978-3-030-19523-6_12

displayed what could be described as a traditional role-conforming behaviour in their play: role conforming in the sense that you would say that the female role is all about nurture and care, and the male role is all about physical presence and, to some extent, violence. I do not subscribe to those roles. However, very often, I see female and male roles described in such a way.

With the same children for a different and unrelated project, I undertook some more research on feminist tales.[2] My key question was to find out what they thought about the tales and their main messages. Almost all children, no matter what their gender, said that girls and boys are the same; basically, there are no differences; they should be allowed to do the same things, play the same games and so on.

At the time, many UK schools had an equal opportunities policy in place. My impression was that the children somehow knew what I wanted to hear. It seemed they had learned what was required from them when asked about equality. There is nothing wrong with that. In my opinion, the words and the actions just differed so strikingly. On a cognitive level, the message seemed to have come across, but it didn't change any of their behaviour.

I didn't take the research any further at the time, so this is a hypothesis based on observation and partial analysis.

This is a story from my early professional life. It led me to one of the core questions that to this day is central to my work: How do I touch people's minds and hearts? How do I bring about not only a change on a cognitive level but also on a behavioural level? How do I really reach people on a deeper level? In my opinion, this is absolutely essential for my work. Ever since the encounter with the group of 10-year-olds over 20 years ago, those are my central questions whenever I prepare for my work, be it leadership training, teaching next-generation health management students or running a workshop.

In the following paragraphs, I am going to share three more recent stories from my work on equality and diversity with groups. I will explore the questions raised above and may have some answers. Here is the first story.

1   Emotions in the Workplace

I am holding a leadership workshop on equality and diversity for a leadership team in an international organisation. Most of the day, we talk about the organisation's policies and their implementation in this particular country, share stories and challenges and look into the future. For the last part, I propose a group process because I would like to introduce a different method of working, and I feel that there might be some more issues which haven't been talked about yet which are present and working in the background anyway.

---

[2]Jay Williams (1978) *The Practical Princess, and other Liberating Fairy Tales.* Basingstoke: Macmillan Education.

I started by collecting topics for the group process. The topics were suggested by the group, and I wrote them on a flipchart. There was something about the smoking corner: some had the impression that all important information seemed to be shared there. There was confusion about the process of how new desk chairs were being distributed. But there was also an important issue about a change in the senior leadership team, and many in the team were concerned about a good hand over. A leadership meeting was planned, but it didn't give people enough reassurance. People didn't think this would guarantee a smooth transition. It wasn't an obvious diversity-related topic, but it was overwhelmingly important to the team. Hence, we went with this topic.

The group process started very well. People got engaged, took sides and spoke what was on their minds, the best leader they've had so far, no one can ever match that, lots of concerns on the transition. At some point, it almost seemed like all was lost; this was the end of the world. More voices came in, appreciating what they were about to lose, honouring the good work the leader had done. People were nodding, and it was getting quieter and quieter. I felt a shift in the room atmosphere and suddenly a great sadness. Someone well respected and dear is leaving. This is sad. I said it aloud, and most people agreed and nodded, and we fell silent.

We stood for perhaps 20 seconds, which is a long time in a group, in silence and shared the great sadness.

Having created this 20-second shared moment of feeling the loss and the sadness that goes with it was such a precious moment. I feel it is always difficult to truly show emotions, particularly emotions that are perceived negatively, like anger and sadness. In a work context, this is even harder. I am very grateful to the group for joining me in the group process, to unearth that feeling and to share it.

The whole group process took about an hour. In that hour, we managed to hear very diverse voices on the topic, had a shared moment of sadness and appreciation and agreed on the next step, which was that it needed a much longer meeting on the transitioning process, and with all colleagues and not just the leadership team, to get everyone on board.

2   Reflecting on/in Confusion

I teach diversity management to an international group of health management students. Strengthening the students' (self-)reflective skills is central to my work with them. It is an important management skill generally but even more vital in diversity management. You need to know yourself and reflect upon yourself and your behaviour, feelings and thoughts. They need to learn to be flexible and adjust to various norms and values, thus need to know about their own norms and values too. One part of the exam is a reflective essay with the aim to assess their reflection skills. Students need to write about something they learned, something that was surprising, new, they agree/don't agree with. I am interested in the process that they are describing, their learning journey. In that exercise, I am not interested in abstract knowledge. One of the best essays I have had so far was three pages of confusion.

Why did I enjoy it so much? The student described himself as a very open and tolerant person. He has a liberal view on the world. On my course, he learned to question all his beliefs and who he really was. A lot of his assumptions about the world fell apart. He didn't really know anymore what to believe and what was right and wrong. In the essay, he described that journey in much detail. He is now in a position to re-evaluate his world view, his thoughts and, with that, his behaviour. He was also brave enough to let me and the other people in the course shake up his world. As the responsible person, I and everyone else in the room created a conducive learning and growing environment. This is an excellent starting point, and I am grateful in this story, too, for the student's trust and courage to join me on a journey with an unclear outcome and, in the student's case, great uncertainty.

3   Building Community While Processing Histories

I co-organise workshops on East-West German issues with some fabulous colleagues. This topic is very close to my heart. Firstly, I grew up in East Germany, and the developments that led to the German reunification and everything that followed from that had a great impact on me personally, on my family and friends and the 16.4 million people living in the GDR (German Democratic Republic—East Germany) in 1989. Of course, it did have an impact on 60.5 million people living in the former FRG (Federal Republic of Germany—West Germany) too, just not as profound. There is still a lot of misunderstanding, even though we speak the same language. There is still a lot of missing knowledge about individual stories, the impact it had on people across Germany, but particularly on people in East Germany. There is still a lot of unspoken anger, hurt, sadness and frustration.

In my opinion, a lot of the issues in Germany today are connected to the process of reunification in the 1990s and how it was conducted. We bring people together in the workshops to explore past and current issues related to East-West-Reunited German history. We explore individual stories, histories and various voices in the field, then and now, through Deep Democracy methodology. This includes listening to as many voices and roles as possible, to let them speak to each other, to conflict with each other and to find a resolution together, where possible. Everybody is encouraged to also utter voices that are not necessarily their own. That way, people experience different views and feelings. People develop the ability to switch perspectives.

The learning for me is huge. In one of the workshops, I experienced my inability to forgive. Right now, I lack the ability to forgive, and this is hindering me in moving forward. Right now, I am still processing that new knowledge about myself, so it is work in progress/process.

In a different workshop, we collectively arrived at a moment of experiencing loss: again, a moment, not long. We had all lost a lot in the process of reunification, some the certainties of their homes or basic knowledge of society's functioning. Some had lost dreams of a better way to shape communities for people to live in. The losses had been very different. The moment of sharing, itself, was more important than sharing the same kind of loss. There was space for loss. That space has healing power. Healing is a crucial element in building a community.

4 Key Ingredients in All Three Stories

I take time. It takes time. It is no secret to all diversity workers that it is all about the process. Processes take time. Processes, contrary to projects, also do not have an official end date. They are ongoing, whether they are facilitated or not. This holds true for me as a human being. I continuously process the world around me, my relationships to other people, hopefully until the day I die. This holds also true for organisations and companies. Diversity is a fact in any given organisation or company, whether there are any policies and practices to facilitate and manage that diversity in place or not. As an organisation, considering yourself as being on a journey, in a process rather than a project with a fixed end date and clear outcomes, might be helpful in the overall management of diversity. It is ongoing learning, not always straightforward learning, and not always intended learning, with success and failure close by. As an individual, organisation or company, allow yourself the space and time to hold that learning process for the benefit of all.

I am looking for minimal shifts. When venturing into deeper levels, the changes or what is actually happening might seem small—20 seconds of sadness? A whole semester teaching and there is confusion? Yes! This is what I am looking for, and I feel honoured and grateful to experience this now and again. People are making themselves vulnerable, and I am in a position to hold that space for them. This goes with a lot of responsibility, too. I try to create safe spaces, as much as possible. What may seem a tiny shift might turn out to have great potential for healing and community building.

In all three stories, I am partly or wholly working with Deep Democracy methodology. Ever since I started learning about Deep Democracy a couple of years ago, I feel that I am getting closer to answering that one question: How do I reach people on a deeper level with my work. It is at the same time both a set of methods and tools that I use in my work and a life philosophy. How do I want to be in this world? How do I want to shape my relationships?

What is Deep Democracy all about? Here is a very brief introduction.

5 Deep Diversity with Deep Democracy

Deep Democracy has one of its main roots in process-oriented psychology, which was founded by Arnold Mindell in the early 1980s. The interdisciplinary root system is widely branched, ranging from Carl Gustav Jung's psychology, quantum physics, communication theory, system theory and gestalt work to shamanism and Taoism. The approach is under constant further development by Arnold Mindell, together with Amy Mindell, Max Schupbach, Ellen Schupbach and a whole community of process workers around the world.

Why is Deep Democracy a deep democracy? It is based on the assumption that it is not enough to prescribe democratic processes of majorities and minorities when it comes to forming permanently functioning communities. In the model of Deep Democracy, all people are present with all emotions. In addition, communities that are not necessarily consensus-building but have learned how to deal with dissent and conflict can generate energy and community from it. For this to happen, it is necessary to dig into deeper layers, particularly emotionally (Mindell, 2002).

Central concepts deal with polarities, rank (e.g. social, psychological or spiritual rank), privileges, power, roles and ghost roles. Ghost roles are of particular interest, because they contain information that is marginalised—information that is not out in the open but which is still very powerful and working under the surface. Identifying ghost roles and giving them space allow us to deal with them (Mindell, 2014). Those or similar concepts are familiar to many in their work on diversity and inclusion. Here, they are connected and used in the interaction of inner work and interaction in small and large groups for the temporary resolution of conflicts.

An important approach in the work is to go straight into the conflict, to welcome it as an opportunity to build or deepen a relationship.

Deep Democracy work assumes that each group has the potential and ability to resolve any conflict—literally, any conflict. One of the key magic ingredients is that it is not about the conflict's solution for all eternity, but a temporary solution, only ever for this moment. Now, at this point in time, we are on the same side.

The Deep Democracy paradigm assumes that I carry all the diversity of the world in me. I am the gentlest person in the world, and I am the terrorist. It is a lifelong process to recognise the different roles in me, especially the marginalised, oppressed ones. The inner work allows me to change roles on the outside, taking different perspectives, to develop empathy within me towards seemingly opposing emotional states. This is where the great potential lies in the concrete work in the field of diversity and inclusion. My inner diversity serves me as the key to me—and to you.

6   Conclusion

Three stories and one very brief introduction to Deep Democracy further, where does this lead me? Here are the three main takeaways for this chapter.

Digging deep inside myself and confronting myself with all my inner diversity, however, full of conflict and contradiction, love and hurt, allow me to let myself be touched by other human beings on a deeper level. I develop the ability to be fully on my side and to be fully on their side.

I need to be able to deal with conflict. In my view, this is essential for good equality and diversity work. People are diverse, and we want to bring them together because firstly this is a reality of humanity and secondly we believe in the power of a diverse humankind. I more and more believe that one of the keys to a prosperous society for all is conflict and being able to deal with it—to be able to throw yourself into it with all your might and heart.

Shifts and developments are often tiny and do not come with a huge bang. Changes take time, are not linear and often rather messy, particularly in the field of equality, diversity and inclusion. Sometimes one has to be alert and able to listen with all one's senses to actually notice the change. So we're in it for the long run.

This is the way to deepen all relationships, build communities and successfully manage companies.

This is deep diversity for me.

This is how I reach people's hearts, for a few seconds, one heart at a time.

What more can I wish for.

References

Mindell, A. (2002). *The deep democracy of open forums*. Charlottesville, VA: Hampton Roads.
Mindell, A. (2014). *Sitting in the fire: Large group transformation using conflict and diversity*. Florence, OR: Deep Democracy Exchange.

Making the Creative Case for Diversity Across Arts and Culture: An Outsider Looking in

Abid Hussain

Abstract
This chapter tells the story of Arts Council England's Creative Case for Diversity and how it impacts on him and the wider arts and cultural sector in England.

Back in the autumn of 2001, I was working in the unglamorous regulatory department at TRANSCO (now the National Grid), the company responsible for managing the gas pipeline network for the United Kingdom. It was during my time there that I was introduced to Zoe Partington who, at the time, was running the West Midlands Disability Arts Forum. To this day, I'm incredibly indebted to the late James Farquhar for making a personal introduction to Zoe, who completely changed my career trajectory. A few months later, I left TRANSCO and accepted a very different job as an assistant officer working at the Arts Council England.

Volunteering with West Midlands Disability Arts Forum was my introduction to the world of arts and culture, but, more crucially, it opened my eyes to the bias, barriers and discrimination that so many talented disabled artists face. Through Zoe, I was introduced to the social model of disability, highlighting the preventable barriers that too often exist without challenge in society. What I have learned to love about the social model approach is that every perceived barrier or block has a solution. Sometimes, those solutions require resources, at other times willpower and culture change, but, more often than not, they just need a bit of common sense!

This is an updated version of a feature originally written for Disability Arts International—http://www.disabilityartsinternational.org/

A. Hussain (✉)
Arts Council England, London, UK
e-mail: abid.hussain@artscouncil.org.uk

© Springer Nature Switzerland AG 2019
M. F. Özbilgin et al. (eds.), *Global Diversity Management*, Management for Professionals, https://doi.org/10.1007/978-3-030-19523-6_13

I'm glad I discovered the forum and met Zoe before I even knew what Arts Council was. They inspired my curiosity, made me fall in love with the arts and gave me the confidence to apply for a job in an industry that I was completely new to. I liked being an outsider; it gave me permission to ask left-field questions, and it helped to shape the purpose that drives me as a policy-maker, simply to make the arts and cultural sector in England inclusive and representative of wider society across our programming, audiences and workforce.

1   Making the Creative Case for Diversity

Equality and diversity discourse is nothing new in England. In 1976, the much-loved and missed Naseem Khan published her ground-breaking report 'The Arts Britain Ignores'. At the heart of her work was a simple observation; the arts and cultural life of England would be significantly enriched by increasing platforms and opportunity for underrepresented artists. Naseem focused on themes of ethnic identity, but her call for change could equally resonate with disabled artists who have faced far too many barriers to opportunity.

This principle was reflected in the Arts Council's 'Creative Case for Diversity', which we launched in 2011 as a catalyst to reframe an increasingly stagnant and unproductive approach to policy and practice that too often centred almost exclusively on the legal imperative for equality and diversity. We had lost sight of the art.

The Creative Case for Diversity articulated a new paradigm for diversity that retains the fundamental diversity principles of equality, access and opportunity but also recognises and celebrates the importance of diversity as a source of artistic excellence and advantage. It argues that, far from diluting quality, diversity increases innovation and excellence, creating compelling new work and narratives that amplify the voice and presence of communities that for too long have been missing, ignored or underrepresented across arts and culture. It directly challenges directors, curators and programmers at publicly funded arts and cultural organisations to take ownership of and accountability for how the diversity of wider society is reflected in the work that they programme, curate or present. Having a conversation about diversity that is interconnected and inseparable to the process of commissioning and creating work ensures that resources are allocated from the outset and that diversity is intrinsic to the process of realising artistic ambition, rather than a long-forgotten afterthought doomed to reside on the pages of well-meaning equality action plans gathering dust in filing cabinets around the country.

2   2012 and the Birth of Unlimited

The Cultural Olympiad and the London Games in 2012 were a game-changer for disabled artists. You may not have thought it or even dared to imagine it in the years preceding the games. A number of disability-led arts organisations in the late 2000s had lost their funding, forums were closing around the country and the voice and presence of disabled artists seemed to be increasingly on the periphery of the sector. We weren't in need of a step change; we needed a revolution and a radical new approach. That revolution started to take shape in 2007, when colleagues at Arts Council England, including Joyce Wilson (Area Director, London), entered into conversations with the London Organising Committee for the Olympic Games (LOCOG). The timing couldn't have been more fortuitous, as Joyce recalls:

> We had ringfenced funding for a different approach to investing in disabled artists—artist led, focusing on investing in and supporting disabled artists directly and encouraging experimentation. When LOCOG approached us offering to back a programme of commissions and showcasing, we were delighted; here was an opportunity to pool resources and hang work on a hook that had heft and profile.

> LOCOG also gave us an opportunity to work collaboratively with other home-nation Arts Councils, and with the British Council also joining in, the net result was an increase in the commissioning funds available, from £150,000 to £2.2m, and we had the birth of Unlimited.

A decade later, Unlimited continues to flourish through the festival on the South Bank and the arts commissioning programme delivered jointly by Shape Arts and Arts Admin. Our direct investment in Unlimited continues to grow and pay artistic dividends, with a further £1.8m invested in the commissioning programme in 2016. In 2018, the festival hosted the first ever Unlimited Symposium, which attracted delegates from over 40 countries to explore themes of art, equality, attitude and the future.

Unlimited has validated the decision to take an artist-centred approach to invest directly in the ideas and talent of disabled artists. One of the more notable successes of Unlimited has been its international impact, both in terms of the festival attracting international delegates supported by our partnership with the British Council and also in terms of securing international bookings for disabled artists from England, whose work has travelled to Europe, South America, Asia, North America and Australasia.

This work has been further strengthened by the Arts Council investing an additional £759,949 to Unlimited via our Ambitions for Excellence fund, to support a new 3-year international programme with further support from the British Council. The next edition of the festival will take place in London in 2020.

One frustration born out of this success is that, for many disabled artists in England, their work has received greater support and artistic recognition in international markets than back home in England. This is a challenge that we need to address head on through our work with publicly funded organisations in England. The talent is there; all it needs is the opportunity. How can we have a situation where artists from England are recognised better internationally than at home?

The Creative Case for Diversity has to serve as a catalyst for arts and cultural organisations in England to take seriously their responsibility to diversify their programmes. For our part, we need to ensure that there are robust measures in place for accountability and, where necessary, action, if that change is not forthcoming.

The success of Unlimited can be attributed to a number of different factors, from its commitment to collaborative working to the brilliant artistic leadership and passion of its senior producer, Jo Verrent. Its success also owes much to the talent, vision and imagination of disabled artists from the United Kingdom and abroad who have inspired us and moved us to moments of joy, laughter, despair and tears through their work.

It has helped to change the way that we do things at the Arts Council, too, and increased our scale of investment significantly, paving the way for other major investments. Most notable are two awards totalling over £4m (our two biggest strategic touring investments ever) to the Ramps on the Moon consortia to support new touring work, and over £700,000 through our Ambitions for Excellence programme to support the integrated circus company Extraordinary Bodies. This additional investment hasn't just come from our diversity-focused programmes, which highlights progress in embedding diversity as a priority across all our funding programmes.

There have been drawbacks, too, as more needs to be done to encourage artists who submitted proposals to Unlimited to consider submitting applications for grants to the Arts Council. We've still got work to do to encourage more disabled artists to apply for funding directly to the Arts Council.

I don't want opportunities for disabled artists to be available only when we run or support initiatives such as Unlimited. A more significant cultural shift needs to take place, where programming diversity becomes part of the very DNA of our arts and cultural organisations and is part of the norm rather than being the exception.

We continue to make changes to remove barriers to access for disabled artists applying to our grants for the arts programme, who can receive financial support for someone to assist them with writing and submitting their applications. We've also introduced an access budget line as part of project costs, recognising the importance of ongoing access and addressing barriers when projects receive funding.

These were vital changes to the way in which we administer and process grant applications and embed our commitment to equality, diversity and the social model of disability at the heart of our open-access funding programmes. By removing barriers to access, we create a more equitable application process. It has also allowed us to address diversity as a priority across our funding programmes, and not just to address it through bespoke initiatives. It has been important to be open about the support that is available as, too often when applying for funding, applicants may not be aware of what they can ask or budget for. What has been incredibly empowering is the conversations that we've opened up with other funding agencies to share our learning and experience. For any funder who wants to increase investment to support the ambition of disabled artists, there are ways to achieve this through refining their existing programmes and processes.

3 Diversity Strategic Funds

Unlimited was the first flagship strategic programme that we developed to engage specifically with disabled artists. We also launched our Elevate and Change Makers programmes, which collectively invested over £7.5m to support diverse artists and organisations.

Our Elevate programme was designed to strengthen the resilience of diverse organisations not in receipt of regular national portfolio funding. Through an investment of £5.3m, we have supported 40 organisations across the country to develop their resilience and to build new partnerships and collaborations with other arts and cultural organisations. Elevate has had a significant impact on helping to diversify our national portfolio, with 20 Elevate organisations joining our national portfolio, including Disability Arts Online, Venture Arts and Together 2012!, which will each receive regular funding over a 4-year period.

Our Change Makers programme supported 20 BAME and disabled leaders to take part in a leadership development programme, working in collaboration with national portfolio organisations. Over half the cohort is comprised of disabled leaders, including Jess Thoms, Andrew Miller and James Rose.

It is my aspiration that our Change Maker cohort will be at the vanguard of a new wave of artistic and executive leaders who are representative of the diversity of contemporary England in the years ahead. There are no excuses for the low number of disabled people working in the arts and cultural sector. Collectively, as a sector, we need to do more, much more.

4 Hitting Reset and Prioritising Data

Taking on the leadership role for our equality and diversity agenda provided a timely opportunity to hit the reset button. Much of my first year in the role was spent in the company of artists and arts organisations across the country, and it helped me to see things from their perspective, which is crucial as a policy-maker. Those conversations helped shape my focus and set priorities for the change I wanted to see. The inspiration for our Elevate and Change Maker programmes emerged directly from open, inspiring and sometimes difficult conversations.

In December 2014, the starting gun was shot on the reset when our chair at the time, Sir Peter Bazelgette, delivered a landmark speech that served notice to the sector that diversity had to be the responsibility of all funded organisations, not just the few. A year later, in 2015, we published our first 'Equality, Diversity and the Creative Case' report which, for the first time, openly published data on our investment and the arts and cultural workforce across the age, disability, ethnicity and gender classifiers.

Some of what we've published has made for uncomfortable reading, particularly in relation to disability. The workforce is not reflective of England, the leadership of the sector even less so. Publishing the data has been critical, as it gives us benchmarks and highlights where we need to improve. It holds us to account, as well as the organisations that receive public funding. We still face challenges around getting better quality data, as for disability we still have too many 'prefer not to say' and 'unknown' responses. We're working with the sector to change things to improve rates of response. Looking forward, we plan to introduce new questions to focus on the barriers that disabled people face, rather than impairment categories. Beyond disability, we're looking at how we can capture and report on socio-economic background and social mobility. Without data, we couldn't have developed programmes like Elevate and Change Makers, as data give us the evidence to respond to things that need our resources and our attention. No one likes tick boxes, but, now more than ever, capturing meaningful data is critical. As organisations look to capture data, it's our job to ensure that people understand the reasons why we ask for the information and why it's so important for them to share it.

5   The Dawn of a New National Portfolio

Our current national portfolio (arts and cultural organisations that receive 4-year funding) for 2018–2022 genuinely excites me. Looking back to the summer of 2014, the equality analysis that accompanied the announcement of our 2015–2018 national portfolio made for heavy and difficult reading. The number of disability-led organisations in the portfolio was on the decline; we were concerned at the lack of representation, in particular of disabled and BAME staff across arts organisations and museums, and there were genuine concerns around the future pipeline of diverse organisations that could help to refresh and revitalise future investment rounds. Our portfolio for 2018–2022 feels fresh and vibrant, and we've seen a significant influx of new disability-led organisations, including Disability Arts Online, Bamboozle, Diverse City and Together 2012! We've also awarded significant increases in investment to existing organisations, including Attitude is Everything, Extant, Heart N Soul, Dash, StageText, Vocal Eyes, Mind the Gap and Deafinitely Theatre.

Just as importantly, we've committed to ensuring that diversity and equality is a shared responsibility across the national portfolio. All funded organisations will be required to evidence their contribution to the Creative Case for Diversity and receive an annual performance rating that will hold them to account. For our larger organisations (Bands 2 and 3[1]), there is a clear expectation that we want them to be rated 'strong' by October 2021. The rating process allows us to look at how organisations are responding to the Creative Case in practice against what they articulated in their National Portfolio Organisations applications. It is vital that aspirations are matched by action. The ratings take into consideration the programme of work presented, talent development initiatives, addressing barriers to artistic involvement and the level of buy-in from board members to hold organisations to account. Ratings are determined on an annual basis by Arts Council relationship

---

[1]http://www.artscouncil.org.uk/national-portfolio-2018-22/our-investment-2018-22-helpful-documents

managers. To support organisations to understand and respond to the Creative Case, we have published the ratings prompts and evidence framework relationship that managers use to determine a rating.

We've set out clear expectations on the changes that we would like to see to diversify the workforce, boards and audiences as part of our funding agreements with organisations. I want the aspirations that we see in applications to manifest itself into tangible action during 2018–2022, demonstrated through disabled people playing a prominent role in arts and cultural programming, the workforce and boards across all arts organisations, libraries and museums that are part of our national portfolio.

Promoting Cultural Awareness: A Means of Managing Global Diversity

Doirean Wilson

Abstract

Global diversity management has resulting in the growth in national and international laws fashioned as a means to address discrimination and the rise in high-profile cases against many international firms. These occurrences are indicative of an inability to understand different cultures, which is a must when doing business abroad in different cultural environments. Research evidence suggests that cultural misunderstandings can result in hostility and suspicion. This can affect an organisation's reputation, sustainability and quest for success, thus arguing a need to be culturally aware. This chapter draws on findings of a study that explored cultural meanings of respect and how these meanings manifest among culturally diverse business students in the classroom. The aim is to provide insight into the cultural awareness practices addressing team conflict that are used to manage diversity among national and international learners.

Global diversity is a topic of much debate and of significant importance today, resulting in a growth in national and international laws, fashioned as a means of addressing discrimination, and a rise in high-profile cases against many international firms.

These occurrences are indicative of an inability to understand different cultures, which is a must when doing business abroad in different cultural environments. Research evidence suggests that cultural misunderstandings can result in hostility and suspicion. This can affect an organisation's reputation, sustainability and quest for success, thus arguing a need to be culturally aware.

D. Wilson (✉)

Middlesex University Business School, The Burroughs, London, UK

e-mail: d.wilson@mdx.ac.uk

© Springer Nature Switzerland AG 2019

M. F. Özbilgin et al. (eds.), *Global Diversity Management*, Management for Professionals, https://doi.org/10.1007/978-3-030-19523-6_14

This chapter draws on findings of a study that explored cultural meanings of respect and how these meanings manifest among culturally diverse business students in the classroom. The aim is to provide insight into the cultural awareness practices used to manage diversity among national and international learners who address team conflict.

1   The Implications of Global Diversity Today

Globalisation is a significant and ongoing twenty-first-century phenomenon that has left an indelible mark on most societies. If we were to define this marvel, then it could be referred to as 'the rapidly developing process of complex interconnections between societies, cultures, institutions and individuals world-wide' (Tomlinson, 1996). This notion is acknowledgement of the diverse aspect of globalisation. Furthermore, the term (globalisation) 'is a social process which involves a compression of time and space, shrinking distances through a dramatic reduction in the time taken either physically or representationally—to cross them' (Tomlinson, 1996), thanks to inventions such as aeroplanes that make it easier and cheaper for people to travel more frequently from one society to another. This privilege also makes 'the world seem smaller and in a certain sense bringing human beings 'closer' to one another' (ibid.).

The impact of globalisation is ever-present today, as seen across different communities and observed in many classrooms and, not least, in a variety of different work environments. Shen, Chanda, and D'Netto (2009) acknowledge that 'increasing globalization, as well as national concerns about growing demographic diversity, have enhanced the need for understanding heterogeneity in organizations'.

What has become increasingly evident is a lack of understanding of people's differences, particularly their culture, which has resulted in a rise in complaints of discrimination and high-profile litigation cases, which not only tarnishes an organisation's reputation but can threaten its sustainability nationally and, for those that operate abroad, internationally.

2   High-Profile Discrimination Cases

Since the mid-1970s, there has been a spate of high-profile discrimination cases against several international firms to their detriment. One such company was Southern California Edison, which had a class discrimination claim filed against it back in 1974 and again in 1994. This latter claim resulted in a settlement that cost the firm $11 million plus an order for diversity training. This was followed by another lawsuit in 2010 brought by a group of Black employees for what they claimed was 'consistently denying them promotions and not paying them fairly' (Nittle, 2019).

Wal-Mart Stores agreed to pay a settlement sum of $17.5 million, despite denying any wrongdoing, to 'approximately 4500 Black truck drivers' who claimed that they were 'turned away in disproportionate numbers' after applying for work with the firm between 2001 and 2008 (Nittle, 2019).

In 2003, a discrimination claim was lodged against the clothing retailer Abercrombie & Fitch for prejudice against 'African Americans, Asian Americans, and Latinos'. However, it was mainly the Latinos and Asians who complained that the company would assign them jobs in the stockroom, where they could not be seen, which they believed was because 'Abercrombie & Fitch wanted to be represented by workers who looked classically American' (Nittle, 2019). Several minority ethnic staff also complained of being sacked, only to be replaced by White employees, which resulted in Abercrombie & Fitch having to pay a $50 million lawsuit to settle the case.

These are not the only types of discriminatory cases that suggest a need for organisations to be culturally aware, as it also includes incidences of genetic discrimination. Genetic discrimination occurs when a person is treated differently to others because of a gene that they might have 'that predisposes them to developing a particular disease or condition such as cancer' (Ellis, 2002: 1071). This revelation can render such individuals being denied life or health insurance, as well as being subjected to discrimination in the workplace (ibid.).

Natowicz, Alper, and Alper (1992) referred to a survey that was conducted among individuals regarded as having a genetic condition that they said 'was designed to gain information about the variety and significance of genetic discrimi- nation' and which revealed incidences of genetic discrimination. What was identified from this survey was, for example, that those who were diagnosed with Charcot-Marie-Tooth disease, a collection of *hereditary conditions that cause dam- age to peripheral nerves*, 'were denied life insurance, automobile insurance, or employment' (Natowicz et al., 1992). This was despite knowing that their condition was not fatal or was very mild.

As acknowledged in a document published by the US National Library of Medicine (2018), there are some disorders that are likely to be more evident among individuals who can track their ancestry to a specific part of the world. Furthermore, those who belong to a particular ethnic group tend to share certain gene types inherited from common ancestors. Furthermore, what was also recog- nised was that if one gene had a disease-causing mutation, then it was likely that the particular ethnic group would be beset with a specific genetic disorder. Sickle cell anaemia is one such disorder that is more commonly found in people of African, Afro-Caribbean or African American decent (US National Library of Medicine, 2018). Thalassemia is another similar blood disease, usually affecting people of Mediterranean origin, and Gaucher disease type 1 is prevalent among Ashkenazi Jews (Beutler et al., 1993). These medical insights could result in genetic discrimi- nation, which would also be discrimination based on a person's culture or race.

3   Diversity Legislation and Implications

The Equality Act 2010 is the legislation that covers England, Scotland and Wales, and this makes it evident that it is unacceptable and illegal to discriminate against a person or group, whether intentionally, unintentionally or due to a lack of understanding. This relates to those who reflect any of the nine protected characteristics specified in the Equality Act 2010, namely, age, disability, gender reassignment, marriage and civil partnership, pregnancy and maternity, religion or belief, sex, sexual orientation and race (Legislation.gov.uk, 2018).

Race discrimination can occur from more than one perspective. An example of this is where the legislation states that 'people born in Britain to Jamaican parents could be discriminated against because they are British citizens, or because of their Jamaican national origins'. Another example of this type of discrimination is a person born in Wales to Nigerian parents who are members of the Yoruba tribe, who might be discriminated against because they are Welsh and of Nigerian origin or because of their Yoruba heritage.

These insights make evident the need to be aware of the significance of global diversity today, which Nishii and Özbilgin (2007) acknowledge is an issue that 'has been increasing due to the expansion of national laws and international policies aimed at eliminating discrimination, as well as a concomitant rise in the number of high-profile litigations against global firms'. Nevertheless, the portent is 'the forms of discrimination that are considered unlawful diverge across countries, and there is extensive national variation in interpretation and implementation of equal opportunities laws' (Özbilgin, 2002).

An example of this scenario is provided by the employment and labour law team at global law firm Eversheds Sutherland, a company that offers legal advice and solutions to a range of international businesses, from small and medium enterprises to larger, multinational firms. The firm's employment and labour law team has put together a summary of employment discrimination law, based on 12 key jurisdictions, which:

- Covers a widespread of countries spanning Africa, North America, Europe and Asia
- Adopts a risk-based approach, providing a snapshot risk rating of each jurisdiction's 'red flag' points to note
- Sets out the types of penalties that non-compliant employers might face
- Indicates where a jurisdiction has not ratified the ILO's (International Labour Organization's), discrimination (employment and occupation) and convention (ratification is assumed unless otherwise stated), while also offering insights into the ILO's overall assessment of each country's employment discrimination regime (www.eversheds-sutherland.com, 2018)

This information is detailed in Table 1.

As documented in Table 1, the employment discrimination law in India protects female applicants against sex discrimination in recruitment and female employees

Table 1 A summary of employment discrimination law, based on 12 key jurisdictions

Who is protected?	Protected characteristic (on what grounds is discrimination unlawful?)	What type of discriminatory treatment is unlawful?	Employer penalty for unlawful discrimination	Discrimination risk	Risk rating
Brazil					
All types of workers, from recruitment until termination of employment	Colour (including race, national and ethnic origin), gender (including pregnancy and sterilisation), religion, disability, age, marital status and social condition	Direct, indirect and positive discrimination Unequal treatment in relation to pay	Compensation for pain and suffering and, where the employee has been dismissed, lost wages and a severance payment. Reinstatement may be an additional remedy, depending on the nature of the discrimination	Racism is treated as a serious criminal offence. It is also a criminal offence for employers to require female employees/applicants to verify non-pregnancy Sexual orientation discrimination is not expressly outlawed, and pressure is rising for such a law to be introduced Two-thirds of all employees in any company having three or more employees must be Brazilian citizens; two-thirds of the payroll must be paid to Brazilian citizens. There are rules providing for foreign employees to be laid off before Brazilians	High → Medium → Low
Canada					
Job applicants, employees, former employees as a minimum	Race, national or ethnic origin, colour, religion, age, sex, sexual	Based on one or more of the above protected characteristics:	Depending on the jurisdiction, complaints may be taken to the local	Federal and provincial laws protect workers on various, slightly different,	High → Medium

(continued)

Table 1 (continued)

Who is protected?	Protected characteristic (on what grounds is discrimination unlawful?)	What type of discriminatory treatment is unlawful?	Employer penalty for unlawful discrimination	Discrimination risk	Risk rating
	orientation, marital status, family status, disability, a conviction for which a pardon has been granted or a record suspended. This list is not exhaustive—check local legislation as it differs across Canada	Failing to hire a job applicant and terminating employment Failing to reasonably accommodate job applicants and employees Unfair treatment of an applicant or employee Following policies/practices that deprive people of employment or advancement opportunities or adversely affect employees that possess a protected characteristic Retaliating against an employee who has filed a complaint Harassment	human rights commission or to a tribunal. A tribunal may order corrective measures including payment for lost wages, severance pay, compensation for emotional injury, implementation of policies, reinstatement, and training	specific grounds. For example, some protect workers from discrimination on additional grounds, such as language, political belief or social status. Local advice is needed Mandatory retirement is generally viewed as a form of age-related discrimination unless the employer can show a justifiable occupational requirement why an employee must retire at a certain age	→ Low
China					
Job applicants, some workers	Race, ethnicity, gender, religion, migrant status, disability, carriers of infectious diseases (e.g. people with hepatitis B or HIV)	No discrimination in recruitment on the grounds of race, ethnicity, gender, religion, migrant status, disability or infectious disease (some exceptions apply with the	Small fines may apply. Claims for damages may be made under tort law	The retirement age for employees is 60 for men and 50 for women (or 55 for those holding a management position or working for the public sector). It can impact on	High → Medium → Low

				High → Medium → Low
			cultural expectations and the treatment of older workers and women Companies must hire disabled employees as directed by local regulations (approx. 1.5% of total headcount) or pay into a disabled fund (e.g. 1.6% of average payroll for the previous year) Fines have been introduced for employers illegally testing job applicants for hepatitis B (a common recruitment practice in China)	
	latter, and women are excluded from some jobs which are deemed not suitable by the state) No discrimination during employment against women and the disabled Employers must prevent and prohibit sexual harassment against female workers			
European Union				
Job applicants, former employees, former employees as a minimum	Gender including pregnancy, maternity and gender reassignment, race or ethnic origin, religion or belief, age, disability and sexual orientation Member states typically go further and have broader grounds	Direct and indirect discrimination, harassment and victimisation (retaliation), although limited exceptions apply (e.g. where treatment can be justified)* Direct and indirect discrimination on grounds of sex with regard to pay for equal work or for work to which equal value is	Penalties vary across member states and typically include payment of compensation linked to the financial loss suffered and to mental distress. In some countries discriminatory acts, such as a dismissal, may be declared void, and reinstatement may be ordered (e.g., France, Spain, Netherlands)	There is strong protection against pregnancy and maternity discrimination. In contrast, there is greater scope to justify age discrimination The burden of proof is reversed: the employer must prove it has not discriminated, once the worker shows facts from which discrimination can be presumed

(continued)

Table 1 (continued)

Who is protected?	Protected characteristic (on what grounds is discrimination unlawful?)	What type of discriminatory treatment is unlawful?	Employer penalty for unlawful discrimination	Discrimination risk	Risk rating
		attributed* With disability discrimination, an employer is under a reasonable accommodation duty (to take reasonable measures to provide access, etc.) *Some countries outlaw such treatment more widely, e.g. France protects against general harassment, victimisation and unequal pay	Criminal sanctions including fines and, occasionally, imprisonment may also apply (e.g. France, Spain, Netherlands)	Many EU countries prohibit discrimination on grounds broader than the EU minimum, e.g. political opinion is common. A minority have open-ended grounds providing for greater protection, e.g. on 'other status' grounds Disability quotas which vary according to company size exist, e.g. Germany and Italy	
India					
Female applicants: sex discrimination in recruitment Female employees: sexual harassment at work All employees: discrimination on grounds of sex or untouchability Applicants for/holders of state/government jobs: discrimination on the	Under the Constitution: religion, race, caste, sex, place of birth, descent. Constitutional rights are only enforceable against the state Under separate legislation: sex (all employees), pregnancy and maternity (all employees), disability (state employees only).	Direct discrimination, sexual harassment, indirect discrimination, dismissal on the ground of victimisation	Penalties range from monetary fines to imprisonment. Courts may award damages based on actual loss suffered New sexual harassment legislation: repeat offences could result in revocation of operating licences. Fines of up to INR 100,000	All employers must by law set up an Internal Complaints Committee to redress complaints of sexual harassment at the workplace and spread awareness Female employees are protected from sex discrimination in recruitment and in relation to terms of service (e.g. promotion, training,	High → Medium → Low

basis of religion, race, caste, sex, place of birth or residence	caste and tribal origin (all employees)			job mobility). All employees are protected from sex discrimination in respect of remuneration. Female employees cannot be dismissed during maternity leave. Certain classes of company must have at least one female director on the board	
United States					
Job applicants, employees, former employees	Race, colour, religion, sex including pregnancy, national origin, disability or genetic information (applies to employers with 15+ employees) Age: age 40 or older (applies to employers with 20+ employees) Military service or affiliation and employees who have exercised other protected rights (e.g. taking protected leave)	Direct and indirect discrimination, harassment and retaliation (victimisation) An employer must reasonably accommodate an employee/job applicant's disability or religious beliefs or practices Men and women in the same workplace are entitled to equal pay for equal work	Penalties may include reinstatement, the payment of lost wages and costs (including paying the employee's reasonable lawyers' fees), noneconomic damages (e.g. emotional harm) and punitive damages (max. $300,000 for some malicious or reckless acts)	Employers are explicitly prohibited from making pre-employment inquiries about a disability. An employer may make a job offer conditional on the applicant answering certain medical questions but only if the same condition applies to all new employees in the same job Many US states prohibit discrimination based on wider grounds than federal law, including but not limited to sexual orientation, marital or parental status, credit history and criminal arrest or conviction record	High → Medium → Low

from sexual harassment at work, while all employees are protected against discrimination on the grounds of sex or untouchability. Applicants employed in government
roles or applying to work with the state in India are protected against discrimination
on the basis of religion, race, sex, place of birth, residence or caste, which 'in India is
described as a fatalistically-accepted system of discrimination' (Elder, 2003).

India's caste system is based on four different parts of the body, referred to in
Sanskrit texts as *var.na*, born 'of the primeval man, Puru.sa', who allegedly
'sacrificed himself on a cosmic funeral pyre at the dawn of creation' (Elder, 2003).
According to the Shabdkosh English Hindi Dictionary (2018), *var.na* is the original
social division into four distinct groups of the Vedic people who lived c.1500–c.500
BCE (Elder, 2003) or caste. These groups were later incorporated in the Laws of
Manu, which require men and women to marry only those within their *var.na* (group
or caste) and work only in occupations that reflect their *var.na* as listed in descending
order, from Puru.sa's head to his feet. For example, those who belong to the
Brahman *var.na* were said to have emerged from Puru.sa's mouth, so were the
highest caste members whose occupations were either priests or teachers; the
Kshatriyas were born of Puru.sa's arms, so could become warriors, rulers and
administrators. Puru.sa's thighs produced the Vaishyas *var.na*, who are merchants,
farmers and traders. The lowest *var.na* caste members were the Shudras, who were
expected to serve members of the other three castes and work as labourers.

According to Hindu myth, it was an act of gross violation for Brahman women to
be impregnated by Shudras men, and such inter-*var.na* or caste sexual relationships
are not permitted under the Laws of Manu. The offspring and their brood were
regarded as social pariahs who were barred from entering sacred places and events.
Furthermore, they were expected to undertake the least desirable occupational tasks,
such as toilet cleaning. These members were perceived as outcastes, otherwise
known as *dalits* or untouchables, because they were not recognised as a group or
as part of the caste system that emerged from Puru.sa's body (Elder, 2003). This
group of people is now protected under Indian law.

Arguably, less-traditional generations today are less likely to comply rigidly to
such Indian cultural mores. However, a lack of awareness of their significance,
particularly for organisations operating internationally and in the Indian region,
could result in them falling foul of the law. An example of such a scenario would
be where a local applicant or employee perceives themselves as being a victim of
employer discrimination due to their sex or caste when they fail to secure a post or
promotion. This might not be the case, but employers who are not culturally aware
may find it difficult to defend themselves in such instances.

Baruch, Humbert, and Wilson (2016) said that the term 'perceived discrimination' is one based on an 'individual's belief that they are being treated less favourably compared to another', which is also a concept that Schmitt and Branscombe
(2002) believe would be subject to a person's position in a social structure.

As recognised by Sue (1991), 'we are fast becoming a multicultural, multiracial,
and multilingual society', which is why these 'demographic changes are having a
major impact on economic, social, legal, political, educational, and cultural
systems'. Businesses need to be warned that if they are to survive in the global

economic playing field, then 'they will need to meet the inevitable challenge of cultural diversity', which arguably can only be achieved by becoming more culturally aware (ibid.).

4   A Study of Cultural Meanings of Respect

A qualitative action research study began in 2005 to explore cultural meanings of respect and how these meanings manifest in behaviours in the classroom. This helped to identify that respect is a key, commonly shared value for all that is culturally situated (Haydon, 2006; Wilson, 2010). The study was carried out collaboratively with undergraduate interdisciplinary business students enrolled on a final-year business consulting module at Middlesex University Business School, London. Students on this module were required to form diverse consulting teams of four to six people, using the criteria of mixed gender, ethnicity, age, programme of study and spatial proximity based on where they lived. The aim was to identify solutions for addressing 'real' business issues, but the ongoing conflict that arose among these students made it difficult for them to work and learn effectively. My predecessors found it difficult to manage this team conflict scenario, which is why I was approached to take over as module leader.

My first task was to identify what was causing the team conflict. This was revealed in the students' Individual Learning Review (ILR) essays, which required them to write about their module learning experience. Ninety-eight percent of the students chose to write about the conflict that arose among them, accusing those who were always of a different culture, although sometimes from the same ethnic group, of treating them disrespectfully. However, none of the students explained what they meant by respect, so in order to gain insight to their respect meanings, at the beginning of the academic year, I asked for two teams to join me in forming two research focus groups to share our stories based on our experiences of respect and disrespect. These stories related to a range of different topics such as work, upbringing, assumptions and peoples' attitudes.

The focus groups met once weekly for an hour, and the students agreed for these sessions to be audio-visually recorded. This exercise was repeated over 6 annual research phases and involved 732 students (399 female and 333 male), born overseas and in the United Kingdom; aged 21–49; of mixed ethnicity; of different social backgrounds, learning abilities and family responsibilities; and with some working part-time. This study enabled the participants to recognise that they gave others their respect and expected their respect back without realising it and that respect in one culture could be disrespect in another.

An example of this was where Nigerian students who were older than the others in their team expected the younger students to respect them by, for example, asking their advice first and taking on duties that they assigned to them without complaint. As one male Nigerian student who participated in the study reported, 'If the elders say go outside and clean the bins or whatever, you do that no arguments'. However, conflict arose with younger students whose cultural meanings of respect differed from those of the older Nigerian students. For example, the British and American students cited 'respecting each other's beliefs', regardless of age, as being one of their core meanings of respect; hence, they regarded the behaviour displayed towards them by the older Nigerian students as being disrespectful. As acknowledged, 'Nigeria is a hierarchical society' where 'age and position earns and even demands, respect' (Embassy of the Federal Republic of Nigeria, 2018). Older Nigerians are revered and in social settings are greeted and served first. They are also expected to 'make decisions that are in the best interest of the group' (ibid.).

In conclusion what was evident from this study is that a lack of awareness of culturally situated beliefs regarding what is perceived as respectful and disrespectful behaviour creates disharmony among those of difference, which can result in conflict. As Shen, Chanda, and D'Netto (2009) acknowledge, 'increasing globalization as well as national'—and international—'concerns about growing demographic diversity have enhanced the need for understanding heterogeneity in organisations' among employees of cultural difference. This is crucial for promoting not only the success of a business but its very survival.

5   Conclusion

As Tomlinson (1996) acknowledged, globalisation is the rapidly developing process of interconnections between people, societies and cultures worldwide. This occurrence has resulted in the growth in organisations doing business abroad, with many not realising how important it is to be culturally aware.

A lack of cultural awareness can lead to suspicion, hostility and complaints of discrimination, albeit not intended. This renders the need for international laws that make evident the rules of the land that transnational businesses would need to ensure they are able to respect. Notwithstanding, to know how to respect employees recruited locally is subject to understanding that respect is a key value for all that is culturally situated, which can have the opposite meaning, namely, disrespect, in another person's culture (Haydon, 2006; Wilson, 2010). Furthermore, if respect is culturally situated, then to understand what it means requires insight to the culture to know how to nurture an environment of respect, promote harmony and boost performance and, in turn, business sustainability to survive in today's volatile, uncertain, complex and ambiguous global climate.

References

Baruch, Y., Humbert, A., & Wilson, D. (2016). The moderating effects of single vs. multiple-grounds of perceived-discrimination on work-attitudes: Protean careers and self-efficacy roles in explaining intention-to-stay. *Equality, Diversity & Inclusion, 35*(3), 232–249. https://doi.org/10.1108/EDI-05-2014-0045.

Beutler, E., Nguyen, N. J., Henneberger, M. W., Smolec, J. M., McPherson, R. A., West, C., & Gelbart, T. (1993). Gaucher disease: Gene frequencies in the Ashkenazi Jewish population. *American Journal of Human Genetics, 52*(1), 85–88.

Elder, J. (2003) *Enduring stereotypes about Asia: India's caste system. The dalit solidarity forum in the USA.* http://www.dalitusa.org/es.html

Ellis, A. M. (2002). Genetic justice: Discrimination by employers and insurance companies based on predictive genetic information. *Texas Law Review, 34*, 1071.

Embassy of the Federal Republic of Nigeria Bucharest–Romania. (2018). *Nigerian society and culture.* Retrieved from http://nigerian-embassy.ro/about-nigeria/culture/

Haydon, G. (2006). *Acknowledges that "respect itself is in part a cultural phenomenon".*

Legislation.gov.uk. (2018). *The Equality Act 2010.* Retrieved from https://www.legislation.gov.uk/ukpga/2010/15/contents

Natowicz, M. R., Alper, J. K., & Alper, J. S. (1992). Genetic discrimination and the law. *American Journal of Human Genetics, 50*(3), 465–475.

Nishii, L. H., & Özbilgin, M. F. (2007). Global diversity management. *Human Resource Management, 18*(11), 1883–1894.

Nittle, N. K. (2019). *5 big companies sued for racial discrimination* (p. 1). ThoughtCo. https://www.thoughtco.com/big-companies-sued-for-racial-discrimination-2834873

Özbilgin, M. (2002). The way forward for equal opportunities by sex in employment in Turkey and Britain. *International Management, 7*(1), 55–67.

Schmitt, M. T., & Branscombe, N. R. (2002). The meaning and consequences of perceived discrimination in disadvantaged and privileged social groups. *European Review of Social Psychology, 12*, 167–199.

Shabdkosh English Hindi Dictionary. (2018). Retrieved from www.shabdkosh.com/translate/varna/varna-meaning-in-Hindi-English

Shen, J., Chanda, A., & D'Netto, B. (2009). Managing diversity through human resource management: An international perspective and conceptual framework, *Human Resource Management 20*, 235–252.

Sue, D. W. (1991). A model for cultural diversity training. *Journal of Counselling & Development, 70*, 99–105. https://doi.org/10.1002/j.1556-6676.1991.tb01568.x.

Tomlinson, J. (1996). Cultural globalisation: Placing and displacing the west. *The European Journal of Development Research, 8*(2), 22–35.

US National Library of Medicine. (2018). *Why are some genetic conditions more common in some ethnic groups?* Retrieved from https://ghr.nlm.nih.gov/primer/inheritance/ethnicgroup

Wilson, D. (2010). What price respect – Exploring the notion of respect in a 21st century learning environment. Contemporary issues in education research. *Journal of College Teaching & Learning Clute Institute, 3*, 11. ISSN: 1544-0389.

Part III
Conclusion

At the Core of Diversity Is Compassion

Paul Gibbs

Abstract

Compassion is not the entirety of justice; but it both contain a powerful, if partial, vision of just distribution and provide imperfect citizens with an essential bridge from self-interest to just conduct (Nussbaum, M. C., *Social Philosophy and Policy* 13:27–58, 1996, 38).

The world has become, in many respects, a better place for many of its inhabitants. This has led to better welfare and living conditions for those fortunate enough to directly benefit from the globalisation of the world's economies and the social power derived from rising incomes. Yet at the turn of the twenty-first century, with the world's wealth at the highest level that it has been in history, we are faced with a situation of uneven development, basic need and disenfranchisement. The perception is that globalisation has created greater wealth than at any time previously and corresponding high levels of consumption, yet deficits have emerged in the areas of human and ethical values, resulting in moral hazards and excesses. As Nussbaum suggests, it is compassion with wisdom that success in management can really mean.

The world has become, in many respects, a better place for many of its inhabitants. This has led to better welfare and living conditions for those fortunate enough to directly benefit from the globalisation of the world's economies and the social power derived from rising incomes. Yet at the turn of the twenty-first century, with the world's wealth at the highest level that it has been in history, we are faced with a

P. Gibbs (✉)
Centre for Education Research and Scholarship, Middlesex University, London, UK
e-mail: p.gibbs@mdx.ac.uk

© Springer Nature Switzerland AG 2019
M. F. Özbilgin et al. (eds.), *Global Diversity Management*, Management for Professionals, https://doi.org/10.1007/978-3-030-19523-6_15

situation of uneven development, basic need and disenfranchisement. The perception is that globalisation has created greater wealth than at any time previously and corresponding high levels of consumption, yet deficits have emerged in the areas of human and ethical values, resulting in moral hazards and excesses. As Nussbaum suggests, it is compassion with wisdom that success in management can really mean. Clearly, compassion is insufficient on its own, but together with care, empathy, belonging, respect and trust, organisations can craft governance structures in which organisational decision-making can reflect and benefit from the diversity that shapes our worlds.[1] In the main study, much of what is reported was grounded in moments of truth, trust, empathy and compassion.

As Berlant (2004) directly asserts in the opening sentence of her book, *Compassion*, 'There is nothing clear about compassion except that it implies a social relation between spectators and sufferers, with the emphasis on the spectators experience of feeling compassion and its subsequent relation to material practice' (ibid.: 1). Reflecting on the United States, Laurent considers the ethics of privilege that expects the judgement of distress not to be held against the sufferer (although see Nussbaum, 2001) but a claim on the spectator to become an 'ameliorative actor' (ibid.). These norms of obligation are tied up with the state as an economic and moral actor and addressed through the state's instruments of power, its businesses, its educational institutions, its government offices and its religious ideology. Such collective action is seen at global level with foreign aid (that which does not expect enriched returns), national welfare programmes and local action based on community and often faith. Organisational veracity and philanthropy are coupled in ways that might seem cynical, and the media play a significant part in how we frame those for whom our institutions should show compassion. Such exposure accelerates what has become known as 'compassion fatigue' and is based on the assumption that there is a finite resource of compassion available to us.

1   But What Is Compassion?

As White points out, 'compassion literally means "feeling with", and it involves the idea of suffering in response to the anguish of someone else' (2017: 20). Compassion tends to involve the desire to *help* another person who is in suffering. Compassion is by no means the same thing as pity. Pity involves looking down on someone from a position of superiority. This is why we typically reject the pity of others—we say 'I don't want your pity'—and self-pity, or looking down on oneself as an object, is the most contemptible thing. Compassion involves respect and a sense of identification with the other person. However, compassion goes beyond empathy. With empathy, the focus stays on person being empathic, but in compassion one

---

[1]Gibbs (2017) has edited a collection of essays on compassion in one higher education that has parallels with these studies.

recognises the other person as the one who is suffering *now*. Empathy can be self-involved, but compassion implies respect for the other person and some recognition of the difference between us.

Compassion as *compassion for others* (a concept that is present in nearly all cultures and spiritual/contemplative traditions) and *self-compassion* (being open to and moved by one's own suffering) is covered thoroughly in this book. Compassion, it appears, is also good for us, and recent research has helped to support this point with psychosocial interventions, cultivating positive emotional states and qualities. In what might be best considered an indicative study, Jazaieri et al. (2013) have shown that targeted compassion training results in significant improvements in three domains of compassion: compassion for others, receiving compassion from others and self-compassion. The amount of formal meditation practised during the training was found to be associated with increased compassion for others. Additional studies, such as that by Mongrain, Chin, and Shapira (2011), suggest that practising compassion can result in lasting improvement in happiness and self-esteem and may be beneficial for anxious individuals in the short term.

Compassion is usually conceived as a personal response to the vulnerable and those that suffer. It is a strong emotion and one that is more likely to lead to action than sympathy or empathy, although all three prove a compelling mix for a humane society. There are caveats on who deserves compassion, and personal carelessness and triviality play a part in how we engage in compassionate acts. There has been a significant increase in the literature relating to compassionate organisations and compassion in organisation, which is a shift to the former from the latter. I do not intend to cover this work, as it is discussed well elsewhere (Kanov et al., 2004). But there are two respects that I do want to consider. These are the relationship of compassion, care and justice within and beyond the organisation and the type of organisational frame and context that relates to its establishment and functioning. These issues were dominant in the main study reported here and in the small case studies that followed.

Care, empathy and compassion require people to have the skills to notice, to feel and then to respond to the suffering of others: to notice them, to respect their dignity and to empathise with their plight. It is about recognising these skills, developing and supporting them and creating an organisational structure that has processes, networks and policies to facilitate them. Compassionate caring for colleagues, both within their working lives and for their circumstance beyond the institution, has proven to be critical to the way in which persons, regardless of their diversity, respond to the institution and to their own responsibility to engage. This is caring that cannot be covered by any obligation of care but is emergent from authenticity in the well-being of others through respect, to empathy to compassion. Compassion, then, is the empathetic reaction to another's suffering and, articulated with a degree of criticality, can become a transformative management catalyst for channeling creative human passion and energy to facilitate justice and solidarity and upholding humanity dignity in diverse settings.

Respecting diversity, equality and inclusion is about understanding the vulnerability of change and its unexpected consequences. It is about merit and recognition that respect the talented but do not do so at the expenses of those less able. To be frank, Hussain argues that 'The talent is there, all it needs is the opportunity'. To fully appreciate, and better understand, how a range of social identities—race, gender, sexuality, class, etc.—contribute to systemic and structural oppression and the discrimination experienced by an individual requires compassion. To find this appreciation, the philosophical writings of thinkers such as Bourdieu (Özbilgin & Tatli, 2011; Tatli, 2011), Foucault (Ahonen & Tienari, 2009; Ahonen, Tienari, Meriläinen, & Pullen, 2014), Schopenhauer (Köllen) and Nussbaum's (2001) theory of emotion as a constituent part of thought, and her proposal that emotion is the form of compassion (Brewis, 2017), have all been called upon to help to understand and underpin the management of diversity.

Yet, compassion cannot be contracted, although it can be facilitated by organisations' structures and procedures. Coupling personal flourishing with compassion is viable, and coupling with top jobs will always deter those who fail in response to this credo. This was also the conclusion of Frost, Dutton, Worline, and Wilson (2000), whose study of compassionate narratives was one of the first to take emotions in the workplace seriously. This ground-breaking study showed how compassion can help others in an institution to 'feel cared for, seen, felt, known and not alone' (2000: 27). They propose an ecology of compassion where care and human connections are enabled. This work chimes with what Tietze argues in her chapter about her professional life, where her challenges in diversity management training are about how she can get in touch with people's minds and hearts. She asks 'How do I bring about not only a change on a cognitive level, but also on a behavioural level? How do I really reach people on a deeper level?'

Diversity also takes time. As Tietze so elegantly puts in in her chapter, 'I take time. It takes time. It is no secret to all diversity workers, that it is about the process. Process takes time.' It is time for all participants to build diversity of being into work schedules. All can be encouraged, and even rewarded, for taking time to respond to others whose needs are greater than their own, within a class and outside it. This inclusion's theme is illustrated both personally and in his own practice by Crabtree, where he introduces us to classroom drama as a methodology to awaken the needs of others in our practice. Curriculum, work practices and social norms can embed ideas of compassion in the substance, context and application of the learning hoped for. For Hussain, the more significant cultural shift needs to take place where programming diversity becomes part 'of the very DNA of our arts and cultural organisations and is part of the norm rather than being the exception'. Compassionate acts can be recognised, large and small, in various ways that are recognised. Students can be encouraged to seek to be settled with themselves and with others. This requires self-trust and self-compassion within the realm of social justice.

2   The Case for Compassion in the Workplace (Especially in Multicultural Organisations)

Values shared in Eastern and Western traditions include compassion, courage, trust and dignity. Compassion is central to Confucian and neo-Confucianism through the role of the benevolent actions of a good person and, as Opdebeeck and Habisch (2011) discuss in terms of empathy, in the monotheist Western spiritual tradition as well. For example, in the Golden Rule in Judaism, 'Whatever you wish that men would do to you, do so to them' (Leviticus, 19.18); in Christianity, 'Not one of you is a believer until he loves for his brother what he loves for himself' (Matthew 7.12); and in Islam, 'A man should wander about treating all creatures as he himself would be treated' (Zia, 2015: Forty *hadiths* of an-Nawawi). These values garner their meaning in action, and the workplace can provide a place where these values can dominate. Such a place is where diversity is seen as a virtue, and individuals are recognised as people in their own right, worthy of, and showing, these values just outlined. It needs leaders who care not just for the rhetoric of their organisational mission but who have the courage to disengage from policy, where it is ill thought out, hypocritical or manipulative. Suffering in the workplace is detrimental to humanity, dignity and motivation and is an unrecognised and costly drain on organisational potential. Leaders who ignore this do so at their peril. Alleviating such suffering confers measurable competitive advantages in areas including innovation, collaboration, service quality, talent attraction and retention. To do so is at the core of diversity management (Worline & Dutton, 2017), and as Mullen suggests in his chapter, 'smart organisations recognise the value of diversity in relation to both team effectiveness and to servicing customers'.

Compassion breeds compassion—those who experience it are then more likely to demonstrate it towards others (Goetz, Keltner, & Simon-Thomas, 2010), and supervisors who perceive that their organisation values their well-being are more likely to show supportive behaviour towards the people whom they manage (Eisenberg, Fabes, & Spinrad, 2006). This extends beyond the recipient of the compassion, for it has positive effects for the compassionate giver. The consequences for such engagement lead to relationships that are stronger and more positive, and therefore there is more collaboration in the workplace (Dunn, Aknin, & Norton, 2008; Dutton, Workman, & Hardin, 2014). It also reduces employee turnover and increases organisational citizenship (Fryer, 2013; Lilius, Kanov, Dutton, Worline, & Maitlis, 2011). There has been considerable research to suggest that those who experience compassionate leadership are more likely to talk about their workplace in positive terms (Lilius et al., 2008), show higher organisational commitment and remain with the organisation longer (Lilius et al., 2011; Moon, Hur, Ko, Kim, & Yoo, 2016). Perhaps the most critical issue is that, when compassion is at the core of organisational values, there is a measurable increase in productivity and financial performance (Kim & Brymer 2011). Bíró, in answering her question, 'Where is the evidence that homogenous teams, organisations and societies perform better?' replies from her own experience and insists, 'Nowhere'! However, I think I am being too instrumental here, for it reads as if I am suggesting that the root of compassion in diversity management is organisational gain.

In an interesting study by Mills (1999), the topic of investigation was being someone who one is not: not for oneself but for others. The motivation is socially derived for what one might be—gay, foreign or even religiously devout. To unbelievers, this last is a cause of discomfort, finding disfavour in those in the social context in which one finds oneself. This desire to belong is taken to be on the terms of others, not on one's own. When environments are not conducive to acceptance, to empathy or to compassion to those who are different, pressures can lead one to self-deception, to anxiety and to displacement, which are negative for all those involved. Here, the advantages of diversity for the multicultural contribution to a group are lost, and a poorer homogeneity is woven and pressed out. Bíró, in her commentary on her personal tales of this hiding of difference, recounts the school *iskolaköpeny* to cover her own clothes to give an illusion of sameness or to hide her and her friends' whole selves in class. Everyone loses, for the consequences are more than normal purpose talk. They are engendered by malice and are a defence mechanism that affects the dignity of all involved. In oppressive environments, it is difficult and courageous to retain one's identity, yet not to do so does hold, I feel, some moral accountability, notwithstanding that a much stronger moral obligation falls on the oppressor to desist from such oppression, whether the oppressor is an individual, group or organisation. This is at the core of managing diversity and is not simply for the goals that it can score but for the moral and stronger reason: that it is the right thing to do. As Mills states, the central moral issue does not turn on the reaction of the oppressed but 'How we should work to foster conditions of justice under which we can all create to revise our own best selves, whatever these may be' (Mills, 1999: 49).

Minty's chapter draws on the hiding of disabilities, and he writes that his work 'encompasses showing people the benefit of sharing necessary information, rather than fighting to hide something and having to work twice as hard just to keep up'. Hiding a disability can be a job in itself! Similarly, Mullen offers an example of a meeting that he held in Moscow, where he noticed that every time a woman in the room spoke, she was either interrupted or the men broke into side conversations. 'I pointed this out to the team; the men were surprised and apologetic but the women did not react at all. The women had become accustomed to that behaviour in the executive committee.' Such acceptance of the hiding of one's contribution by oneself in contexts where such behaviour is not recognised is oppressive and ought to be called out as requiring organisational change, not personal, resulting in benefits to both parties. Mullen offers some really good examples of this.

We might not go so far, as Schopenhauer calls this the virtue of loving kindness. This, he suggests, does not make a difference between different humans, for diversity management approaches would be motivated by such loving kindness and 'would aim at being as comprehensive as possible. Diversity management, then, would not limit itself to only a few dimensions of diversity, such as gender or ethnicity' (Köllen, 2016: 228). Boulaye's graphic discussion of diversities seen in the war of her childhood shows that diversity is not solely an issue for organisations but is one that can have profound influences on our whole lives. Her advocacy for the emergence of compassion, tolerance and integration in society, encouraged by leaders, might equally apply to organisations. Minty offers us another example of a gay Italian friend of his, who spoke of the development of gay rights and suggested: 'Sometimes you have to make it an issue, and only then can it become a non-issue.'

Here, I would like to introduce a warning, not in the Nietzschean sense but in the idea of *receiving compassion from others.* This is how we might deal with being recipients of compassion from others and feeling that one does not deserve, or should not accept, care and kindness from others, which has been associated with self-criticism. Insecure attachment has been explored by Gilbert, McEwan, Matos, and Rivis (2010) and offers a disturbing insight into society in general (Gerhardt, 2010). Gilbert et al. (2010) found that fears of compassion were associated with self-criticism, in that self-critical people actually have a fear of being kind to themselves: 'In addition, fears of compassion were strongly linked to depression, anxiety and stress' (p. 386). So compassion might cause distress, as well as alleviating it,[2] by providing feelings of contentment, safeness and connectedness that we are not prepared for, in our prudence that is encouraged by our social worlds. Surely, then, the issue of compassion is more than the individual nature of our being in the world and is also the nature of the work that we are engaged in. Schopenhauer is right that 'only in as far as action has sprung from compassion does it have real value' (1995: 144). Ruiz and Vallejos (1999) hold this view, especially with regard to moral education. Quoting Arteta, they argue that in a society that is technologically dominated by instrumentalism and consumerism, 'only from a compassionate point of view (and the mutual recognition of personal dignity) can we become moral subjects and not mere subjected objects' (ibid.: 16).

Finding compassion within ourselves is one thing, but accepting it when we need it seems potentially much more difficult, and when an institution allows anxiety and fear to flourish, embracing a functional discourse of compassion just might not be enough. In such institutions, 'caring for' students is replaced by 'caring about', with an accompanying loss of sensitivity and action. Sadiqi offers insights into how a global financial firm might go about achieving this. He warns us, however, that certain cultural understanding of diversity might not be universal. These differences also have to be respected. He offers examples of gender, ethnicity, disability, LGBTQ+ and faith. Taking one example of balancing gender opportunities in Saudi Arabia, he illustrates how local problems can occur and need to be resolved when a global directive requires specific but diverse action that recognises local cultural conditions. Wilson's wide-ranging chapter offers us, from her perspective as an academic, the complex global legal framework for employment discrimination and also an insight into how common terms carry a culturally different meaning. As she says, 'lack of awareness of culturally situated beliefs regarding what is perceived

---

[2]See Gilbert (2010, 2014) for a discussion of compassion centre therapy.

as respectful and disrespectful behaviour creates disharmony among those of difference, which can result in conflict'.

Turning finally to the main project in chapter 'Five Nations: A Diversity Study—Alex, Paul Gibbs, Kate Maguire & Alison Scott-Baumann', compassion did not emerge in the sense of an explicit term in the analysis of the stories that were told, which informed the analysis. Yet, should it be used as a meta-thematic tool, the rather functional approach to diversity management evident in the tension between a values system and the business model might find resolution: a resolution of compassion as a way of dispositional engagement, as a way of recognising the emotional issue and as a way of enframing solutions. This, too, would have helped to resolve the structural ambiguity 'inside–outside' dissonance between what was expected of internal staff (in terms of their behaviour and practices) and what was considered appropriate to their external cultural context. It would have given a way to confront the issue of the colonising of values, presented in a dry, prosaic way, stripped of the emotional power of compassion. This is also true of the finding that conversing in the local language, regardless, is more embracing and conducive to a sense of belonging and respect. Belonging seeks to understand the laminated layer of reality that exists in the organisation and is set against the ethos of managerial directives. Understanding belonging as an exploration intends to reveal what is worthy and valuable to those who are members of the organisation as a community and how collective engagement can be achieved and enjoyed. Indeed, such an understanding will highlight some of the ambiguities of practices that might be changed or, if central to the sustainability of the institution, need to be openly managed in the expectation of all.

3   What We Might Do?

The same realisation of the underlying quality of compassion applies to the general recommendation that we articulated at the end of chapter 'Five Nations: A Diversity Study—Alex, Paul Gibbs, Kate Maguire & Alison Scott-Baumann'. Compassionate leadership is associated with a valuing of all voices in a team, ensuring a climate that encourages team members to listen carefully to each other, understand all perspectives in the team, empathise and help and support each other. It often requires compromise, and this in turn needs flexibility. As Bothwick suggests, when we are talking about flexibility, we are talking about people having the ability to work when they need to and where they need to, to meet business needs and to also be able to balance other demands on their time. It's about empowering our people by making sure that they know what is required of them and when it is due and then trusting them to deliver. This enables compassionate, collective and inclusive leadership with regard to diversity management, to inclusion and to creativity and innovation. It helps to promote a culture of learning, where risk-taking (within safe boundaries) is encouraged and where there is an acceptance that not all innovation will be successful—an orientation diametrically opposite to a culture characterised by blame, fear and bullying. Worline and Dutton (2017) and Amabile and Khaire (2008) see compassionate leadership as an enabling condition for innovation across sectors.

Compassion can be understood as having four components: noticing, appraising, empathic concern and acting (Atkins & Parker, 2012). These are based on two preconditions: the first being mindful of others and their needs and the second a commitment to values-directed action. It is the latter that is often the route that an organisation takes, but the former that, as has already been said, is where the heart follows the mind. In a report relating to healthcare, where diversity is central, West et al. (2017: 20) interpret these in the following ways:

- Paying attention to the other and noticing their suffering—*attending*
- Understanding what is causing the other's distress by making an appraisal of the cause—*understanding*
- Having an empathic response, a felt relation with the other's distress— *empathising*
- Taking intelligent (thoughtful and appropriate) action to help to relieve the other's suffering—*acting by helping*

Applying these four approaches to our recommendation in chapter 'Five Nations: A Diversity Study—Alex, Paul Gibbs, Kate Maguire & Alison Scott-Baumann', we might suggest the following, as shown in Table 1.

Table 1 Capitation implementation of recommendation from chapter 'Five Nations: A Diversity Study—Alex, Paul Gibbs, Kate Maguire & Alison Scott-Baumann'

Recommendations	Compassionate agency
Senior managers should fully embody the organisation's diversity values in all that they do, both internally and externally	Attending, acting by helping
Organisations need to be open and honest between embedding the diversity areas in all that they do and ensuring that the organisation's activities are sustainable and achievable	Empathising, understanding
More attention needs to be given to both the values and the skills of local staff—identifying where there might be dissonance, as well as fully understanding the richness of staff experiences and the skills that they can contribute	Understanding, empathising
Organisations should consider how to best integrate and work with those who are not able to speak English fluently	Attending
Good diversity practices should be shared horizontally across the organisation, both within and between country offices, so that colleagues can learn from each other directly	Acting by helping
Organisations should consider whether its diversity approach is applicable to all countries in the current form or whether it should reflect the different cultural contexts in which it is implemented	Acting by helping

4 Any Closure?

We hope this book has offered ideas for practice, ideas to consider and ideas to open opportunities for innovative thinking. What is for sure is that diversity management is central to our development of a human democratic and enlightened society. It is perhaps the most significant contribution that organisations can bring to the stability of world of complexity, uncertainty and danger, yet of great care, love and compassion. We hope that you have found the book worthwhile.

References

Ahonen, P., & Tienari, J. (2009). United in diversity? Disciplinary normalization in an EU project. *Organization, 16*(5), 655–679.

Ahonen, P., Tienari, J., Meriläinen, S., & Pullen, A. (2014). Hidden contexts and invisible power relations: A Foucauldian reading of diversity research. *Human Relations, 67*(3), 263–286.

Amabile, T. M., & Khaire, M. (2008). *Creativity and the role of the leader.* Boston, MA: Harvard Business School Press.

Atkins, P. W. B., & Parker, S. K. (2012). Understanding individual compassion in organisations: The role of appraisals and psychological flexibility. *Academy of Management Review, 37*(4), 524–546.

Berlant, L. (2004). *Compassion: The culture and politics of an emotion.* New York: Routledge.

Brewis, D. N. (2017). Social justice 'lite'? Using emotion for moral reasoning in diversity practice. *Gender, Work and Organization, 24*(5), 519–532.

Dunn, E. W., Aknin, L. B., & Norton, M. I. (2008). Spending money on others promotes happiness. *Science, 319,* 1687–1688.

Dutton, J. E., Workman, K. M., & Hardin, A. E. (2014). Compassion at work. *Annual Review of Organizational Psychology and Organizational Behavior, 1,* 277–304.

Eisenberg, N., Fabes, R. A., & Spinrad, T. (2006). Prosocial development. In N. Eisenberg (Ed.), *Handbook of child psychology: Social emotional, and personality development* (Vol. 3, 6th ed., pp. 646–718). Hoboken, NJ: Wiley.

Frost, P. J., Dutton, J. E., Worline, M. C., & Wilson, A. (2000). Narratives of compassion in organisations. In *Emotion in organizations* (Chap. 2) (pp. 25–45). London: Sage.

Fryer, B. (2013). *The rise of compassionate management (finally).* Boston, MA: Harvard Business School Blog Network.

Gerhardt, S. (2010). *The selfish society: How we all forgot to love one another and made money instead.* London: Simon & Schuster.

Gibbs, P. (2017). *The pedagogy of compassion at the heart of higher education.* Geneva: Springer.

Gilbert, P. (2010). *Compassion focused therapy.* London: Routledge.

Gilbert, P. (2014). The origins and nature of compassion focused therapy. *British Journal of Clinical Psychology, 53,* 6–41.

Gilbert, P., McEwan, K., Matos, M., & Rivis, A. (2010). Fears of compassion: Development of three self-report measures. *Psychology and Psychotherapy: Theory, Research and Practice, 84,* 239–255.

Goetz, L., Keltner, D., & Simon-Thomas, E. (2010). Compassion: An evolutionary analysis and empirical review. *Psychological Bulletin, 136*(6), 351–374.

Jazaieri, H., Jinpa, G. T., McGonigal, K., Rosenberg, E. L., Finkelstein, J., Simon-Thomas, E., et al. (2013). Enhancing compassion: A randomized controlled trial of a compassion cultivation training program. *Journal of Happiness Studies, 14,* 1113–1126.

Kanov, J. M., Maitlis, S., Worline, M. C., Dutton, J. E., Frost, P. J., & Lilius, J. M. (2004). Compassion in organizational life. *American Behavioral Scientist, 47*(6), 808–827.

Kim, W. G., & Brymer, R. A. (2011). The effects of ethical leadership on manager job satisfaction, commitment, behavioral outcomes, and firm performance. *International Journal of Hospitality Management, 30*(4), 1020–1026.

Köllen, T. (2016). Acting out of compassion, egoism, and malice: A Schopenhauerian view on the moral worth of CSR and diversity management practices. *Journal of Business Ethics, 138*, 215–229.

Lilius, J. M., Kanov, J. M., Dutton, J. E., Worline, M., & Maitlis, S. (2011). Compassion revealed: What we know about compassion at work and where we need to know more. In K. Cameron & G. Spreitzer (Eds.), *Oxford handbook of positive organizational scholarship*. New York: Oxford University Press.

Lilius, J. M., Worline, M. C., Maitlis, S., Kanov, J., Dutton, J. E., & Frost, P. (2008). The contours and consequences of compassion at work. *Journal of Organizational Behavior, 29*(2), 193–218.

Mills, C. (1999). Passing: The ethics of pretending to be what you are not. *Social Theory and Practice, 2*(1), 29–51.

Mongrain, M., Chin, J. M., & Shapira, L. B. (2011). Practicing compassion increases happiness and self-esteem. *Journal of Happiness Studies, 12*, 963–981.

Moon, T. W., Hur, W. M., Ko, S. H., Kim, J. W., & Yoo, D. K. (2016). Positive work-related identity as a mediator of the relationship between compassion at work and employee outcomes. *Human Factors and Ergonomics in Manufacturing & Service Industries, 26*(1), 84–94.

Nussbaum, M. C. (1996). Compassion: The basic social emotion. *Social Philosophy and Policy, 13*, 27–58.

Nussbaum, M. C. (2001). *Upheavals of thought: The intelligence of emotions*. Cambridge: Cambridge University Press.

Opdebeeck, H., & Habisch, A. (2011). Compassion: Chinese and Western perspectives on practical wisdom in management. *Journal of Management Development, 30*(7/8), 778–788.

Özbilgin, M., & Tatli, A. (2011). Mapping out the field of equality and diversity: Rise of individualism and voluntarism. *Human Relations, 64*(9), 1229–1253.

Ruiz, P. O., & Vallejos, R. M. (1999). The role of compassion in moral education. *Journal of Moral Education, 28*(1), 5–17.

Tatli, A. (2011). A multi-layered exploration of the diversity management field, diversity discourses, practices and practitioners in the UK. *British Journal of Management, 22*(2), 238–253.

West, M., Eckert, R., Collins, B. & Chowla, R. (2017) Caring to change: How compassionate leadership can stimulate innovation in healthcare. The Kings Fund. Accessed January 29, 2019, from https://www.kingsfund.org.uk/sites/default/files/field/field_publication_file/Caring_to_change_Kings_Fund_May_2017.pdf

Worline, M., & Dutton, J. (2017). *Awakening compassion at work: The quiet power that elevates people and organizations*. Oakland, CA: Berrett-Koehler.

Zia, S. H. (2015, February 9). Forty *hadiths* of the sayings of the Prophet Muhammad about compassionate living. *Muslim Times*. Accessed 6 November 2016.

A Reflection on Compassion

Jason De Santolo

Abstract

A poetic statement on wise action and the urgency of compassionate reorientation in the just transition.

1 Starving for Compassion/*Marrkar Murrwar*[1]

The Elders full of compassion, tummies full,
 sitting in stillness with fire, thousands of years passing,
 through flood times, isolation—compassion lifts spirit,
 through droughts, desolation—compassion holds resolve.
 The Earth breathes in compassion, breathes out life.

The Elders see children shipping guns, disease, war,
 children holding their breath uninvited,
 murdering, raping, stealing, trailing a stench of death,
 the children slit Elders tummies, eat their entrails.
 The children lost to hatred, tummies full.

The Elders full of compassion, tummies eaten,
 sitting in stillness with fire, hundreds of years pass,
 embracing the weeping children, starved of compassion,
 drinking poisonous tears, waters without flow.
 The Earth breathes in death, coughs out blood.

---

[1]With kind permission of author

J. De Santolo (✉)
School of Design, Faculty of Design Architecture & Building, UTS, Ultimo, NSW, Australia
e-mail: jason.desantolo@uts.edu.au

© Springer Nature Switzerland AG 2019   173
M. F. Özbilgin et al. (eds.), *Global Diversity Management*, Management for
Professionals, https://doi.org/10.1007/978-3-030-19523-6_16

The Elders wisdom stirs, singing life into the land,
    gathering their entrails, a constellation of scars,
    the children sense their first breath, a wise action,
    marrkar murrwar, happiness resides inside tummies.
The Earth breathes in love, breathes out hope.

Jason De Santolo

2   Notes

Compassion is a happening, when I sit peacefully on country—marrkar murrwar, I am happy inside my tummy. Elder Nancy McDinny

It's not just us blackfellas that are real worried, but whitefellas too.
    We all gotta lined-up together, black and white, to protect our country.
    It's what gives us life. Elder Jack Green

Garrwa and Yanyuwa Elders sit in their homelands, on Country peacefully, for thousands and thousands of years, literally eternally, since the Yigan, since (dreamtime) creation. I remember, my Elders wearing white hats, singing, laughing, in full lotus beyond body, in full wisdom, on Country, un-phased. Their compassion both an emotional space dwelling in the stomach and a happening, a renewal (De Santolo 2018). It springs from movement, body, mind, spirit and through the shared breath of country. Compassion gives life and hope in times of immense violence and chaos.

Compassion is linked to the emphasis of 'just transition' as a beacon amidst the chaos of neoliberalism. Here wise action strives for life, comes from a deep reflection of unfinished business and a challenging of colonialism, paternalism, patriarchy. Yet we are still lost to a united meaning, still bound by a counter colonial narrative. We exist in a paradox of reason as Naomi Klein puts it: 'we are, in fact, a mess of contradictions, with our desire for self-gratification coexisting with deep compassion, our greed with empathy and solidarity'. Compassion helps us understand the meanings behind this shared sense of loss and of becoming/being lost. A grief driven by disconnection—the weeping oppressor. Compassion is one way to feel the Earth's pedagogy, a songline logic, a form of relational, emotional resonance. In looking inwards, we see beyond the illusions, beyond renewables as energy, beyond liberation as a voice to parliament, an act, an amendment. We disrupt the domination of Western rights transitions as recontextualisation of self-determination, as the only pathway to a 'new' and 'newer' reality. In looking deep within our sensory emotional selves, we search the void of shared experience and potential. This is a reorientation beyond mapping, where we touch the source, overcome crisis and move into transformational praxis (Smith, G 2015). Transformation of self, of higher being, of connectedness, of shared humanity. Breathing in compassion, breathing out life, a 'black transition' calls for resurgence and wise action that is centred around love for all children, unity, truth and liberation of country.

Index

A

Action, 2, 14, 18, 27, 46, 48, 58, 70, 72, 73, 97–99, 107, 112, 113, 124, 130, 138, 139, 142, 155, 162, 163, 165, 167, 169, 174
Administration, 60, 101
Advocacy, 167
Africa, 6, 16, 18, 20, 56, 93, 115, 121, 124, 148
Anthropology, 4, 18, 42, 46, 48, 57, 58
Arts Council, 7, 137–140, 142
Attending, 63, 169

B

Belonging, 17, 20, 43, 45, 82, 83, 88, 89, 122, 127, 162, 168
British Council, 1, 3–6, 12, 13, 21, 43, 45–48, 50, 56–61, 64, 65, 67, 69, 71, 72, 74–76, 82, 84, 103, 139

C

Care, 130, 162–165, 167, 170
Challenges, 1–8, 17, 19–21, 26, 29–33, 35, 36, 42, 49, 56, 60, 63, 66, 69, 70, 74, 76, 86, 98, 112–114, 116, 118, 120, 121, 123, 124, 126, 127, 130, 137–139, 142, 155, 164
Change, 5, 29, 43, 59, 83, 92, 104, 117, 124, 130, 137, 154, 164
Clarity, 15, 17, 20
Codes, 64
Colonisation, 113
Compassion, 2, 3, 8, 161–170, 173, 174
Compromise, 2, 14, 70–72, 74, 75, 92, 168
Contexts, 2, 12, 26, 45, 56, 96, 104, 115, 122, 131, 163
Creativity, 56, 86, 168

Culture

Culture, 5, 6, 8, 12, 16–20, 27, 43, 45, 47–49, 56, 58, 61, 64, 67, 69–71, 83–85, 87, 91, 92, 94, 106–108, 114, 123–125, 127, 137–143, 145–147, 155, 156, 163, 168

D

Democracy, 7, 132–134
Deregulation, 4, 31–33, 36
Dignity, 13, 163, 165–167
Directives, 116, 167, 168
Disability, 6, 18, 26, 33, 45, 60, 63, 65, 67, 85, 93, 95, 103–109, 119, 124–125, 137, 138, 140–142, 148–151, 153, 166, 167
Discrimination, 8, 12, 13, 21, 26, 29, 43, 64, 82, 83, 100, 112, 118, 119, 124, 137, 145–150, 152–154, 156, 164, 167
Diversity, 1, 11, 26, 42, 56, 81, 87, 107, 111, 121, 130, 138, 145, 162
Diversity management, 1–8, 12–13, 16–18, 26–36, 46, 61, 75–76, 81–86, 111, 120, 131, 164–166, 168, 170

E

Economies, 16, 28, 36, 161
Effectiveness, 16, 26, 28–31, 65, 68, 75, 99, 107, 111, 114, 116, 165
Efficiency, 65, 68, 75
Egypt, 4, 56, 59, 68, 69, 73
Emergence, 58, 167
Emotions, 7, 11, 71, 129–135, 163, 164
Empathy, 44, 117, 134, 162, 163, 165, 166, 174
Entertainment, 92
Equality, 2, 4, 6, 11–21, 26, 28–31, 34–36, 43, 45, 56, 72, 82, 111, 112, 118–120, 122–125, 130, 134, 138–142, 148, 164

© Springer Nature Switzerland AG 2019
M. F. Özbilgin et al. (eds.), *Global Diversity Management*, Management for Professionals, https://doi.org/10.1007/978-3-030-19523-6

F
Fear, 43, 49, 69, 72, 90, 105, 106, 118, 167, 169
Financial returns, 119
Flexibility, 12, 27, 122–124, 168

G
Ghana, 4, 56, 59, 62, 68, 69, 71–73
Global, 1, 12, 26, 43, 59, 82, 113, 121, 145, 162

H
Harassment, 26, 29, 150–154
Hate, 82, 125
Heart and mind, 106, 130, 164, 169
Helping, 47–49, 63, 70, 92, 113, 141, 169
Hidden, 44, 49, 85, 105
Human resources (HR), 6, 15, 18, 20, 27, 33,
      60, 85, 86, 108, 118, 125
Human rights, 2, 12, 26, 43, 48, 67, 71, 73, 81,
      126, 149

I
Identity, 12, 13, 34, 47, 63, 83, 115, 118, 122,
      138, 164, 166
Imagination, 18, 58, 140
Implementation, 2–4, 7, 11–21, 29, 31–33, 35,
      36, 49, 56, 63, 73, 76, 125, 130, 148, 150
Inclusion, 2, 4, 5, 7, 11–21, 27, 29, 34–36, 43,
      45, 56, 72, 82, 84, 86, 94, 95, 98, 99,
      101, 106, 118, 120–122, 124–127, 134,
      135, 164, 168
Individualism, 4, 31–33
Innovation, 13, 26, 28, 86, 95, 119, 122, 127,
      138, 165, 168
Intersectional, 4, 31, 33–36, 100

J
Jordan, 4, 56, 59, 69, 70

K
Kenya, 4, 56, 59, 69, 72, 122

L
Leadership, 6, 16, 20, 27, 28, 59, 60, 65, 73, 82,
      84–86, 112–117, 119, 130, 131, 140,
      141, 165, 168
Learning, 5–7, 46–49, 59, 62, 66, 82, 84, 86, 88,
      94, 97–101, 105, 112–113, 119,
      131–133, 140, 155, 164, 168
Legal, 16, 17, 20, 28, 29, 31, 32, 76, 107, 108,
      138, 148, 154, 167

Lesbian, gay, bisexual, transgender, queer,
      plus (LGBTQ+), 18, 112, 118, 125,
      126, 167
Listening, 18, 48, 58, 126, 129, 132
Literature, 1, 3, 4, 13–21, 27, 44, 46, 48–50, 57,
      58, 75, 163

M
Management, 1, 12, 26, 43, 60, 81, 111, 124,
      130, 150, 162
Marginalisation, 99, 119
Middlesex University, 1, 17, 45, 58, 155
Multiculturalism, 18

N
Narrative inquiry, 17, 21, 42–50, 58
Nigeria, 87, 88, 156

O
Oppression, 100, 107, 164, 166
Others, 2, 11, 26, 42, 56, 82, 87, 93, 104, 113,
      123, 130, 137, 147, 162
Özbilgin, M., 1–8, 13, 16, 19–21, 26–36, 61,
      148, 164

P
Pain, 149
Paradox, 42, 44–46, 174
Philosophy, 133
Policy, 2, 3, 6, 14–21, 27, 30, 43, 45, 48, 49,
      56, 72, 85, 95, 98, 106, 111, 118,
      122–124, 126, 130, 133, 138, 141, 148,
      150, 163, 165
Politics, 4, 45, 46, 107
Power, 2, 7, 13, 14, 17, 19–21, 28, 32–35,
      42–44, 47, 49, 61, 62, 70, 74, 82–86, 95,
      112, 114, 116, 124, 125, 133, 134,
      161, 168
Practices, 2, 14, 27, 42, 56, 92, 94, 111, 133,
      138, 146, 162
Prejudice, 83, 86, 147

R
Religion, 12, 34, 45, 63, 64, 70, 83, 85, 126,
      148–150, 152–154
Research, 2, 12, 29, 42, 56, 84, 125, 129, 133,
      145, 163
Resolve, 62, 63, 71, 99, 109, 134, 167, 168, 173
Respect, 1, 8, 31, 47–49, 65, 67, 69–71,
      119, 121, 146, 153, 155–156,
      161–163, 168

S
Saudi Arabia, 4, 56, 59, 70, 71, 123, 167
School of Oriental and African Studies (SOAS),
        1, 45, 58
Self-awareness, 113, 117, 118
Sharing, 27, 50, 76, 84, 85, 97, 105, 132, 166
Society, 26, 28, 36, 42, 49, 56, 63, 69, 86, 92,
        99, 106, 107, 119, 126, 132, 134, 137,
        138, 146, 154, 156, 163, 165, 167
Solidarity, 4, 31–36, 163, 174
Storytelling, 2, 4, 16, 18, 42, 45, 46, 48, 49, 56,
        58, 61, 62

T
Temporality, 69–70
Theatre of the classroom, 5, 93–101
Time, 2, 14, 15, 18, 42, 43, 46–48, 50, 57, 58,
        60, 62–64, 66, 69, 70, 72–74, 82–84, 90,
        92, 99, 103, 105–108, 114, 115, 126,
        130, 131, 133–135, 137, 141, 146, 155,
        162, 164, 166, 168

V
Value chain, 4, 29, 31, 33–36, 123
Values, 1, 15, 29, 43, 56, 86, 94, 111, 121, 131,
        151, 155, 162
Voices, 2, 3, 5, 19, 21, 47, 62, 63, 65, 89, 115,
        131, 132, 138, 168, 174

W
Workers, 7, 28, 31, 33, 34, 56, 67, 125, 133,
        147, 149–151, 164

Printed by Printforce, the Netherlands